506173

SEMANTICS

KT-458-707

401.43 KEA

ST

6930247)

MODERN LINGUISTICS SERIES

Series Editors

Professor Noël Burton-Roberts
University of Newcastle upon Tyne

Dr Andrew Spencer
University of Essex

Each textbook in the **Modern Linguistics** series is designed to provide a carefully graded introduction to a topic in contemporary linguistics and allied disciplines, presented in a manner that is accessible and attractive to readers with no previous experience of the topic, but leading them to some understanding of current issues. The texts are designed to engage the active participation of the reader, favouring a problem-solving approach and including liberal and varied exercise material.

Noël Burton-Roberts founded the **Modern Linguistics** series and acted as Series Editor for the first three volumes in the series. Andrew Spencer has since joined Noël Burton-Roberts as joint Series Editor.

Titles published in the series

English Syntax and Argumentation Bas Aarts
Phonology Philip Carr
Linguistics and Second Language Acquisition Vivian Cook
Sociolinguistics: A Reader and Coursebook
Nikolas Coupland and Adam Jaworski
Morphology Francis Katamba
Semantics Kate Kearns
Contact Languages: Pidgins and Creoles Mark Sebba

Further titles are in preparation

Modern Linguistics Series
Series Standing Order
ISBN 0–333–71701–5 hardcover
ISBN 0–333–69344–2 paperback
(*outside North America only*)

You can receive future titles in this series as they are published by placing a standing order. Please contact your bookseller or, in the case of difficulty, write to us at the address below with your name and address, the title of the series and the ISBN quoted above.

Customer Services Department, Macmillan Distribution Ltd
Houndmills, Basingstoke, Hampshire RG21 6XS, England

Semantics

Kate Kearns
Senior Lecturer, Department of Linguistics, University of Canterbury
New Zealand

© Kate Kearns 2000
All rights reserved. No reproduction, copy or transmission of this
publication may be made without written permission.

No paragraph of this publication may be reproduced, copied or
transmitted save with written permission or in accordance with the
provisions of the Copyright, Designs and Patents Act 1988, or under
the terms of any licence permitting limited copying issued by the
Copyright Licensing Agency, 90 Tottenham Court Road, London
W1T 4LP.

Any person who does any unauthorised act in relation to this
publication may be liable to criminal prosecution and civil claims
for damages.

The author has asserted her right to be identified as the author of
this work in accordance with the Copyright, Designs and Patents
Act 1988.

First published 2000 by
PALGRAVE MACMILLAN
Houndmills, Basingstoke, Hampshire RG21 6XS and
175 Fifth Avenue, New York, N. Y. 10010
Companies and representatives throughout the world

PALGRAVE MACMILLAN is the global academic imprint of the
Palgrave Macmillan division of St. Martins Press, LLC and of Palgrave
Macmillan Ltd. Macmillan is a registered trademark in the United
States, United Kingdom and other countries. Palgrave is a registered
trademark in the European Union and other countries.

ISBN–13: 978–0–333–73842–9 hardcover
ISBN–10: 0–333–73842–X hardcover
ISBN–13: 978–0–333–73843–6 paperback
ISBN–10: 0–333–73843–8 paperback

This book is printed on paper suitable for recycling and made from
fully managed and sustained forest sources.

A catalogue record for this book is available from the British Library.

15 14 13 12 11 10 9 8 7 6 5 4
15 14 13 12 11 10 09 08 07 06 05

Printed and bound in Great Britain by
Arrowsmith, Bristol

SOUT.
UNIVERSITY LIBRARY
SUPPLIER Blackw
ORDER No
DATE 71206

Contents

Acknowledgements

I wish to thank the University of Canterbury, New Zealand, for study leave granted in 1998, during which this book was written.

Preface

This book grew out of a semantics course taught at the second-year level in the general Arts or Sciences bachelor's degree at the University of Canterbury. Most of the students are studying linguistics or philosophy as a major subject, but they also come from a number of other fields in the humanities, physical sciences or professional studies. They generally have taken an introductory course in either linguistics or philosophy.

A mixed undergraduate class in semantics presents the dilemma of deciding what to do about the conceptual and notational complexity of formal theories. A detailed formalization procedure is not of the greatest interest to many of the students, and if the full formal apparatus is used, it isn't possible to introduce more than a limited range of data. If a very limited range of data is covered, this leaves a gap in the linguistics programme, particularly for the teaching of syntax, where some acquaintance with semantic issues is increasingly useful and important. The aim of this book is to introduce a wider range of topics in formal semantics with a limited formal apparatus.

Chapters 1–4 are introductory to the rest of the book, but a selection can be made from the remaining chapters. There are several themes that could be followed: Chapters 4–6 cover NP interpretation and Chapters 8–10 cover events and thematic roles. Verbal and nominal aspect is covered in sections of Chapters 6 and 7 and Chapter 9.

The text is intended to be used as a coursebook, accompanied by lectures on the topics covered and by discussion of the exercises. This book is not a 'teach yourself' text for private, unassisted study. The exercises included are of varying difficulty – some are for basic review and are suitable for private revision, but the more demanding exercises may best be used as the basis of class discussion sessions.

As always, students are urged to also read other introductions to semantics which take a different approach.

1 Introduction

The study of linguistic meaning is generally divided in practice into two main fields, semantics and pragmatics. **Semantics** deals with the literal meaning of words and the meaning of the way they are combined, which taken together form the core of meaning, or the starting point from which the whole meaning of a particular utterance is constructed. **Pragmatics** deals with all the ways in which literal meaning must be refined, enriched or extended to arrive at an understanding of what a speaker meant in uttering a particular expression.

This division can be roughly illustrated with (1) below.

(1) I forgot the paper.

Semantics provides the literal meaning of the elements *I*, *forget*, past tense, *the* and *paper*, and the meaning drawn from the order of the words, giving very approximately 'The person who is speaking at some time before the time of speaking forgot a particular item which is a paper'. Pragmatic considerations flesh this out to a more complete communication.

Suppose that it is Sunday morning. Anna, the speaker, has just returned to her flat from the local shops where she went to buy croissants and the Sunday newspaper. In this context her flatmate Frances understands Anna to say that she forgot to buy a copy of the Sunday newspaper for that morning, and the time of her forgetting was while she was at the shops – she presumably remembered her intention to buy a paper when she set out and has obviously remembered it on returning. If the shops are nearby, Anna might also intend Frances to infer that Anna will go back for the paper.

Suppose, alternatively, that a man has been found murdered in the fields near a farmhouse. Two nights before the body was found the farmhouse was broken into, although nothing was reported missing. The owners of the house are renovating a small upstairs room, and the floor of this room is currently littered with sticky scraps of stripped wallpaper. The dead man was found with a scrap of the wallpaper on the sole of his shoe. Two detectives are discussing the case. One has just finished speculating that the murder is connected to another set of recent events in the nearby town, and is not related to the break-in at the farmhouse. She then stops and says 'I forgot the paper'.

In this context her colleague understands her to mean that while she was working through her alternative scenario she forgot the wallpaper scrap on the dead man's shoe. Given the background assumption that the scrap of paper proves the man's presence upstairs in the farmhouse at some stage, her

1

utterance is also understood to mean that she withdraws her speculative alternative scenario, which is probably not correct.

Examples like these demonstrate the enormous contribution of pragmatic information to communication. On the other hand, the starting point from which we arrive at both fleshed-out meanings is the constant contribution of the literal meaning of *I forgot the paper*.

This book will mainly concentrate on literal meaning, the content of words and expressions which is fairly constant from one occasion of use to another. The kind of semantic/pragmatic division illustrated above is discussed in detail in Chapter 11.

1.1 KINDS OF MEANING

1.1.1 Denotation and Sense

There are two most basic ways of giving the meaning of words or longer expressions. The first and most simple way is to present examples of what the word **denotes**. For example, the word *cow* can be defined by pointing to a cow and saying 'That is a cow', or the word *blue* can be defined by pointing to a blue object and saying 'That colour is blue.' Definition by pointing to an object of the kind in question, called **ostensive definition**, appeals directly to the **denotations** of the words defined. The word *blue* denotes the colour blue, or blue objects in the world, and the word *cow* denotes cows. The general point is that linguistic expressions are linked in virtue of their meaning to parts of the world around us, which is the basis of our use of language to convey information about reality. The denotation of an expression is the part of reality the expression is linked to.

The second way of giving the meaning of a word, commonly used in dictionaries, is to paraphrase it, as illustrated in (2).

(2)   *forensic*   'pertaining to courts of law and court procedures'

      export   'to send out from one country to another, usually of commodities'.

This kind of definition attempts to match the expression to be defined with another expression having the same **sense**, or content. The clearest kind of sense-for-sense matching is translation from one language to another. To say that *le train bleu* means 'the blue train' is to say that the French expression and the English expression have the same sense.

The most widely discussed form of the sense/denotation distinction is the **sense/reference** distinction. An expression which denotes just one individual is said to **refer** to that individual. Titles and proper names are common referring expressions.

Suppose, for example, that some of the winners of the Mr Muscle Beach Contest are Wade Rodriguez (1992), Denzel Lucas (1993), Josh Minamoto (1994) and Rob Cabot (1995). The expression *Mr Muscle Beach* has a constant sense which one might paraphrase as '(title of) the winner of an annual body-building competition called the Mr Muscle Beach Contest', but depending on the year in which, or about which, the expression is used it refers to Rodriguez, Lucas, Minamoto or Cabot. This general pattern of a constant sense allied with changeable reference is discussed in more detail in Section 5.5.

Sense and denotation do not have parallel status. In the context of the anecdote above the expression refers at different times to Wade Rodriguez, Denzel Lucas, Josh Minamoto and Rob Cabot. The fact that the expression refers to one of these men at a given time depends on, and follows from, the sense of the expression. It is only because the expression has the sense '(title of) the winner of an annual body-building competition called the Mr Muscle Beach Contest' and Lucas won the competition in 1993 that the expression refers to Lucas in 1993. And given the sense of the expression, it cannot denote anyone who has not won the competition in question. So sense is more basic than denotation, and denotation is dependent on sense.

Sense and denotation are the fundamental aspects of meaning in general. The next two sections review different ways of partitioning complex meanings in terms of their components.

1.1.2 Lexical and Structural Meaning

The meaning of a complex expression such as a sentence is composed of **lexical meaning**, which is the meaning of the individual words, and **structural meaning**, which is the meaning of the way the words are combined.

Structural meaning mainly comprises the meaning derived from the syntactic structure of an expression, for example:

(3)a The rat that bit the dog chased the cat
   b The cat that chased the dog bit the rat
   c The rat that chased the cat bit the dog
   d The dog that chased the rat bit the cat
   e The dog that bit the rat chased the cat
   f The dog that chased the cat bit the rat
   g The dog that bit the cat chased the rat
   h The dog that chased the cat chased the rat
   i The dog that chased the rat chased the cat ... and so on ...

From a vocabulary of seven words (*the, that, rat, dog, cat, chased, bit*) we can construct a large number of different sentences with different meanings, all based on a single syntactic structure with a common 'meaning template':

(4)   [The A [that B-ed the C]] D-ed the E

   x is an A
   x performed the D action
   y is an E
   y undergoes the D action
   x performed the B action
   z is a C
   z is the undergoer of the B action

The meaning components outlined in (4) are examples of syntactic meaning.

Any theory of human language has to be compatible with the fact that human languages are instantiated in human minds, which have a finite capacity. Although the language known by any one person at a given point in time contains a fixed number of words, it can in principle produce, or generate, infinitely many sentences, because the syntax is recursive. **Recursiveness** is the property of embedding a phrase inside another phrase of the same kind, which allows for sentences to be extended in length indefinitely. The examples below illustrate two kinds of recursion many times repeated.

(5)a   The car broke down because Tom forgot to fill the tank because he was running late because Bill rang him just when he was leaving because Bill wanted to sell John a home gym because he doesn't use the home gym anymore and he needs the money because he spent too much money last month because he went for a quick holiday because he needed a break...

   b   This is the maiden all forlorn that milked the cow with the crumpled horn that tossed the dog that chased the cat that killed the rat that ate the malt that lay in the house that Jack built.

The examples in (5) show that recursion can be used to lengthen a sentence by adding to it. For example, the sentence *The car broke down* can be lengthened by adding *because Tom forgot to fill the tank*, giving two sentences, the original one and the longer one. In principle, any sentence can be used to form a new sentence by using a recursive addition, and so the number of sentences is infinite.

Given that the language has infinitely many sentences, our knowing a language cannot possibly amount to memorizing its expressions. Rather, we know the vocabulary and the syntactic rules for generating sentences. The syntactic rules themselves are a finite number, probably a fairly small number.

We can also match meanings to these infinitely many sentences, and again, we can't possibly do this by memorizing sentence/meaning pairs. Most of the sentences we hear and understand are heard for the first time, and could not have been learned ahead. It must be that along with the syntactic rules for forming phrases and sentences, we also know interpretation rules which combine meanings just as syntactic rules combine forms. Accordingly, linguistic meaning is **compositional**. Compositionality is the property of being composed from parts. Syntactic and semantic rules work in parallel.

Structural meaning also overlaps with the meaning of syncategorematic expressions, introduced in the next section.

1.1.3   Categorematic and Syncategorematic Expressions

The distinction between categorematic and syncategorematic expressions applies to individual words, rather than phrases. Meaningful inflections can also be included here, as they are syncategorematic.

Categorematic expressions, which include the vast majority of words, are the descriptive words such as nouns, adjectives and verbs. These words are termed categorematic because their descriptive content, or sense, provides a basis for categorization. For example, the descriptive content of the word *chimney* provides the basis for forming the category of chimneys, the sense of *blue* provides the basis for the category of blue things, the senses of the words *domestic, professional, commercial*, and so on provide the basis for categories of things and activities, and so on.

Syncategorematic words are all the rest, including the examples here.

(6)   *as, some, because, for, to, although, if, since, and, most, all, . . .*

What syncategorematic words have in common is that they do not have independent, easily paraphrasable meanings on their own, and we can only describe their meaning by placing them in a context. Unlike the categorematic words, they are not themselves descriptive of reality, do not denote parts of reality. Rather, they serve to modify categorematic expressions or to combine them in certain patterns.

Examples of modifying expressions are tense, illustrated in (7a–c), and modality, illustrated in (7d–e). (Tense and modality are discussed further in Chapters 3 and 7.)

(7)a   He believed us.
  b   He believes us.
  c   He will believe us.
  d   He might believe us.
  e   He must believe us.

In (7a–c) the tense endings *-ed* and *-s* and the future auxiliary *will* are combined with the same base sentence form *He BELIEVE us*. The basic sentence form describes a state of affairs, and semantic tense locates this state of affairs in the past, present or future. The past, present or future content of the tense expressions (*-ed, -s, will*) doesn't stand alone, but must combine with a sentence to be given a particular interpretation. These expressions do not in themselves denote the past, present and future – that is, they do not have the same senses as the expressions *past/the past, present/ the present, future/the future*.

The same base sentence *He BELIEVE us* appears in (7d–e), but here the state of affairs of his believing us is not located in the past, present or future. Rather, the modal (*might, must*) expresses a qualification on whether or not there is such a state of affairs. There is room for doubt in (7d) but not in (7e).

An example of a syncategorematic expression combining descriptive expressions is *all* in the examples below.

(8)a　All diamonds are hard.
　　b　All dogs like icecream.
　　c　All zinks neb.
　　d　*All* A B.　　　　(*All As are B* or *All As B*)

The general form of the framework for *all,* given in (8d), is just as clear when filled with nonsense words as in (8c). *All* sets up a relationship between A and B. Thinking in terms of categories, we can say that 'All A B' places the A category inside the B category – the Bs include the As. For example, the category of hard things includes the category of diamonds (8a), the category of icecream-likers includes the category of dogs (8b), and the category of nebbers, whatever they are, includes the category of zinks, whatever they are (8c). The meaning of *all* is defined in terms of the way it relates the meaning of the A predicate to the meaning of the B predicate, rather than being defined apart from a context, and this gives *all* a syncategorematic character. (The quantificational determiners, including *all*, are discussed in Chapter 4.)

In summary, lexical meanings may be either categorematic or syncategorematic. Syncategorematic expressions, both words and inflections, group naturally with structural meaning, because they must be defined in terms of the constructions they appear in.

(9)
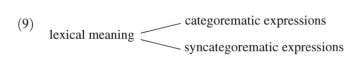

lexical meaning　　＜　categorematic expressions
　　　　　　　　　　　　syncategorematic expressions

1.2　STUDIES BASED ON SENSE

In the anatomy of a complex expression such as a sentence the categorematic words make the clearest contribution to sense. These are the words which generally have the most recognizable or identifiable senses when considered in isolation, and so they seem to be the best starting point for studies of sense.

1.2.1 Lexical Sense

Certain aspects of lexical sense involving relationships among word senses are readily analysable. Some illustrations from this area are given in this section, and references for further reading are at the end of the chapter. The discussion of antonyms below is based on Cruse (1986).

One of the most familiar sense relations is opposition or **antonymy**. Young children can identify opposites, or antonyms, such as *black* and *white*, and opposition is the basis of many doublet sayings and rhetorical devices such as *from top to bottom, hither and yon, by night and day*, and so on. Various uses of words in antonym pairs reveal that there are several different kinds of antonym with different internal sense structures.

Perhaps the most basic antonyms are **complementaries**, such as *open/shut, dead/alive*, and *hit/miss*. The entities these terms apply to are either one thing or the other.

(10)a   A door is either open or closed.
  If the door is open then it is not closed.
  If the door is not closed then it is open.
  If the door is closed then it is not open.
  If the door is not open then it is closed.
  (A door which is slightly open is still open.)

Similarly, a life-form (animal or vegetable) is either alive or dead, and if you shoot at a target you either hit it or miss it. Complementaries are anomalous in sentences like (11). The sign '#' indicates semantic anomaly.

(11)a   # The door is neither open nor closed.
  b   # He shot at the target and he neither hit it nor missed it.
  c   # The dog is neither alive nor dead.

Most opposites are not complementary, for example:

(12)a   The water is neither hot nor cold.
  b   The performance was neither good nor bad.
  c   He is neither short nor tall.

Non-complementary opposites are based on a scale with opposite poles and a neutral middle zone. The difference between the two kinds can be represented as in the diagrams below.

(13)

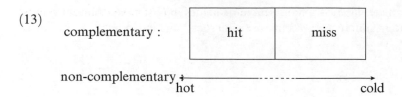

Non-complementaries are further subdivided according to how the terms are used for different parts of the scale.

Polar antonyms, such as *heavy/light*, *fast/slow*, *high/low*, and *wide/narrow* give the opposite poles on a scale for a particular property which commonly has a separate neutral term.

(14) heavy/light   weight
      fast/slow   speed
      long/short   length
      high/low   height

The basic statements *It is long* and *It is short* place an object at or near one pole for the property of length. The actual measured values, for example in centimetres, which count as long or short depend on perceived norms for the kind of object described.

In a simple question one of the terms stands for the neutral property the whole scale relates to. For example, the question *How long is it?* carries no expectation that the object concerned is either long or short, but the question *How short is it?* is appropriate where the object is expected or known to be short. *Long* stands for the neutral property of length in this kind of question, but *short* covers only the short end of the length scale.

Polar antonyms like *long/short* are characterized by the generality of their comparative forms, in that the comparisons *A is longer than B* and *B is shorter than A* can be used naturally of any two objects, whether they are long or short.

(15) A and B are both long.   A is longer than B.
                               B is shorter than A.

      A and B are both short.   A is longer than B.
                               B is shorter than A.

Comparatives like these are called **pseudocomparatives**. Suppose we make a contrast between longness, the property of being long, and length, the property of having linear extent (whether long or short). The pseudocomparative *longer* can be used to relate two short objects because it relates different degrees of length or linear extent rather than different degrees of longness. Then the two underlined morphemes in (16) have different senses, 'linear extent' in (16a) and 'longness' in (16b).

(16)a A and B are both short, but A is <u>long</u>er than B.
   b It is <u>long</u>.

Another set of antonyms, termed **overlapping antonyms** by Cruse, is largely based on the *good/bad* opposition, and includes evaluative terms such as *pretty/plain, kind/cruel,* and *polite/rude.* In this set the positive pole comparative is a pseudocomparative and the negative pole comparative is a true comparative, for example:

(17)a   A and B are both rude, but A is more polite than B.
   b   A and B are both rude, but B is ruder than A.
   c   A and B are both polite, but A is more polite than B.
   d # A and B are both polite, but B is ruder than A.

There isn't really a neutral term for a property covered by the whole *polite/ rude* scale, but suppose there is such a property – call it 'demeanour'. Then the pseudocomparative *more polite* means 'a greater degree of demeanour' rather than 'a greater degree of politeness', and can be used of polite or rude people, while the true comparative *ruder* means 'a greater degree of rudeness' and can only be used of rude people.
   There are also **equipollent antonyms**, including *hot/cold, nice/nasty,* and *happy/sad.* Both poles of equipollent antonyms form true comparatives.

(18)a   A and B are both nice, but A is nicer than B.
   b # A and B are both nice, but B is nastier than A.
   c   A and B are both nasty, but B is nastier than A.
   d # A and B are both nasty, but A is nicer than B.

Here niceness and nastiness are not coded as poles on a continuous scale but as distinct properties. If something is nice it can't be said to have any degree of nastiness, and vice versa.
   Hot and *cold* form a mixed scale. They resemble equipollent antonyms because they fit the pattern shown in (18). But *hot* and *cold* also resemble typical polar antonyms in describing a measurable property with a neutral term *temperature,* so one might expect *hot* and *cold* to form pseudocomparatives, as pseudocomparatives are typical of polar antonyms. In this case the pseudocomparatives would express greater or lesser degrees of temperature, rather than of heat or cold (that is, hotness or coldness). In fact, pseudocomparatives on the temperature scale are formed from the intermediate terms *warm* and *cool.*

(19)   A and B are both hot:
                   A is hotter than B   'a greater degree of hotness'
                   B is cooler than A   'a lesser degree of temperature'
               #   B is colder than A

       A and B are both cold:
                   A is colder than B   'a greater degree of coldness'
                   B is warmer than A   'a greater degree of temperature'
               #   B is hotter than A.

Other major sense relations studied in traditional lexical semantics are
synonymy, hyponymy and meronymy. If A and B are **synonyms** they have
the same sense – in fact true lexical synonymy is rare, but *oculist* and *eye-doctor* are candidates for synonymy. If A is a **hyponym** of B then an A is a
kind of B. *Dachshund*, *spaniel* and *terrier* are hyponyms of *dog*. If A is a
meronym of B then an A is part of a B. *Finger* and *palm* are meronyms of
hand; *sole, heel, upper, tongue* and *insole* are meronyms of *shoe*.

1.2.2   Semantic Features

Word senses may also be analysed in terms of sense components, also called
semantic markers or **semantic features**, particularly those which determine
classifications like the system illustrated in (20).

(20)

human	man	woman	child	girl	boy
horse	stallion	mare	foal	filly	colt
sheep	ram	ewe	lamb		
cattle	bull	cow	calf		
swan	cob	pen	cygnet		
pig	boar	sow	piglet		
hare	buck	doe	leveret		
deer	buck	doe	fawn		
cat	tom	queen	kitten		
dog	dog	bitch	puppy		

All the terms in the system can be defined in terms of species and the
components or features ADULT/JUVENILE and MALE/FEMALE. So,
for example, the word *stallion* might be defined as [EQUINE, ADULT,
MALE], *lamb* as [OVINE, JUVENILE] and *pig* as [PORCINE].

1.2.3   Basic Category Words

Word sets like those in (20) demonstrate the plausibility of the semantic
components MALE/FEMALE and ADULT/JUVENILE, but components

like EQUINE and PORCINE are more controversial. Given that the property of being equine is simply the property of being a horse, if EQUINE is a semantic marker then it must be the whole content of the word *horse*. Intuitively this seems mistaken, as the sense of the word *horse* is felt to be far more complex than such an analysis would indicate.

In fact, the sense of basic category words such as *horse*, *pig* and *bird* is difficult to analyse further. Take a dictionary definition for *horse*:

> a solid-footed perissodactyl quadruped (*Equus caballus*), having a flowing mane and tail; its voice is a neigh. In the domestic state used as a beast of burden and draught, and especially for riding upon.
> (*Shorter Oxford English Dictionary*, 3rd edn, reprinted 1968, p. 923)

The three types of information given here – zoological classification, physical description and general information – would also appear under *horse* in an encyclopaedia. Information listed in an encyclopaedia is offered as general knowledge about <u>things in the world</u>, in this case about horses, while information listed in a dictionary is offered as information about <u>words and their senses</u>. With species terms it is very difficult to separate encyclopaedic knowledge about the thing denoted from dictionary knowledge about the sense of the word – there seems to be no separately statable sense which is not simply a description of the typical object.

In cases like these the definition given is a bit like ostensive definition rather than definition by sense matching. The information given, particularly the species' Latin name *Equus caballus*, identifies what the word *horse* denotes. If you aren't familiar with the zoological classification, the information 'solid-footed ... quadruped ... , having a flowing mane and tail; ... used as a beast of burden and draught, and especially for riding upon' might be enough to single out horses, and you can then conclude that the word *horse* denotes that kind of animal. Arguably, this is what the word *horse* means – it means little more than that it has a certain denotation, similarly with words like *pig* and *bird*. To say what *horse* means is to say what a horse is, and ultimately this can only be done by a kind of ostension – 'a horse is one of those'.

If the sense of words like *horse*, *pig* and *bird* is little more than the fact of having a certain denotation, there must be some other role for all the information which seems to attach to these words. The point is easily illustrated with *bird*.

(21) *BIRD* 1 flies, has wings
        2 sings sweetly
        3 is small and light
        4 lays eggs in a nest
        5 is timid

Points 1–3 are quite likely to come to mind as components of the sense of *bird*, particularly because these properties are the basis of metaphors and similes such as *fly/sing like a bird*. But although these seem to be obvious bird properties not all birds have them. Many birds do not fly (kiwi, ostrich, emu, pukeko, moa, takahe, penguin), many birds are not small and light (Emperor penguin, moa, ostrich, emu) and many birds do not sing sweetly. Not all birds are timid – swans, geese and magpies can be very aggressive.

These properties of birds contrast strongly with semantic components such as MALE/FEMALE and ADULT/JUVENILE, which are always present in any use of a word containing them. 'This is a stallion' entails 'This is male' and 'This is adult', and 'This is a piglet' entails 'This is juvenile'. The bird features, on the other hand, are not always present with the word – 'This is a bird' does not entail 'This flies' or 'This sings sweetly'. The contrast indicates that the bird features listed in (21) are features of a cognitive concept, not semantic features of a word sense.

Findings in cognitive psychology indicate that mental concepts of concrete entities such as birds are structured around prototypes. The central bird prototype, for example, is a generalized average or prototypical bird. The prototypical bird flies and sings, has a fairly small roundish body and round head, a small beak, short legs and dull-coloured plumage. Real birds fall at various distances from the prototype depending on their similarity to that prototype. Thrushes, sparrows, starlings and blackbirds are close to the prototype. Birds like parrots, turkeys, emus, flamingos, cranes, kiwis and penguins are further from the prototype in features like size, body shape, colour and lack of flight.

If you are asked to quickly visualize a bird, the chances are that you will visualize something near the prototype, such as a sparrow, or the prototype itself, which isn't any particular bird species. If you are shown pictures of assorted objects including birds and asked to pick out those that are birds, it takes a moment longer to recognize non-prototypical birds, such as flamingos or penguins, as birds, even though they are well known. The prototype is like a mental template for recognizing birds which works better (or faster) for some birds than for others.

Were we to identify conceptual prototypes with word senses, we would be led to conclude that senses themselves reflect the inner grading which ranks sparrows and thrushes as more birdlike than emus and turkeys. One might say that a sparrow is 100 per cent a bird but a turkey is only 70 per cent a bird, or that the statement *This turkey is a bird* is only 70 per cent true.

However, this conclusion seems to confuse prototypes with **vague predicates**, such as *bald*, *crowd* or *orange*. How many hairs can a bald man have and still be bald? How small can a group of people be and still be a crowd? Vague predicates have undefined boundaries. Suppose you have a coloured ribbon which is red at one end and yellow at the other, changing gradually from one shade to the other through the length of the ribbon. The middle zone is orange. There is no clear-cut boundary between orange and red or between orange and yellow. The region bordered by yellow on one side and orange on the other is likely to be called 'yellowy-orange' or 'orangey-yellow' or 'halfway between yellow and orange'. It isn't quite true to call the colour 'yellow' but it isn't quite false either – it's yellow to some extent.

Birds are different. A turkey is a bird – it is 100 per cent a bird. If it were only 70 per cent a bird, what would the other 30 per cent of it be? Either a thing is a bird or it isn't. The slight delay in recognizing a turkey as a bird compared with recognizing a sparrow is not like the decision of whether or not orangey-yellow is yellow. Despite the momentary hesitation, once you realize that a turkey is a bird you are absolutely certain of it, but you cannot ever be certain that orangey-yellow is not yellow, or that it is yellow – there is no sure conclusion to be reached.

The mental concept *BIRD* may be compared to the dictionary entry for *horse* quoted earlier. Both the concept and the dictionary entry give information about a word's denotation or information about a kind and its instances, but these are not the same as senses. For words like these a sense distinct from denotation is very difficult to define. To know the meanings of these words is to know what objects they denote. To know further facts about those objects, such as that horses are used for riding upon, is to have more general knowledge about the world. Searching for the senses of many categorematic words leads us to mental concepts, which are not themselves senses, or to denotations. The pure sense, if any, is elusive.

1.2.4 Family Resemblances

A different kind of problem for sense analysis arises with words like *game*, which the philosopher Ludwig Wittgenstein described in terms of **family resemblances**. The activities which are called games do not have any features common to all, but a number of different features occur in certain clusters of games, for example:

(22) soccer, basketball, hurling, etc.
       rules for play
       competition/contest
       scoring system
       physical skill/strategy
       pastime

       chess
       rules for play
       competition/contest
       mental skill/strategy
       pastime

bridge, mah jong, poker, backgammon, etc.
rules for play
competition/contest
scoring system
mental skill/strategy
pastime
commonly with gambling – rules for play may specify payments

roulette
scoring system
chance – no skill
pastime
gambling

young children's games (18 months–3 years)
physical activity
pastime? (not a recreation from work)

psychobabble 'games' (e.g. Poor Little Me, I'm Only Trying to Help,
   etc.)
rules for play?
competition/strategy
pastime?

Although many of the features, such as 'competition', 'rules for play' and
'pastime', are recurrent, no one feature must occur in all types of game.
'Pastime' seems to be a defining feature of *game* in uses like 'This isn't a
game, you know!' (implying 'This is serious' or 'This is work'), but it isn't
a necessary feature of the many games in the first three groups which can be
played professionally, in which case they ARE work.

   The distinction between *game* and *sport* is difficult to define. Despite their
other similarities, archery is a sport but darts is a game. The Olympic Games
originally included only events commonly described nowadays as sports but
not as games (for example, discus, javelin, foot races), and the events which
are described as games (hockey, netball) were later additions, but all are
competitive sporting events. Perhaps the difference is that games tend to
have a greater mental strategy component than sports and more detailed
rules for play, rather than just the exercise of physical strength and skill, but
this characterization of games clearly cannot apply to games of the roulette
type. The casino industry promotes use of the term *gaming* as a euphemism
for gambling, and it may be that use of the word *game* is euphemistic or
trivializing in other instances as well.

   Wittgenstein suggested that the different activities which come under
game are related by family resemblances, just as different physical features
may make members of a family alike as a group although no feature is

shared by all. A resembles B, B resembles C, A does not really resemble C, but nevertheless they are alike overall.

It might seem that *game* is polysemous. A **polysemous** word has two or more distinct but related meanings, so polysemy is akin to ambiguity. For example, senses of the word *fork* cluster around two main centres. The first is the shape of the letter 'Y', exemplified by a fork in the road, a fork in a tree or tree branch, a forked tongue, forked lightning, and so on. The other sense is 'implement or tool with sharp tines' exemplified by kitchen forks, garden forks, pitchforks, and so on. The two senses are related by a loose similarity of shape, but the uses of the word fall into two clearly defined senses.

The different uses of *game* are clearly related to each other, like uses of *fork*, but unlike *fork*, the uses of *game* do not fall into clear clusters illustrating the presence of precisely definable alternative senses. We can sort individual games themselves into clusters according to their salient characteristics, but we can't give a plausible paraphrase of the sense of *game* each group illustrates. We cannot identify a determinate sense or cluster of senses for *game*.

1.2.5 Review of Lexical Sense

As I said earlier, sense seems to be more basic to 'real' meaning than denotation, as the actual denotation of an expression depends on what the sense of the expression is. For example, the expression *Mr Muscle Beach* denotes Josh Minamoto in 1994 because the sense or descriptive content of *Mr Muscle Beach* accurately describes Josh in that year. The denotation relationship – *Mr Muscle Beach* denotes Josh Minamoto – can't be established without going through the link established by the sense or descriptive content of the expression.

Given that sense is prior to denotation, it seems that the search for the nature of meaning in general should focus on sense, rather than on denotation, and denotation will follow on. But as the preceding section illustrates, the analysis of sense can be very uncertain.

Some areas of vocabulary, such as sense relations like antonymy, or word sets classified by species, age and gender, yield quite plausible analyses of their senses up to a point. For other areas of vocabulary, however, word senses are difficult to determine. Family resemblance terms like *game* reveal no basic sense components common to all uses. It seems that the sense of words like *game* cannot be more closely defined than to say, for example, that the sense of *game* is whatever determines for any activity whether or not that activity is a game. What this is, exactly, cannot be isolated. Differences like the *darts/archery* contrast suggest that this may be partly a matter of customary usage rather than principle.

With words for basic species, like *bird*, candidates for sense components are more likely to be components of mental concepts, which are not the same as senses. It may be that words like *bird, horse* and *pig* have no determinate sense beyond what might be expressed as [AVIAN], [EQUINE], and [POR-CINE], which are just abbreviated ways of expressing '*bird* denotes birds', *horse* denotes horses', and '*pig* denotes pigs'.

Given problems like these, the most widely used formal semantic theories today are not based on the traditional notion of sense, but define meaning in terms of denotation. Denotational theories are discussed in the next section.

An important alternative approach to linguistic meaning focuses on the cognitive character of human language, and explores the mental concepts associated with linguistic expressions. Recommended readings in this area are given at the end of this chapter.

1.3   DENOTATIONAL THEORIES

1.3.1   Denotations

A long-standing and influential view about language is that the meaningful-ness of language amounts to its 'aboutness'. Words and expressions symbol-ize and describe – and are thus about – things and phenomena in the world around us, and this is why we can use language to convey information about reality. Accordingly, the meaningfulness of language consists of connections between words and expressions and parts of reality.

As we saw earlier, the part of reality a linguistic expression is connected with is the expression's denotation.

A **name**, such as *Midge, Rinny,* or *Keeper* has the thing it refers to as its denotation. Suppose that the names in (23) all refer to dogs.

(23)   name: *Midge*
       denotation of *Midge* = Midge   (she is a small brown dog)

       name: *Rinny*
       denotation of *Rinny* = Rinny   (he is a fox terrier)

       name: *Keeper*
       denotation of *Keeper* = Keeper   (he is a faithful hound)

Names don't describe the things they refer to. Most personal names are coded as male or female by convention, but the convention can be broken, as in the case of the American actress Michael Learned, who has a first name usually given to boys; female forms of the name include *Michaela* and *Michelle*. Names which are based on meaningful expressions don't have to be given to people who fit the meaning; an ugly man can be called *Beau-regard* and a blonde woman can be called *Melanie*. In short, the apparent descriptive content that some names have isn't relevant to their denotation.

In contrast to names, descriptive words like *brown, coughs, skyscraper, indignant* can only denote things that they do describe – words like these, which are categorematic, are called **predicates**. Predicates are mainly expressed by nouns, adjectives and verbs, and their denotations are the sets of things they apply to or are true of, for example:

(24)   word (noun): *dog*
        denotation of *dog* = the set of dogs

        word (adjective): *brown*
        denotation of *brown* = the set of brown things

        word (verb): *grin*
        denotation of *grin* = the set of creatures that grin

At first, this analysis for the meaning of predicates seems a bit thin. Take, for example, the meaning of *brown* as the set of brown things in the world. Is that all there is to it?

Suppose the world was exactly the way it is except for one detail a certain brown pottery bowl on a windowsill in Ladakh is blue instead of brown. If the world was like that instead of how it is, then the set of brown things would be different, but surely the word *brown* wouldn't have a different meaning. This seems to make the word meaning depend on accidents of fate. We want to take into account the way the word *brown* would relate to the world even if things were a bit different from the way they actually are.

We want to take into account not only the objects a predicate happens to apply to in fact, but also all the hypothetical objects that it would apply to, meaning what it does mean, if things were different. *Dog* applies to all actual dogs and hypothetical dogs, *grin* applies to all actual and hypothetical creatures that grin, and so on. We need to consider hypothetical versions of the whole of reality to state what individual predicates would apply to in virtue of their meaning. Words connect not only with the real world, but also with other possible worlds.

1.3.2   Possible Worlds, Extension and Intension

The term **possible worlds** is used in semantics for hypothetical ways reality might be or might have been. The way things actually are is the actual world, and it is included in the possible worlds because it is obviously a possible reality. A possible world different from the actual world is a whole alternative universe, not just an alternative version of Planet Earth. There are infinitely many possible worlds.

Many possible worlds have dogs in them, which the word *dog* applies to. We can collect together all the dogs in the real world to form the set of all

real dogs – this set is the **extension** of *dog*. To get closer to what we think of
as the 'real meaning' of the word *dog* we need the **intension**, which is the set
of all dogs in all possible worlds, or simply, the set of all possible dogs. This
comprises the full possible range of doghood. So there are two kinds of
denotation for predicates:

(25)   word (noun): *dog*
       extension: the set of all dogs in the actual world
       intension: the set of all dogs in all possible worlds

       word (adjective): *brown*
       extension: the set of all brown things in the actual world
       intension: the set of all brown things in all possible worlds

       word (verb): *grin*
       extension: the set of all creatures that grin in the actual world
       intension: the set of all creatures that grin in all possible worlds

1.3.3   Truth Conditions

The analysis of sentences centres on declarative sentences – declarative
sentences are the sort that can be used to make statements.

For example, we need to establish how the whole sentence *Midge is
grinning* connects with the world. The sentence describes part of the world,
if in fact it is the case that Midge is grinning. If she is, the sentence is true. To
find out whether the sentence is true you have to know what it means so that
you can identify which facts are relevant: in this case, you have to find Midge
and check her facial expression.

So a sentence is true or false depending on whether or not its meaning
'matches' the way reality is. If you know the relevant facts about reality and
you know what a sentence means, then you know whether it is true or false.
If you know what a sentence means and you know that it is true, then you
know the relevant facts. If you know a certain fact, and you know that the
truth of a particular true sentence depends precisely on this fact, then you
know what that sentence means.

Extensions and intensions for sentences establish connections with reality
in terms of truth. They work a little differently from extensions and intensions for predicates. The **extension of a sentence** is its **truth value** – that is,
either true or false, depending on whether or not the sentence is true in the
actual world. The **intension of a sentence** is the set of all possible worlds in
which that sentence is true, for example:

(26)   **sentence**: *Midge is grinning*
       extension: truth value (true or false) in the actual world
       intension: the set of all possible worlds in which *Midge is grinning* is true

The intension of a sentence is also called the **truth set** for the sentence.

In theories of this kind the sense of a predicate is analysed as its intension. Correspondingly, a sentence intension (or truth set) stands for the sense, or meaning, of a sentence, which seems odd – how can the meaning of a sentence be a set of universes? The example *Midge is grinning*, if true, directly describes a state of affairs in the actual world of Midge having a certain expression on her face. Why isn't that state of affairs the semantic value of the sentence?

A few more examples will show that the actual world is not enough to pin down a sentence meaning, and that other worlds are also needed.

Suppose the sentences below are true, and think of the situations they relate to.

(27)a Midge isn't purple.
   b Midge isn't white.

First locate the situations – presumably they are wherever Midge is. Now, how can you tell the difference by looking at the world between Midge's not being purple and Midge's not being white? The actual situation of Midge's being brown gives you the truth of both (27a) and (27b). The sentence meanings can't be told apart just from looking at the actual world, in which they are both true. But they can be separated if all the possible worlds are brought into play.

There are possible worlds containing Midge in which she is purple – call the set of all those worlds WP. Then there are worlds in which she is white – call the set of all those worlds WW. Now *Midge isn't purple* is true not only in the actual world, but also in every other possible world containing Midge except the worlds in WP. Similarly, *Midge isn't white* is true in all possible worlds containing Midge – including the actual world – except the worlds in WW. So although these two situations can't be told apart in a single situation where they coincide, they can be distinguished if we consider all the worlds where those situations occur. The truth set for *Midge isn't purple* is a different set from the truth set for *Midge isn't white*, which shows that the two sentences have different meanings.

The worlds in which the situation of Midge's not being purple occurs are the worlds in which *Midge isn't purple* is true – in other words, the intension or truth set of *Midge isn't purple*. The truth set for *Midge isn't purple* is like a complete specification of every possible version of a situation of that kind, combined with every other possible way that reality, apart from Midge's colour, might have been. The truth set for *Midge isn't purple* will be different from the truth set for any other factual sentence, unless it means the same thing. (A factual sentence is any sentence which is true or false according to how things actually are.)

Sentence X in (28) stands in for any factual sentence at all that does not mean the same as *Midge isn't purple*. Whatever sentence X is, there will always be at least one world where one of these combinations of truth values occurs:

(28)   Sentence X   *Midge isn't purple*

     true   false
     false   true

Suppose that sentence X is *Midge is coloured*. Then in all the worlds where Midge is purple, *Midge isn't purple* is false and *Midge is coloured* is true. Suppose sentence X is *Midge is green*. In any world where Midge is brown, *Midge is green* is false and *Midge isn't purple* is true.

So long as they differ by at least one world, the truth sets or intensions for two sentences are different, and the sentences have different meanings. This argument applies to any factual sentence at all in the place of sentence X. *Midge isn't purple* has a different intension, by at least one world, from any other factual sentence – it is unique. If a factual sentence turns out to have the same intension as *Midge isn't purple* then it has the same meaning. *Midge n'est pas violette* and *Midge ist nicht violett* are sentences with the same intension as *Midge isn't purple*.

Using all the possible worlds, we can also deal with *Midge is purple*. Given that Midge is brown, this sentence is false, and doesn't match up to any situation in reality. Even if we locate Midge in reality, as we have seen, her brownness is evidence for the falsity of *Midge is green* or *Midge is yellow* just as much as for *Midge is purple* – the actual world has no particular relationship with any false sentence, and can't help us pin down its meaning. To give the meaning of *Midge is purple* (or any false sentence) we need the set of all worlds where it is true.

To say that a sentence is true if and only if a certain circumstance or state of affairs is actually the case is to state the conditions under which the sentence is true. Accordingly, to state the required circumstance is to state what is called the **truth condition** for a sentence. Many theories analyse sentence meaning in terms of truth conditions, and such theories are called **truth-conditional theories**. Theories which analyse meaning in terms of referring to, denoting or describing things, situations and events in the world (or in possible worlds) are **denotational theories**. Most formal semantic theories are both denotational and truth-conditional.

So far, the tools we have to analyse meaning are these: we have reality itself, also called the actual world, and all the infinitely many possible alternative ways reality might have been – these are the possible worlds (including the actual world). Given the possible worlds, we have both extensions and intensions for linguistic expressions.

- The **extension of a name** is its actual referent.

- The **extension of a predicate** is the set of things in actuality that the predicate applies to, or is true of.
- The **extension of a sentence** is its actual truth value, true or false.
- The **intension of a name** is its actual referent wherever it occurs in any possible world. (This point will be discussed further in Section 5.5.)
- The **intension of a predicate** is the set of all things the predicate is true of in all possible worlds.
- The **intension of a sentence** is the set of all worlds in which the sentence is true – the truth set or truth condition.

We saw earlier that lexical sense is quite difficult to pin down, and so it would be difficult (perhaps impossible) to come up with an analysis of the sense of every word in the language. Even if we could analyse all the word senses, it seems that different kinds of words would have different kinds of senses. This presents a problem for a theory of syntactic meaning, which needs some kind of uniform analysis for word meanings in general. Word meanings have to be analysed in a uniform way so that general rules for syntactic meaning can apply to all sentences of the same form, regardless of the individual words they contain.

As we have seen, extensions and intensions are uniform analyses of word meanings in terms of sets of things. In this kind of theory sense is analysed as intension. Even if intension is not absolutely the same as sense, and does not seem to capture the 'real meaning' of words, it is a good substitute for sense in theories which focus on structural meaning.

The next section illustrates a formal analysis of sentence meaning, showing how sentence meaning is composed from its parts.

1.3.4 A Simple Illustration of a Compositional Formal Theory

The basic expressions of the language are given with their denotations. For the sake of simplicity, here we use only one world, standing for the actual world. The semantic value of any expression x, written 'SVal(x)', is the extension. Tense is also ignored for now.

(29) *Midge*   SVal(*Midge*) = Midge
      Keeper SVal(*Keeper*) = Keeper
      barks   SVal(*barks*) = the set of creatures that bark
      grins   SVal(*grins*) = the set of creatures that grin

Syntactic rules for forming phrases and sentences are stated, along with semantic rules for interpreting the combinations formed.

(30) noun phrase (NP) → name
      verb phrase (VP) → intransitive verb (V)
      sentence (S)   → NP + VP

The following sentences are generated by the rules:

(31)a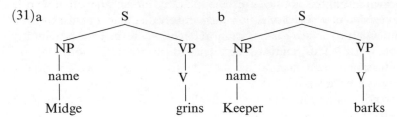

Here the interpretation for VP is the same as for V as no other expression is added – similarly for NP. The semantic rule for S in (32) states how the truth condition is calculated:

(32)   SVal(S) = true iff SVal(NP) ∈ SVal(VP)
       ('x ∈ A' is read as 'x is a member of A')

The rule in (32) is read as follows:

> The semantic value of S is 'true' if and only if the semantic value of NP is a member of the semantic value of VP.

Applying rule (32) to (31a) gives (33).

(33)   SVal(*Midge grins*) = true iff SVal(*Midge*) ∈ SVal(*grins*)

which reads as in (34).

(34)   The semantic value of *Midge grins* is 'true' if and only if the semantic value of *Midge* is a member of the semantic value of *grins*.

(34) is simplified to (35):

(35)   *Midge grins* is true if and only if Midge is a member of the set of creatures that grin.

Applying rule (32) to (31b) gives (36).

(36)   SVal(*Keeper barks*) = true iff SVal(*Keeper*) ∈ SVal(*barks*)

From (36) we get the truth condition shown in (37).

(37)   *Keeper barks* is true if and only if Keeper is a member of the set of creatures that bark.

If we add *and* to the lexicon we can generate complex sentences. *And* is syncategorematic, and is not given a semantic value alone. The semantic rule for *and* interprets *and* in construction with any two sentences. The syntactic and semantic rules for *and* are:

(38) S → S *and* S
      SVal(S$_1$ *and* S$_2$) = true iff SVal(S$_1$) = true and SVal(S$_2$) = true.

Now we can interpret *Midge barks and Keeper grins*.

(39)

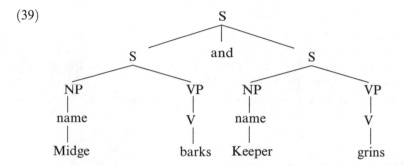

   SVal(*Midge barks and Keeper grins*) = true iff SVal(*Midge barks*) = true and SVal(*Keeper grins*) = true.

   SVal(*Midge barks*) = true and SVal(*Keeper grins*) = true iff SVal(*Midge*) ∈ SVal(*barks*) and SVal(*Keeper*) ∈ SVal(*grins*).

   Midge barks and Keeper grins is true if and only if Midge is a member of the set of creatures that bark and Keeper is a member of the set of creatures that grin.

This brief illustration shows the way semantic rules mirror syntactic rules, and sentence meanings are mapped compositionally from sentence structures. Most formal semantic theories concentrate on the compositional analysis of syntactic and syncategorematic meaning. The compositional mapping of sentence structures to sentence meanings is not discussed in any further detail in this book.

1.4 REVIEW

Semantics is a somewhat varied and divided field, partly because of the very different ways meaning itself can be defined. It may not be possible to form a synthesis of the sense-based, conceptual and denotational approaches to meaning, and the nature of meaning itself remains mysterious when we try to analyse it in more detail.

Part of the difficulty with finding an adequate theoretical answer to the question *What is meaning?* is that meaning itself is not a theoretical notion. The word *meaning* is part of the common language, and refers to WHAT-EVER, if anything, is the essential nature common to all individual expression meanings, such as the meaning of *pylorus*, the meaning of *coracle* and the meaning of *Don't put it there!* Frequently, common terms are not defined by the theories that seem to be about the phenomena that the terms refer to. For example, the hardness of a diamond and the softness of cornsilk are physical properties of matter, and physics is the science of matter, but the terms *hard* and *soft* are not technical terms in the science of physics, and physics does not define these terms.

In practice, sense, denotation, truth conditions and mental concepts are used to give accounts of individual meanings, and a unified definition of the word *meaning*, or analysis of meaning in general, is not forthcoming. This book is an introduction to properties of sentence meanings, drawing on analyses which are not generally confined to any particular theoretical framework, although a truth-conditional account of meaning is assumed.

FURTHER READING

On the nature of meaning, see introductions to general semantics. Recent textbooks include Allan (1986), Chierchia and McConnell-Ginet (1990), Frawley (1992), Larson and Segal (1995) and Saeed (1997).

Chierchia and McConnell-Ginet, and Larson and Segal are introductions to compositional formal theories.

Bach (1989) is an introduction to formal semantics.

Carston (1995) is an introductory summary of truth-conditional semantics.

For lexical semantics see Cruse (1986) and references cited there.

For an introduction to meaning and the mental representation of meaning see Chapter 11 in Clark and Clark (1977), Chapter 5 in Anderson (1995), and Chapter 18 in Johnson-Laird (1988).

Ungerer and Schmid (1996) is an accessible introduction to cognitive linguistics.

For conceptual semantics see particularly Jackendoff (1983), especially Chapters 1–3, Jackendoff (1988), Lakoff and Johnson (1980), and Lakoff (1987).

For a brief review of semantic theory see Ladusaw (1988), and ter Meulen (1988) for a review of issues in the study of meaning. General issues in semantic theory are also discussed in some of the readings listed at the end of Chapter 5.

For pragmatics, see Chapter 11 of this book and references given there.

Encyclopaedias and dictionaries of linguistics and philosophy are very useful to clarify key terms and concepts.

2 First Order Logic

2.1 REPRESENTATIONS FOR MEANINGS

To discuss the meanings of sentences and other expressions, we need a way to represent them. Sentences written in ordinary writing are not reliable representations of their meanings, as written forms do not always capture sameness and difference of meaning, for example:

(1)a Rameses ruled Egypt.
   b Egypt was ruled by Rameses.
   c Visiting relatives can be boring.
   d Visiting relatives can be boring.

Sentences (1a,b) have different written forms but the same meaning. Sentences (1c,d) have the same written form but different meanings – one means 'Relatives who are visiting one can be boring' and the other means 'It can be boring to visit relatives'. So we need to represent meanings directly, and for this we shall use a notation based on first order logic.

Logic is chiefly concerned with relationships between meanings, particularly the meanings of declarative sentences, in processes of reasoning. The meaning of a declarative sentence – the kind that can be used to make a statement and can be true or false – is a **proposition**. To explore how propositions are related to each other in reasoning, logic analyses their inner structure. **Propositional logic** analyses certain ways of combining propositions to form complex propositions. The expressions which are used to combine propositions are the connectives, discussed in Section 2.2. **Predicate logic** analyses the inner structure of simple propositions, which are formed of predicates and their arguments, discussed in Section 2.3, and may also contain quantifiers, which are discussed in Section 2.4.

2.2 THE LOGICAL CONNECTIVES

The logical connectives combine propositions to form more complex propositions in ways which correspond to certain uses of *and*, *or*, and *if*. We begin with conjunction.

2.2.1 Conjunction

Conjunction is expressed by certain uses of *and*, illustrated below.

(2) Moira left and Harry stayed behind.

In this sentence *and* joins the two sentences *Moira left* and *Harry stayed behind*. The whole sentence is true if both the joined sentences are true, and false otherwise. That is, it is false if they both left, or both stayed behind, or if Harry left and Moira stayed behind. This pattern holds for any two sentences joined by *and*: the truth value for the whole sentence depends on the truth values for the parts.

(3)a   Alfred sings alto and Paul sings bass.
    b   There were lights showing and the door stood open.
    c   The airport was closed and all ferry trips were cancelled.

This general pattern is characteristic of logical connectives, which are **truth-functional**: the truth value for a complex proposition formed with a truth-functional connective can be calculated simply from the truth values of the joined propositions, without referring to the content of the propositions.

Most natural language expressions for connecting sentences are not truth-functional. The difference can be illustrated with *because*, as in (4).

(4)a   Jill was late for work because her car broke down.
    b   Jill was late for work because she was caught in a traffic jam.

Suppose that Jill was late for work, her car broke down, and she was caught in a traffic jam, so the component propositions in (4a) and (4b) are true. In fact, Jill's car broke down long before she had to leave for work so she took a taxi, and if it hadn't been for the traffic jam she would have arrived on time, so (4a) is false and (4b) is true. We can't calculate the truth or falsity of (4a,b) simply by knowing whether or not the component propositions are true. We have to know the CONTENT of the propositions combined by *because* to judge whether or not the circumstances described in the *because*-proposition really caused the circumstances described in the other proposition. In short, the truth of a proposition with *because* depends on more than just the truth or falsity of the propositions which are combined, so *because* is not truth-functional.

Propositional logic deals with truth-functional expressions. Four of these, including conjunction, are connectives, because they connect two propositions. Propositional logic also deals with negation because it is truth-functional as we shall see below, although it does not combine propositions and therefore is not strictly a connective.

The conjunction connective is written with the symbol '&' or '∧'. The symbol '&' is used in this book. Propositions are represented by **propositional variables**, traditionally *p* and *q*, with *r* and *s* added if needed. Complex propositions formed by conjunction are also called conjunctions. Conjunctions in general are represented by the formula *p&q*, where *p* and *q* stand for any proposition.

We can list all the possible combinations of truth values for p and q and give the corresponding truth value for the conjunction p&q. In effect, this defines the meaning of the conjunction connective. Such a definition is given in the form of a table called a **truth table**.

(5) Truth table for conjunction

p	q	p&q
T	T	T
T	F	F
F	T	F
F	F	F

The order in which p and q are expressed makes no difference to the truth value. The propositions p&q and q&p are **equivalent**: p&q always has the same truth value as q&p, for any combination of truth values for p and q. This doesn't hold for all uses of the word *and*, but it does hold for the examples in (2) and (3), repeated here.

(6)a Moira left and Harry stayed behind.
    Harry stayed behind and Moira left.

  b Alfred sings alto and Paul sings bass.
    Paul sings bass and Alfred sings alto.

  c There were lights showing and the door stood open.
    The door stood open and there were lights showing.

  d The airport was closed and all ferry trips were cancelled.
    All ferry trips were cancelled and the airport was closed.

The conjunction connective only connects propositions, expressed by sentences, but the word *and* can connect a wide range of types of expression. Some of the sentences in which *and* connects expressions smaller than sentences can be analysed as conjunction reduction, illustrated below. **Conjunction reduction** is a linguistic abbreviation for what is logically a conjunction of whole propositions.

(7)a [Moira and Harry] left.
  b Tom saw [Moira and Harry].
  c Moira was [changing her spark plugs and listening to talkback radio].

In (7a) and (7b) *and* connects two names, while in (7c) two verb phrases are joined. Sentences like these can be analysed as instances of linguistic abbreviation:

(8)a　*Moira and Harry left* expresses 'Moira left and Harry left'.
　　b　*Tom saw Moira and Harry* expresses 'Tom saw Moira and Tom saw Harry'.
　　c　*Moira was changing her spark plugs and listening to talkback radio* expresses 'Moira was changing her spark plugs and Moira was listening to talkback radio'.

Not all uses of *and* to join non-sentential expressions can be analysed as conjunction reduction. The commonest exception is the use of *and* to form a complex noun phrase which refers to a group, as in these examples.

(9)a　<u>Sally and Harry</u> met for lunch.
　　b　<u>Sally, Harry, Jeff and Buzz</u> met for lunch.
　　c　<u>Harry, Jeff and Buzz</u> surrounded Charles.
　　d　The gang met for lunch.
　　e　The forest surrounded the castle.

At first sight it looks as if (9a) could be analysed as a conjunction of propositions, 'Harry met Sally for lunch and Sally met Harry for lunch', but the other examples indicate that this won't work generally. In particular, (9d) indicates that it is the group as a whole which meets, and so the noun phrase *Sally, Harry, Jeff and Buzz* in (9b), for example, should be interpreted as referring to the whole group of people. Similarly, (9c) cannot be understood to mean 'Harry surrounded Charles and Jeff surrounded Charles and Buzz surrounded Charles', because 'Harry surrounded Charles' doesn't make sense – the three people as a group surrounded Charles. In these instances the word *and* is not a connective at all as it doesn't join sentences, but forms a complex noun phrase referring to a group, which as a whole performs the described action.

2.2.2　Negation

As above, negation is generally included with the logical connectives because it is truth-functional, being defined by a truth table. Simply, negation combines with a single proposition to reverse its truth value. The symbol for negation is '~'.

(10)　Truth table for negation

p	~p
T	F
F	T

Negation is expressed in several ways in English, most commonly by *not* or *n't* after the first auxiliary verb. For example, if *p* represents the proposition expressed by *Moira left*, then $\sim p$ is expressed by *Moira didn't leave*. If 'Moira left' is true, then 'Moira didn't leave' is false, and if 'Moira didn't leave' is true, then 'Moira left' is false.

2.2.3 Disjunction

The **disjunction** connective corresponds to the use of the word *or* which is commonly glossed as 'and/or' or described as 'inclusive disjunction'. The symbol for disjunction is the lowercase letter *v*.

(11)   Truth table for disjunction

p	q	pvq
T	T	T
T	F	T
F	T	T
F	F	F

A logical disjunction is true if either or both of the combined propositions is true.

Where two propositions joined by disjunction have some content in common, the sentence expressing the proposition (with the word *or*) is usually abbreviated in the form of **disjunction reduction**, much like conjunction reduction. For example, *That job will take two or three tins of paint, depending on the weather* is interpreted as 'That job will take two tins of paint or that job will take three tins of paint, depending on the weather.'

Inclusive disjunction ('and/or') corresponding to logical disjunction is illustrated in (12).

(12)   You can get there by train or bus
       ('You can get there by train or you can get there by bus')

This sentence is true if there is a bus link and no train link, or a train link and no bus link, or both a bus link and a train link. On the most usual reading both are available, although in any single journey you will choose one or the other.

The sentence in (12) can also be understood to express exclusive disjunction, commonly glossed as 'either/or', Sentence (12) with exclusive disjunction would express something like 'You can get there somehow, either by train or by bus, (but I can't remember which)'. Exclusive disjunction is also illustrated in (13).

(13)   The agent arrived in Berlin on the 9.25 or the 11.10.
       ('The agent arrived in Berlin on the 9.25 or the agent arrived in Berlin
       on the 11.10').

Here one or the other of the connected sentences is true, but not both. This
sentence cannot be understood to mean that the agent arrived on both
trains.

As the truth table indicates, logical disjunction is inclusive ('and/or',
'either or both'). The exclusive disjunction use of *or* ('either but not both')
can be represented by adding the qualification 'but not both' to logical
disjunction, for example:

(14)   p = you take the money
       q = you take the bag
       Either you take the money or you take the bag = (pvq) & ~(p&q).

Note here that brackets are used to indicate which proposition, simple or
complex, is combined by a particular connective or combined with negation.
The disjunction pvq is itself the first part of the whole conjunction. Negation
combines with the conjunction p&q, then the whole negative proposition
~(p&q) is the second part of the whole conjunction.

2.2.4   The Material Implication Connective

Conditionality is mainly expressed by certain uses of *if* or *if... then* –
sentences with *if* are called **conditional sentences** or conditionals for short.
There are two logical connectives corresponding to conditionals, the material implication connective and the biconditional connective, which is discussed in the next section. As we shall see, these two connectives only partly
fit the usual ways we understand *if* sentences.

The material implication connective is represented by the symbol '→'. The
proposition p in p→q is the **antecedent**, and q is the **consequent**. In a
conditional sentence the antecedent is the sentence to which *if* is attached,
although it may appear first or second in the whole sentence. For example, in
both sentences in (15) the antecedent is *if Marcia invited John/him* and the
consequent is *John/he will go*.

(15)a   If Marcia invited John, (then) he'll go.
    b   John will go if Marcia invited him.

The main point with implication is that where the antecedent is true, the
consequent must also be true. If the antecedent is true and the consequent is
false, then the whole implication is false. So the first two lines of the truth
table for implication are:

p	q	p→q
T	T	T
T	F	F

The remaining lines of the truth table, where the antecedent is false, are not so clearly related to ordinary uses of *if*. Where the antecedent is false the implication is true no matter what the truth value of the consequent, as shown in the full truth table below.

(16) Truth table for material implication

p	q	p→q
T	T	T
T	F	F
F	T	T
F	F	T

Using the example in (15), the lines of the truth table give these truth values:

(17) p = Marcia invited John
q = John will go
p→q = If Marcia invited John, he'll go

Line 1: Marcia did invite John and John will go: the implication is true.

Line 2: Marcia did invite John, but actually John won't go: the implication is false.

Line 3: Marcia didn't invite John, but he will go anyway: the implication is true.

Line 4: Marcia didn't invite John and John won't go: the implication is true.

Lines 1 and 2 give the results we would expect from the ordinary use of *if*. Line 3 seems odd. If John will go (to some understood destination) whether Marcia invited him or not, why bother to say 'if Marcia invited John' at all? All that is communicated here is 'John will go'. In fact, an utterance of *If Marcia invited John, he'll go* is more likely to be intended to mean 'If Marcia invites John he'll go, but not otherwise' – explicitly, 'If Marcia invited John he'll go, and if she didn't invite him, he won't go'. On this reading the whole sentence on line 3 should be false. This use of *if* is more like the biconditional connective, to be reviewed in Section 2.2.5.

The chief general difference between material implication and conditional sentences is that *if* is commonly not simply truth-functional in actual use. Given that material implication is truth-functional, the truth of an implication proposition depends only on a certain combination of truth values for the contained propositions, and the actual content or subject matter of those propositions is irrelevant. Logically, (18) expresses a perfectly fine (and true) implication, but it is odd as a conditional sentence.

(18)   If the number 1960 is divisible by 5 then 1960 was a leap year.

antecedent (1960 is divisible by 5)	true
consequent (1960 was a leap year)	true
implication	true

But many of us would dispute the truth of (18), because we don't calculate leap years by dividing by five. The problem here is that we frequently use *if... then* to express some **causal** relationship between the antecedent and consequent – the antecedent describes some event or state of affairs which causes what is described by the consequent – in other words, the consequent describes the consequences. Sentence (18) reads most naturally as stating that the status of 1960 as a leap year depends on the year's number being divisible by five, whereas in fact divisibility by four is the criterion for leap years. For the implication to be true, it is sufficient that the antecedent and consequent are both true. For the conditional sentence to be true as we normally understand it, the status of 1960 as a leap year would have to depend on, or be caused by, the fact that the number 1960 is divisible by 5.

These uses of *if* carry extra aspects of meaning, such as causality, but note that they also include the truth-value combinations given by the first two lines of the truth table. Even with the causal use of *if*, if the antecedent is true the consequent must also be true. For example, *If the number 1960 is divisible by 4 then 1960 was a leap year* expresses the causal connection accurately. In addition, given that the antecedent is true, the conditional is true only if the consequent is also true and 1960 was a leap year – if 1960 was not a leap year the conditional is false. That is, the causal meaning associated with *if* is extra content added to the meaning of logical implication.

There is a common rhetorical use of *if... then* that fits well with the logical analysis, requiring no causal or commonsense connection between the sentences, as illustrated in (19).

(19)   If that's a genuine Picasso then the moon is made of longlife food product

p = That's a genuine Picasso
q = The moon is made of longlife food product.

Assume (by conversational conventions discussed in Chapter 11) that a sentence like (19), when uttered, is taken as being true. The rhetorical device requires that the consequent be obviously false. This gives the combination of values:

(20)

p	q	p→q
?	F	T

Checking the truth table for implication, repeated here, we see that this combination of truth values occurs only on line 4, where the antecedent is false.

p	q	p→q
T	T	T
T	F	F
F	T	T
F	F	T

So this rhetorical device is used to convey that the antecedent is false. Here, (19) is used to convey that that's not a genuine Picasso. Routines of this form include the cliché *if... I'll eat my hat*.

The extra aspects of meaning found with *if*, such as causality, are generally analysed as a layer of meaning which is added to the literal meaning of *if* by pragmatic processes. Sentence conjunction with *and* is also commonly interpreted with extra pragmatic content, in addition to the truth-functional meaning of logical conjunction, which is assumed to be the core literal meaning of *and*. This issue is discussed further in Chapter 11. Other kinds of conditional are also discussed in Chapter 3.

2.2.5 Equivalence and the Biconditional Connective

The biconditional connective, represented by the symbol '↔' or '≡', expresses the relation of equivalence between propositions. Two propositions are equivalent if, in any given circumstances, they have the same truth value, either both true or both false. Accordingly, the biconditional p↔q is true if p and q have the same truth value, and otherwise false.

(21)   Truth table for equivalence/biconditional connective

p	q	p↔q
T	T	T
T	F	F
F	T	F
F	F	T

The corresponding English expression is *if and only if*, often abbreviated in writing to *iff*. Unlike *and*, *or* and *if*, these paraphrases are not common English expressions, being largely confined to 'philosopher talk'. This relation is commonly used in technical contexts, particularly in statements of truth conditions:

(22)a   'Snow is white' is true if and only if snow is white.
   b   'Schnee ist weiss' is true if and only if snow is white.
   c   'La neige est blanche' is true if and only if snow is white.

In (22b), for example:

p = 'Schnee ist weiss' is true
q = snow is white

As we saw in Chapter 1, the truth set for q (the set of all possible worlds in which q is true) is the set of all the possible and actual circumstances of snow being white. The whole biconditional in (22b) asserts that 'Snow is white' and ' "Schnee ist weiss" is true' are either both true or both false in all circumstances, therefore in all possible worlds. Obviously the truth set for ' "Schnee ist weiss" is true' is the same as the truth set for 'Schnee ist weiss'. In effect, the sentence 'Schnee ist weiss' is true in exactly the same possible worlds as 'Snow is white', and therefore it has exactly the same truth set, or intension. In short, it has the same meaning.

The truth table for equivalence also appears to be part of the meaning of *if* in uses like (15), repeated here as (23a), and (23b), where the rider 'but not otherwise' is understood.

(23)a   If Marcia invited John he'll go.
   b   If you kick me again I'll punch you.

Take (23b):

p = you kick me again
q = I punch you

line 1: you kick me again and I punch you   true
line 2: you kick me again but I don't punch you   false
line 3: you don't kick me but I punch you anyway   false
line 4: you don't kick me and I don't punch you   true

What is added to the equivalence relation in this use of *if* is the notion of temporal sequence and causality – that is, the kicking happens before the punching and also causes the punching, as the punching is in response to the kicking. For example, line 1 would also apply if I punched you first and you kicked me in response, but the sentence *If you kick me again I'll punch you* is not understood in this way. As with other uses of *if* mentioned above, the extra content here, in addition to the truth-functional content, is generally considered to be pragmatic.

For review of this section, see the exercises in Part A at the end of the chapter.

2.3 PREDICATES AND ARGUMENTS

The internal structure of the most simple kind of proposition, an **atomic proposition**, consists of a predicate and its argument or arguments. We begin with so-called two-place predicates as an illustration.

(24)a   Brigitte is taller than Danny.
     b   Alex is Bill's henchman.
     c   Fiji is near New Zealand.

All of these sentences express a relationship between two entities. If we take out the expressions which refer to entities, we are left with the part that expresses the relationship – this part expresses the **predicate**.

(25)a   ... is taller than ...
     b   ... is ...'s henchman.
     c   ... is near ...

In each of these sequences there is one main word which on its own indicates the nature of the relationship, or the content of the predicate. In the notation to be used here the symbol for the predicate is based on the main word, omitting tense, copula *be*, and some prepositions. The entities bound in a relationship by the predicate are its **arguments**, referred to in these examples by names. By convention, names are represented by lowercase letters. The formulae for the sentences in (24) are

(26)   TALLER (b, d)
     HENCHMAN (a, b)
     NEAR (f, n)

These examples illustrate some of the main points about logical predicates.

First, predicates are semantically 'incomplete' if considered in isolation. It isn't possible to paraphrase or explain the meaning of one of these predicates without including the notion of there being two entities involved in any situation where the predicate applies.

Secondly, each predicate has a fixed number of arguments. These predicates must have exactly two arguments to form a coherent proposition – no more and no fewer – hence they are two-place predicates. The argument 'slots' are part of the predicate's meaning.

Predicates are commonly used elliptically in natural language, with one of the arguments not explicitly mentioned. For example, one might say simply 'Brigitte is taller' or 'Alex is a faithful henchman'. But the second, unmentioned argument in elliptical utterances like these is still understood in the expressed proposition. If Danny is a subject of conversation, 'Brigitte is taller' can be interpreted to mean 'Brigitte is taller than Danny'. In another context, it may be interpreted to mean that Brigitte is taller than she used to be. It isn't possible to be taller in isolation without being taller than some comparison standard, and it isn't possible (in modern English) to be a henchman without being someone's henchman. The second argument is still understood to be present in the proposition expressed.

The elliptical use of predicates found in natural language is not well formed in logic, and both the arguments of a two-place predicate must be represented in a logical formula. Although (27a,b) below can communicate complete propositions (because we can usually understand from the context what elements have been ellipted), (27c,d) are not well formed, and don't express propositions. Logical formulae themselves cannot be elliptical.

(27)a   Brigitte is taller.
   b   Alex is a faithful henchman.
   c   TALLER(b)
   d   HENCHMAN(a)

The unmentioned argument is usually clearly identified from the context. Even if no context is supplied with an example to give this information, the argument position can be filled by a general term, for now, *someone* or *something*, as in (28).

(28)a   TALLER (b, someone)
   b   HENCHMAN (a, someone)

The third point about predicates is that the order of the arguments in the formula is significant. Generally (but not always) the order of arguments in a logical representation is taken from the order of the corresponding expressions in the sentence, for example:

(29)a   Brigitte is taller than Danny.
      TALLER(b, d)

  b   Danny is taller than Brigitte.
      TALLER(d, b)

The predicates we looked at in Chapter 1, such as *dog, brown* and *barks,* are all one-place predicates. The most basic subject+predicate sentence of traditional grammar contains a one-place predicate, with the subject of the sentence expressing its single argument, as in (30).

(30)a   Zorba was Greek.   GREEK(z)
  b   Moby Grape is purple.   PURPLE(m)
  c   Perry is a lawyer.   LAWYER(p)
  d   Cyrus coughed.   COUGH(c)

Note that one- and two-place predicates can be expressed by a range of lexical categories, as illustrated in (31).

(31)   adjective: TALL PURPLE GREEK TALLER
      preposition: NEAR ON BESIDE
      noun: LAWYER DOG CORACLE
      verb: COUGH SEE READ

Three-place predicates (and four-place predicates, if there are any) are expressed by verbs, and perhaps by nouns derived from verbs.

Three-place predicates are commonly expressed by so-called double object verbs, for example:

(32)a   Richard gave Liz a diamond.   (double object)
  b   Richard gave a diamond to Liz.
  c   Marcia showed Clive the ad   (double object)
  d   Marcia showed the ad to Clive

      other three-place verbs: *tell, teach, send, pass, offer,* etc.

Although the two sentences in each pair have different word order, they have the same meaning. For examples like these, one word order must be chosen as the basis for the order of arguments in the logical representation – in this case, the order in (32b, d) is used, and the formulae are as in (33).

(33)a   GIVE (r, a diamond, l)   for (32a, b)
  b   SHOW (m, the ad, c)   for (32c, d)

Here two of the arguments are expressed by noun phrases which are not names – *a diamond* and *the ad.* Noun phrases like these are analysed in more detail in the next section and in Chapter 4.

There may not be any real four-place predicates in natural language, although in principle there is no limit on how many arguments a predicate can have. The reason for uncertainty over four-place predicates is covered in the next section.

A couple of likely candidates for four-place predicates are *buy* and *sell*.

(34)a   Marcia sold the car to Clive for $200.
         SELL(m, the car, c, $200)

   b   Clive bought the car from Marcia for $200.
         BUY(c, the car, m, $200)

2.3.1   Predicates, Verbs and the Number of Arguments

As we saw earlier, every predicate has a fixed number of arguments which must be present in a well-formed proposition, and accordingly, a logical form must represent all the arguments of each predicate. Natural language allows for elliptical forms like those in (27a, b), where an argument of the predicate need not be expressed in the sentence, although its presence in the proposition is still understood. Other examples of ellipsis are in (35).

(35)a   Will you pour out?   (the tea)
   b   I gave at the office   (money, to your charity)
   c   Add meat to pan and sauté lightly.   (you, the meat)

On the other hand, there is a general axiom in syntactic theory that all syntactic arguments of verbs (and possibly of other predicates) are obligatory, and must be expressed in a well-formed sentence. Ellipsis is a special exception to this general rule. This principle may be used to test whether or not a phrase is an argument of the verb, for example:

(36)a   Al put the groceries away/on the bench.
   b   * Al put the groceries.

The asterisk before (36b) indicates that the sentence is ill-formed. A sentence with the verb *put* requires a locative phrase expressing where something is put. Sentence (36b) lacks a locative expression and is ill-formed, in contrast to (36a). This is generally taken as evidence that the locative expression is obligatory with *put* and therefore is an argument of *put*. Roughly, an expression which can be omitted without making the sentence ill-formed is not an argument of the predicate. The converse is illustrated in (37).

(37)a   We planned the weekend the other night.
   b   We planned the weekend.

Of the two noun phrases *the weekend* and *the other night*, both referring to intervals of time, only the first is an argument of *plan*. The second noun phrase can be left out, and is not an argument.

The general principle that the syntactic arguments of verbs are obligatory has a number of apparent counter-examples falling into two main groups.

The first group are elliptical sentences. A possible strategy for at least some of these sentences is to include a sort of 'silent pronoun' in the syntactic structure of the sentence to fill the argument slot. This allows the obligatory argument principle to be maintained, as the silent pronoun counts as an expression of the argument in question, even though it is not pronounced. What it refers to is provided by the context, as is commonly the case with pronouns like *he*, *she*, *they*, etc.

Counter-examples of the second kind show what is called **variable adicity**. The **adicity** of a predicate is the number of arguments it takes, derived from the terms *monadic* (= one-place), *dyadic* (= two-place), *triadic* (= three-place), and so on. Verbs with variable adicity seem to have variable numbers of arguments in different sentences, for example:

(38)		
a	They showed the film to the censor on Tuesday	3
b	They showed the film on Tuesday	2
c	He served the soup to the guests first.	3
d	He served the soup first.	2
e	He served the guests first.	2
f	She wrote a letter.	2
g	She wrote him a letter.	3
h	She made a sandwich.	2
i	She made him a sandwich.	3

Discussing data like these, linguists refer informally to optional arguments, although strictly speaking an argument is obligatory by definition. Indispensability is part of what it is to be an argument.

An alternative is to maintain that all arguments are indeed obligatory, and that the sentence groups above do not contain the same verb – for example, the verb *show* in (38a), which has three arguments, is not the same as the two-argument verb *show* in (38b). Although this option protects the obligatoriness principle, it conflicts with the common intuition that the sentence groups do contain the same verb, and it carries the consequence that many common verbs must be classed as highly ambiguous.

For the present purposes, phrases which appear to be so-called optional arguments, in that they are argument-like in meaning but can be omitted, will be analysed as arguments in logical forms.

We are uncertain about the existence of four-place predicates because verbs like *buy* and *sell* have variable adicity.

(39)a Marcia sold the car to Clive for $200.
   b Marcia sold the car for $200.
   c Marcia sold the car to Clive.
   d Marcia sold the car.
   e Clive bought the car from Marcia for $200.
   f Clive bought the car for $200.
   g Clive bought the car from Marcia.
   h Clive bought the car.

With *sell* the buyer and the price can be omitted, and with *buy* the seller and the price can be omitted, even though these entities must be present in a buying or selling event. The meaning of *sell* must include the notion of payment, otherwise it isn't distinguishable from *give*. Similarly, the exchange of payment differentiates *buy* from *take* or *receive*.

There is an important difference between the missing arguments in (39) and the ellipsed arguments in (28) and (35), which is that in general, ellipsed arguments are specifically identified from the general context. In contrast to this, the unspecified price in (39c, g), the buyer in (39b, d) and the seller in (39f, h) are understood to exist, but nothing else need be known about them. This raises doubts as to whether or not the omissible phrases in (39) are arguments at the syntactic level.

The main predicate and its arguments comprise an atomic proposition. Ordinary natural language sentences generally contain more than this, for example:

(40)a Seymour will slice the salami carefully in the kitchen tomorrow to make the canapés.
   b SLICE (s, the salami)

The basic logical representation introduced so far shows only the main predicate, SLICE, and its two arguments, the slicer and the slicee. We omit the tense marker *will*, the manner adverbial *carefully*, the locative adverbial *in the kitchen*, the temporal adverbial *tomorrow*, and the adverbial clause of purpose *to make the canapés*. Tense is covered in Chapter 7 and adverbials in Chapter 8. Until then they will be omitted in logical forms.

2.3.2 Sentences as Arguments

All the arguments in the discussion so far have been expressed by noun phrases, but arguments can also be expressed by sentences themselves, for example:

(41)a Clive said something
      SAY (c, something)

   b   Clive said [that he gave the car to Marcia]
       SAY(c, GIVE(c, the car, m))

   c   Clive thinks [the earth is flat]
       THINK(c, FLAT(the earth))

In (41b, c) the proposition expressed by the embedded sentence is the second argument of the main verb – the proposition is what is said or what is believed. (Sentences about thinking and believing are discussed in Section 5.5.)

The clearest examples of sentential arguments are found with verbs, but plausibly members of other word classes can also have sentential arguments.

(42)a   Shirley was proud [of the new car]
    b   Shirley was proud [that she graduated]
    c   Shirley was proud [to be Miss Lada 1993]

In (42a) it seems that the new car, the source of Shirley's pride, is the second argument of *proud*. In (42b, c) the embedded sentence also expresses the source of pride, the second argument of *proud*, and so the propositions can be represented as in (43).

(43)a   PROUD(s, the new car)
    b   PROUD(s, GRADUATE(s))
    c   PROUD(s, MISS LADA 1993(s))

A sentential argument may also be the only argument of the main predicate in a sentence, for example:

(44)a   [That Clive drove the car] is obvious
    b   It is obvious [that Clive drove the car]
    c   OBVIOUS (DRIVE (c, the car))

For a review of this section, see the exercises in Part B at the end of the chapter.

2.4   THE LOGICAL QUANTIFIERS

2.4.1   The Universal Quantifier

The atomic propositions we have discussed so far have had **individual arguments**, referred to by names or noun phrases like *the dog*, with logical forms like these:

(45)a John saw Mary   SEE (j,m)
   b Fido was barking   BARK (f)
   c The dog was barking BARK (the dog)

Propositions with **quantified arguments** rather than individual arguments (that is, **quantified propositions**) must be treated differently. Take the example below.

(46) God made everything.

The chief point here is that *God* and *everything* have very different kinds of meaning. While *God* is a name referring to an individual, *everything* doesn't refer to a thing, but rather has the potential to refer to any thing considered individually. Suppose it were possible to point to each thing in existence in turn and say 'God made that'. According to (46) each utterance would be true, and (46) can be analysed as a sort of summary of all those propositions about different individuals.

Pronouns like *that*, *this* and *it* are referring expressions which can in principle refer to any individual depending on the circumstances in which they are used – they have **variable reference**, in contrast to names, which have **constant reference**. The logical terms used to translate names are **individual constants**. To analyse quantified propositions we need **individual variables**, comparable to pronouns. Individual variables are traditionally written as x, y and z, with u, v and w added if needed. Like *this* and *that*, individual variables can in principle refer to any individual at all, depending on the context. With an individual variable the logical form for *God made that* can be written as

(47) MAKE (g, x)

As it stands, (47) does not fix the reference for x and so doesn't express a proposition, as it cannot be true or false.

The universal quantifier, written as '$\forall$', fixes how the variable is to be interpreted. The whole logical form for *God made everything* is (48).

(48) $\forall$x (MAKE (g, x))

The quantifier is paired with a copy of the variable which is its target, and the formula with which the quantifier combines is bracketed to fix the scope of the quantifier. (48) can be read as (49).

(49) For any value of x, God made x
    For all values of x, God made x
    Whatever x may be, God made x

Here the universal quantifier fixes the value of x as every thing, taken individually. The quantifier **binds** the variable, which is accordingly a **bound variable** in the whole formula '∀x(MAKE (g, x))'. A variable which is not bound by a quantifier is a **free variable**. The x variable is free in the basic formula 'MAKE (g, x)'. A proposition form with a free variable, such as 'MAKE (g, x)', stands for an **open proposition**. An open proposition by itself is incomplete and cannot have a truth value. A formula with no free variables stands for a **closed proposition**, which is complete and has a truth value. Because there are no free variables in (48) it stands for a closed proposition.

Noun phrases expressing universal quantification are usually more complex than *everything*, as in (50).

(50)a Now is the time for <u>all good men</u> to come to the aid of the party.
   b <u>Every cloud</u> has a silver lining.
   c <u>Every dog</u> is barking.

Take the significance of *dog* in (50c). Suppose 'Every dog is barking' is true. Now you point to each thing in turn and say 'that is barking'. This time the utterance will be false on many pointings, but for any pointing to a dog it will be true. In other words, if the thing pointed to is a dog then 'that is barking' is true. So for 'Every dog is barking', the pointing exercise goes with the utterance of 'If that is a dog then it is barking', and the logical form for (50c) is (51), using the implication connective.

(51) ∀x(DOG(x) → BARK(x))
'For every thing x, if x is a dog then x is barking'

The logical universal quantifier does not express **existential commitment** – that is, a sentence like *Every dog is barking* can be true on the logical analysis even when there are no dogs.

On the logical analysis, if there are no dogs 'Every dog is barking' is true, because the antecedent 'DOG(x)' will be false for any value of x. If there are no dogs, only lines 3 and 4 of the truth table for implication will come into play.

(52)

	DOG (x)	BARK (x)	DOG (x) → BARK (x)
1	T	T	T
2	T	F	F
3	F	T	T
4	F	F	T

On the logical analysis 'Every dog is barking' is equivalent to 'There is no non-barking dog'.

A universally quantified noun phrase in object position or other sentence positions is analysed in the same way, for example:

(53)a   Bill hates all reporters.
        $\forall x(REPORTER(x) \rightarrow HATE(b, x))$
        'For all x, if x is a reporter then Bill hates x'.

   b   Clive gave a bone to every dog.
        $\forall x (DOG(x) \rightarrow GIVE(c, a\ bone, x))$
        'For all x, if x is a dog then Clive gave a bone to x'.

   c   The book was signed by every guest.
        $\forall x (GUEST(x) \rightarrow SIGN(x, the\ book))$
        'For all x, if x is a guest then x signed the book'.

The expressions *a bone* and *the book* are not fully analysed here, but the way we represent NPs like these will be revised.

2.4.2   The Existential Quantifier

The other logical quantifier, the existential quantifier, is written as '$\exists$' and used to translate noun phrases with *a/an* or *some* and for *there is* sentences. The sequence '$\exists x$' is read as 'there is an x' or 'there is at least one thing x'.

Unlike the universal quantifier, the existential quantifier does explicitly express existential commitment. An existential sentence states the existence of at least one thing of the kind specified, for example:

(54)a   A dog barked.
        'There is at least one thing x such that x is a dog and x barked'.
        $\exists x (DOG(x) \& BARK(x))$

   b   There is an antidote to Huntsman venom.
        $\exists x (ANTIDOTE(x, h))$

   c   Some birds were singing.
        $\exists x (BIRD(x) \& SING(x))$

   d   A black limousine awaited Marla.
        $\exists x (LIMOUSINE(x) \& BLACK(x) \& AWAIT(x, m))$

   e   Louise bought some trashy paperbacks.
        $\exists x (TRASHY(x) \& PAPERBACK(x) \& BUY(l, x))$

As these examples show, the existential quantifier is neutral between singular and plural. Note that unlike the universal quantifier, the existential quantifier is not analysed with '$\rightarrow$'.

The determiner *no* is analysed with the existential quantifier and negation, as in (55).

(55)a   There is no antidote to cyanide.
    $\sim \exists x \ (\text{ANTIDOTE}(x, c))$
    'It is not the case that there is an x such that x is an antidote to cyanide'.
    For short, 'there is no x such that ...'
  b   Clive ate nothing.
    $\sim \exists x \ (\text{EAT}(c, x))$
    'There is no x such that Clive ate x.'

In sentences like (55) the negation cancels the existential quantifier's guarantee of the existence of a thing of the kind described. To affect the interpretation of the existential quantifier in this way, the negation must appear before the quantifier. Reversing the order of the existential quantifier and negation gives a different meaning, as in (56).

(56) $\exists x \sim (\text{EAT}(c, x))$
    'There is at least one thing x such that Clive didn't eat x.'

As we saw above, 'Every dog is barking' is equivalent to 'There is no non-barking dog'. For any universally quantified proposition there is an equivalent existentially quantified proposition, and vice versa, as shown in (57) and (58). (57a) is equivalent to (57b), and (58a) is equivalent to (58b).

(57)a $\forall x \ (\text{DOG}(x) \rightarrow \text{BARK}(x))$
    'For every x, if x is a dog then x is barking.'

  b $\sim \exists x \ (\text{DOG}(x) \ \& \sim\text{BARK}(x))$
    'There is no x such that x is a dog and x is not barking'.

(58)a $\exists x \ (\text{DOG}(x) \ \& \ \text{BARK}(x))$
    'There is an x such that x is a dog and x is barking.'

  b $\sim \forall x \ (\text{DOG}(x) \rightarrow\sim \text{BARK}(x))$
    'It is not the case that for all x, if x is a dog then x is not barking'

2.4.3   Scopal Ambiguity

The examples above show that the relative order of negation and a quantifier is significant. This was first mentioned with (55b) and (56), repeated in (59).

(59)a $\sim \exists x \ (\text{EAT}(c, x))$
    'Clive ate nothing'.

 b   ∃x ∼ (EAT(c, x))
     'There is at least one thing Clive didn't eat.'

These examples illustrate a more general point. The internal structure of a simple proposition always contains at least the predicate and its arguments. With quantifiers and negation, we add to the logical forms symbols which combine with a propositional form as a whole. This is represented by placing the symbols for negation and quantification at the beginning of the propositional form. Expressions like negation and quantification are **scopal expressions**. The interpretation of a scopal expression is combined with, or affects, the interpretation of the whole proposition it combines with, which is its **scope**. This is illustrated in (60) and (61).

(60)

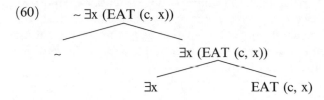

In (60) we say the quantifier is in the scope of negation, or the quantifier has narrow scope with respect to negation, or negation takes scope over the quantifier.

(61)

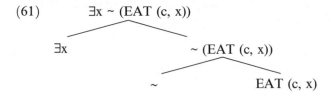

In (61) we say the quantifier has wide scope with respect to negation, or negation has narrow scope.

The representations in (60) and (61) are for the propositions expressed by the sentences *Clive ate nothing* and *There is something Clive didn't eat*, respectively. From the form of the sentences, it is clear which meaning is expressed, and which order is required for negation and the quantifier.

A sentence with two or more scopal expressions doesn't always have a clearly identified single meaning, and is commonly ambiguous between the readings for the different possible scopes – this is called **scopal ambiguity**. Scopal ambiguity with two quantifiers is illustrated in (62).

(62)   Everyone loves someone.

The subject *everyone* is represented with a universal quantifier, and the object *someone* with an existential quantifier. There are two possible orders for the quantifiers, with different readings, as shown in (63).

(63)a   ∀x∃y (LOVE (x, y))

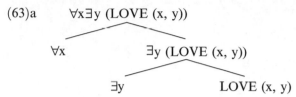

∀x   ∃y (LOVE (x, y))

∃y   LOVE (x, y)

'For every person x, there is at least one person y such that x loves y.'

b   ∃y∀x (LOVE (x, y))

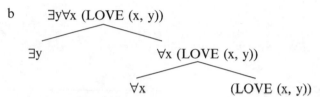

∃y   ∀x (LOVE (x, y))

∀x   (LOVE (x, y))

'There is at least one person y such that everyone loves y.'

Both of these logical forms represent possible readings of the English sentence, which is ambiguous, depending on which scope is assigned to the scopal expressions, the quantifiers *everyone* and *someone*. A sentence can be ambiguous, but a logical form represents a particular meaning and cannot be ambiguous. An ambiguous sentence is associated with two (or more) logical forms.

EXERCISES

SECTION I: THE LOGICAL CONNECTIVES

(A)   Basic Review

Assuming that p is true, q is false and r is true, calculate the truth values for the following formulae. Here is an example: ~ (p&q) v (r→q)

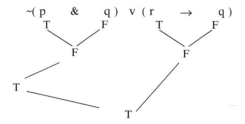

(1)   (p&q) → q
(2)   (p v (qvr)) → (p & (qvr))
(3)   (p&r) ↔ (~r v ~q)
(4)   (p→q) & (p&r)
(5)   q → ((rvp) ↔ (r&p))
(6)   ((p ↔q) ↔ (r↔q)) v ~r
(7)   r → ((~q & p) v ((q → r) v ~ (r↔p)))
(8)   ((rvq) ↔ (q → ((q&r) v p))) →~r
(9)   ((r&~q) → (pv~r)) ↔ ((rv~r) & (p↔~q))
(10)   ((~r → p) & (p →~q)) & ((q↔~p) & (r → q))

(B)   Truth Tables

Construct the truth table for ~(pvq) ↔ (~p&~q).
What can you conclude from this about ~ (pvq) and ~ p& ~q ?

(C)   Truth Tables

Construct the truth tables for ~p v q and ~q →~p.
There is a formula with only three symbols which is equivalent to both of
these – what is it?

(D)   Conditionals and Implications

According to the truth table for implication, what are the truth values for the
sentences below? Do these truth values fit with your normal intuitions about
these sentences?

(1)   If Baltimore is in Singapore then Elvis is dead.
(2)   If Baltimore is in Singapore then Elvis is alive.
(3)   If Ireland is surrounded by sea then it is an island.
(4)   If Ireland is connected to Wales then it is an island.
(5)   If Cain killed Abel then Abel is dead.
(6)   If Abel isn't dead then Cain didn't kill him.
(7)   If humans walk upright then they can use their hands to carry things.
(8)   If humans can't use their hands to carry things then they don't walk
       upright.

(E)   Truth Tables

(1)   The formula

       (~q & ~r) ↔ (r v (p&q))

is true on only one combination of truth values for p, q and r. What are
the values for p, q and r on which the formula is true? (Construct the
truth table for the formula to find this out.)

(2)   There is a simple formula which just says that the truth values for p, q
and r are the values you found as the answer to (1). Can you write this
formula? What is the relationship between this formula and the formula in (1)?

SECTION II: PREDICATES AND ARGUMENTS

(F)   Basic Review

Give the logical forms for the following sentences.

(1)   John gave ten dollars to Mary.
(2)   Mary was given ten dollars by John.
(3)   Toby was under the table.
(4)   Clive showed Maddy the photos.
(5)   China is east of Europe.
(6)   Sheila is a surgeon.
(7)   Max, Clyde and Damien partnered Latoya, Gina and Britt
respectively.
(8)   Jerry is Ben's brother.
(9)   Paul is the brother of Sheila.
(10)   Jerry and Ben are brothers.
(11)   Clive and Marcia embraced.
(12)   Bill was painting in the kitchen.
(13)   Bill was painting the kitchen.
(14)   Mary finally bought the painting yesterday.
(15)   John sat in the chair.
(16)   John sat in the hall.
(17)   Jason picked at his food.
(18)   Clyde told Tom that Bill had left.
(19)   'Bill has left', Clyde told Tom.
(20)   'Ouch!' said Sarah.

(G)   Adding Connectives

Give the logical forms for the following sentences. Some of the sentences are
ambiguous. For each ambiguous sentence give two logical forms showing
the different readings.

Example: Dorothy saw Bill or Alan.
           SEE (d, b) v SEE (d, a)

(1)   Either Sydney or Canberra is the capital of Australia.
(2)   Audrey went to Motueka and visited Rangi or interviewed Cameron.
(3)   Alice didn't laugh and Bill didn't either.
(4)   Alice didn't laugh and nor did Bill.
(5)   Neither Bill nor Alice laughed.
(6)   Frank is not both rich and generous.
(7)   If Adam trusts Eve he's stupid.
(8)   Sue will be rich if Lenny dies.
(9)   If David is Audrey's brother then Fanny's his aunt or Bob's his uncle.
(10)   Claire will hire Burt and Ethel will resign if Lenny leaves Taiwan.

(H)   *Only if*: Discussion

Compare the uses of *only if* in the sentences below. Does *only if* have a constant meaning? Write the logical forms for the sentences.

(1)   Combustion occurs only if oxygen is present.
(2)   Bill will leave only if Mary resigns.
(3)   Bill will leave only if Mary doesn't resign.
(4)   Mary will resign only if Bill leaves.

SECTION III: THE LOGICAL QUANTIFIERS

(I)   Basic Review

Using ∀ and ∃ where appropriate, write logical forms for the sentences below.

(1)   A young woman arrived.
(2)   Ida saw something sinister.
(3)   All roads lead to Rome.
(4)   Utopia welcomes all travellers from Spain.
(5)   There's a castle in Edinburgh.
(6)   Someone murdered Clive.
(7)   Clive got murdered.
(8)   The boat got sunk.
(9)   The boat sank.
(10)   Nobody saw Charles.
(11)   Maxine sent every letter John had written her to Ruth.
(12)   Gina or Boris fed every puppy.

(J)   Negation

Using ∀ and ∃, write logical forms for the sentences below. If the sentence is ambiguous, give a form for each reading.

(1) Everyone doesn't like Bob.
(2) Not everyone likes Bob.
(3) Bob doesn't like everyone.
(4) Bob doesn't like anyone.

(K) Adding Connectives

Using ∀ and ∃, write logical forms for the sentences below. Note that (6) is ambiguous so there are two forms for it.

(1) Grammar A generates all and only well-formed formulae.
(2) Clive gave every child a biscuit or a Batman comic.
(3) Zoe read all the death notices but nothing else.
(4) There's no business like show business. (Treat *show business* as a name.)
(5) Chairman Miaou is heavier and meaner than any spaniel.
(6) Every prize was won by some high school kid.

FURTHER READING

Allwood, Andersson and Dahl's (1977) *Logic in Linguistics* is an accessible introduction to first order logic and is particularly recommended.

3 Modality and Possible Worlds

In this chapter we will see how the logical quantifiers, introduced in Chapter 2, and possible worlds, introduced in Chapter 1, are used to analyse modality. In Section 3.3 we will also see how possible worlds can be used to clarify the relationship between a certain kind of conditional statement and material implication, introduced in Chapter 2.

Modality expresses **necessity** and **possibility**. A **modal proposition** includes the information that the basic proposition it contains is necessarily or possibly true. A necessarily true proposition is one which is true in any circumstances whatsoever, and cannot be false. A possibly true proposition is one which may or may not be true in fact, but is not necessarily false.

In English, modality is most commonly expressed by the modal verbs *shall, should, can, could, may, might, would* and *must*, and sometimes *will*, and by adverbs like *possibly, maybe, perhaps* and *necessarily*. These expressions will be illustrated below.

3.1 KINDS OF MODALITY

3.1.1 Logical Modality

Logical modality concerns the total truth possibilities for a proposition, according to the requirements of logic.

Logical necessity is illustrated in (1) below. The logical symbol for necessity is '□', as shown in (1e), which represents (1a–d).

(1) <u>necessity</u>
    a Necessarily, the diameter of a circle passes through the centre of the circle.
    b It is necessarily the case that the diameter ...
    c It must be the case that the diameter ...
    d The diameter of a circle must pass through the centre of the circle.
    e □ the diameter of a circle passes through the centre of the circle.

The modal statements in (1a–e) all express the proposition that the contained proposition 'The diameter of a circle passes through the centre of the circle' is necessarily true – it is not possible for this contained proposition to be false, in any circumstances. 'The diameter of a circle passes through the centre of a circle' is indeed necessarily true, and so the proposition expressed in (1) is true. Because 'The diameter of a circle passes through the centre of the circle' is necessarily true, obviously it is true in actuality – any necessarily true proposition is true in fact, because it is impossible for it to be false.

Logical possibility is illustrated in (2) and (3) below. The symbol for logical possibility is '◇', as shown in (2c), which represents (2a–b), and (3c), which represents (3a–b).

(2) possibility
    a   Napoleon might have won at Waterloo.
    b   For Napoleon to have won at Waterloo was possible.
    c   ◇ Napoleon won at Waterloo.

(3)a It is possible for there to be a man who is older than his own uncle.
    b   There can be a man who is older than his own uncle.
    c   ◇ there is a man who is older than his own uncle.

A statement of logical possibility states that the truth of the contained proposition is compatible with the requirements of logic, and so the contained proposition is not necessarily false – logic allows it to be true. Whether or not the contained proposition is true in fact can vary.

The modal statement in (2) is true, as it was possible for Napoleon to have won at Waterloo. In fact we know that Napoleon was defeated at Waterloo and 'Napoleon won at Waterloo' is false, but if reality had developed differently he might have won. The modal statement in (3) is also true, as it is perfectly possible for 'There is a man who is older than his own uncle' to be true. Here the contained proposition is also true in fact, as there are many families in which the described circumstance holds.

3.1.2 Epistemic Modality

Epistemic modality is so called because it concerns what is known, from the Greek *epistēmē*, meaning 'knowledge'. Epistemology is the branch of philosophy which explores the nature of knowledge. Epistemic modality expresses the necessity or possibility of a proposition's being true in fact, given what is already known. In other words, epistemic modal statements express conclusions drawn from the actual evidence about the range of possibilities for what is the case in reality.

Epistemic necessity is illustrated in (4).

(4) The dinosaurs must have died out suddenly.

What is expressed in (4) could be paraphrased as 'Given what we already know, it must be the case that the dinosaurs died out suddenly', or 'The evidence we have leads to the inescapable conclusion that the dinosaurs died out suddenly.' Epistemic necessity expresses what follows from our present knowledge, which may be incomplete. So epistemic necessity, unlike logical necessity, doesn't guarantee that the contained proposition is true in fact. Even if we take (4) as true, we can't thereby take it for granted that the dinosaurs died out suddenly.

Epistemic possibility is illustrated in (5).

(5)a There might/could be intelligent life in deep space.
   b It is possible that there is intelligent life in deep space.
   c There is possibly intelligent life in deep space.

The proposition expressed in (5) is that the truth of 'There is intelligent life in deep space' is compatible with our present knowledge. To say (5) is to speculate about how the actual universe might be in fact, not about how it might have been had things been otherwise than they are. Assuming that (5) is true, what we know now about the evolution of life on this planet is compatible with a similar scenario having unfolded elsewhere in the universe, but we don't know whether or not that has in fact happened. In reasoning from the evidence in hand to the conclusion that 'There is intelligent life in deep space' is possibly true, we have to obey the requirements of logic, so 'There is intelligent life in deep space' is also logically possible. Epistemic possibility includes logical possibility.

Until recently the modal form *may have (done)* was used only for epistemic modality, although *might have (done)* can be logical or epistemic. The contrast is shown in (6).

(6)   <u>logical possibility</u>
     a She might have fallen down the cliff – thank goodness the safety harness held.
     b She may have fallen down the cliff – thank goodness the safety harness held.
     <u>epistemic possibility</u>
     c She may have fallen down the cliff – we're still waiting for the rescue team's report.
     d She might have fallen down the cliff – we're still waiting for the rescue team's report.

This distinction seems to be disappearing. A headline such as *Pilot may have averted crash* is now ambiguous: on the epistemic interpretation, evidence now reveals that a plane which did not crash may have been in danger which was averted by the pilot's action. On the emerging non-epistemic interpretation, the plane did crash but the pilot could have prevented it had things happened differently. A somewhat bizarre example of this shift is the headline *GP Criticized over Death: Baby may have lived – Coroner*.

3.1.3 Deontic Modality

Modal auxiliaries also express **deontic modality**, which is concerned with compliance or compatibility with some code of behaviour or set of rules. **Deontic necessity** expresses what is required or compulsory, or what someone is obliged to do, and **deontic possibility** expresses what is allowed or permitted. These are illustrated in (7) and (8).

(7) deontic necessity
    a You must be home by midnight.
    b Buildings erected after September of this year are required to comply with the Revised Building Code.

(8) deontic possibility
    a Visitors may use the downstairs sitting room after 6 p.m.
    b Harry is allowed to drive the tractor.

3.2 MODALITY AND POSSIBLE WORLDS

Recall that a logically necessary proposition is true in any circumstances whatsoever, and for a proposition which is logically possibly true there are circumstances in which it would be true, even if it isn't true in fact. 'Circumstances' here means alternative ways reality might have been – for example, no matter how reality might have been, the diameter of a circle passes through its centre, and given at least one other way things might have gone, Napoleon might have won at Waterloo. As outlined in Chapter 1, these alternative ways of reality are possible worlds.

The discussion of possible worlds in Chapter 1 implied that there is just one set of all the possible worlds, with infinitely many members, and that semantics works with that set. The term *possible world* tells us only that worlds which are possible are in the set. In fact a bit more detail than this is needed for the different kinds of natural language modality, which do not all use the full set of worlds. Some of the differences are reviewed in this section.

Logical modality works with the full set of worlds. A logically necessary proposition is true in any possible circumstances whatsoever, which is the same as being true in all possible worlds. A logically possible proposition is true in at least one possible set of circumstances, even if it isn't true in fact. Accordingly, logical necessity and possibility are analysed as in (9) and (10). The w variable is a restricted variable, and can only have worlds as its value.

(9) logical necessity
     'Necessarily S' is true iff
     ∀ w(S is true in w)

     'Necessarily the diameter of a circle passes through its centre' is true iff
     ∀w ('The diameter of a circle passes through its centre' is true in w)

     'Necessarily the diameter of a circle passes through its centre' is true if
     and only if for every possible world w 'The diameter of a circle passes
     through its centre' is true in w.

(10) logical possibility
      'Possibly S' is true iff
      ∃w (S is true in w)

      'Napoleon might have won at Waterloo' is true iff
      ∃w ('Napoleon won at Waterloo' is true in w)

      'Napoleon might have won at Waterloo' is true if and only if there is
      at least one possible world w such that 'Napoleon won at Waterloo' is
      true in w.

Logical modality is the simplest modality, in that it deals with all the possible
worlds without distinction.
   Epistemic modality is defined in terms of epistemically possible worlds. An
epistemically possible world is one in which everything we know about the
actual world also holds – we don't know of any differences between the
actual world and any epistemically possible world (even though there might
be differences) – for all we know, any epistemically possible world IS reality.
In the definitions below the variable w_e ranges over epistemically possible
worlds.

(11) epistemic necessity
      'The gods must be crazy' is true iff
      $\forall w_e$ ('The gods are crazy' is true in w_e).

      'The gods must be crazy' is true if and only if for every epistemically
      possible world w 'The gods are crazy' is true in w.

   Epistemic *must* conveys that all the evidence we have about some real
situation leads to an inescapable conclusion, but it is far weaker than logical
necessity. *The gods must be crazy* may be true interpreted epistemically, but
even if it is, there are infinitely many logically possible worlds where the gods
are sane and wise, and thus *The gods must be crazy* interpreted as logical
necessity is false.
   Epistemic possibility is analysed as in (12).

(12) epistemic possibility
'She may have fallen down the cliff' is true iff
$\exists w_e$ ('She fell down the cliff' is true in w_e).

'She may have fallen down the cliff' is true if and only if there is at least one epistemically possible world w such that 'She fell down the cliff' is true in w.

According to the definition in (12), what we know about the actual circumstances is consistent with her having fallen down the cliff, and we could subsequently discover that she did fall in fact.

Deontic modality can also be analysed in terms of possible worlds, but in this case the possible worlds at issue are the ones in which the relevant code of behaviour (for example, the ten commandments, the Confucian code, what your mother says) is always adhered to. Exactly which code of behaviour is at issue is a pragmatic matter, as it depends on the context in which a deontic modal statement is made. A deontically necessary action or course of events is found in all such 'perfect obedience' worlds. A permissible action or course of events is found in at least one such world – that is, perfect obedience is compatible with what is permitted, but doesn't require it.

In the definitions in (13) and (14), the variable w_{po} stands for perfect obedience worlds.

(13) deontic necessity
'Children must be seen and not heard' is true iff
$\forall w_{po}$ ('Children are seen and not heard' is true in w_{po}).

'Children must be seen and not heard' is true if and only if for every perfect obedience world w 'Children are seen and not heard' is true in w.

(14) deontic possibility
'A cat may look at a king' is true iff
$\exists w_{po}$ ('A cat looks at a king') is true in w_{po}.

'A cat may look at a king' is true if and only if there is at least one perfect obedience world w such that 'A cat looks at a king' is true in w.

These sayings are deontic generalizations. If a deontic statement applies to a particular situation, then the perfect obedience worlds at issue are the ones which contain that situation. For example, 'He must leave town' is true if and only if he leaves town in all the perfect obedience worlds where he is in town, and whatever it is that makes his departure imperative (in addition to general principles) also holds.

The possible worlds analysis reviewed so far captures two key properties of modal sentences. First, the use of possible worlds captures the fact that modal sentences are about hypothetical states of affairs, and not simply descriptive of actual reality. Secondly, the use of existential and universal quantification gives an elegant account of the way that necessity can be defined in terms of possibility and negation, and possibility can be defined in terms of necessity and negation, as reviewed in the next section.

3.2.1   Interdefinability with Negation

Necessity and possibility are opposed in such a way that each can be paraphrased using the other, with negation, as shown in (15).

(15)a   □p   It is necessarily the case that p
         ~◇~p   It is not possibly the case that not p

    b   ◇p   It is possibly the case that p
         ~□~p   It is not necessarily the case that not p

    c   □~p   It is necessarily the case that not p
         ~◇p   It is not possibly the case that p

    d   ◇~p   It is possibly the case that not p
         ~□p   It is not necessarily the case that p

English sentences to illustrate these patterns are given in (16)–(18). They don't sound equally natural, and it isn't always possible to negate a sentence by simply adding *not*.

(16)   *logical modality*
         □p   A circle's diameter must pass through its centre.
         ~◇~p   The diameter of a circle can't not pass through the circle's centre.
                     It is not possible for the diameter of a circle to not pass through the centre of the circle.

         ◇p   Terry might have hit the bullseye.
         ~□~p   Terry need not have not hit (missed) the bullseye.
                     It wasn't necessary for Terry to not hit the bullseye.

         □~p   Necessarily parallel lines do not meet.
         ~◇p   Parallel lines can't meet.
                     It is not possible for parallel lines to meet.

                     (If he had been in a hurry...)
         ◇~p   He might have not read the note.
                     It might have been that he didn't read the note.

~□p   It needn't have been that he read the note.
       It wasn't inevitable that he read the note.

(17) *epistemic modality*
      □p   The dinosaurs must have died out suddenly.
      ~◇~p   It can't be that the dinosaurs didn't die out suddenly.
                 The dinosaurs can't have not died out suddenly.
                 It is not possible that the dinosaurs did not die out
                 suddenly.

      ◇p   There could be intelligent life in deep space.
      ~□~p   It need not be the case that there is no intelligent life in deep
                 space.
                 It is not necessarily the case that there is no intelligent life in
                 deep space.

      □~p   He must have not seen the note.
                 It must be the case that he didn't see the note.
      ~◇p   He can't have seen the note.
                 It is not possible that he saw the note.

                 (Perhaps he was in a hurry...)
      ◇~p   He might have not read the note.
                 It is possible that he didn't read the note.
      ~□p   He needn't have read the note.
                 It needn't be so that he read the note.
                 It isn't necessarily the case that he read the note.

(18) *deontic modality*
      Assume that p = He leaves town
                  ~p = He does not leave town/He stays in town.

      □p   He must leave town
                 He is obliged to leave town.
      ~◇~p   He may not stay in town.
                 He may not not leave town.
                 He is not permitted to stay in town.
                 He is not permitted to not leave town.

      ◇p   He may leave town.
      ~□~p   He need not not leave town.
                 He need not stay in town.
                 He is not obliged to not leave town.

      □~p   He must not leave town.
                 What he must do is not leave town.
                 He must stay in town.
                 He is obliged to not leave town.

$\sim\Diamond p$ He may not leave town.
         He is not permitted to leave town.

$\Diamond\sim p$ He may stay in town.
         He may not leave town.
         What he may do is not leave town.

$\sim\Box p$ He need not leave town.
         He is not obliged to leave town.

As we saw in Chapter 2, existential and universal quantification are related in the same way. For any universally quantified proposition there is an equivalent existentially quantified proposition with negation, and vice versa. Examples illustrating this are repeated in (19) and (20) below. (19a, b) are equivalent, and (20a, b) are equivalent.

(19)a $\forall x\,(DOG\,(x) \to BARK\,(x))$
         'For every x, if x is a dog then x is barking.'

   b $\sim\exists x\,(DOG\,(x)\ \&\ \sim BARK\,(x))$
         'there is no x such that x is a dog and x is not barking.'

(20)a $\exists x\,(DOG\,(x)\ \&\ BARK\,(x))$
         'There is an x such that x is a dog and x is barking.'

   b $\sim\forall x\,(DOG\,(x) \to \sim BARK\,(x))$
         'It is not the case that for all x, if x is a dog then x is not barking.'

As we see in the schematic representations below, in the possible worlds analysis of modality, the interdefinability of necessity and possibility follows automatically from the interdefinability of universal and existential quantification.

(21)a $\Box p$ It is necessarily the case that p
              $\forall w\,(p$ is true in w$)$

   $\sim\Diamond\sim p$ It is not possibly the case that not p
              $\sim\exists w\,(\sim p$ is true in w$)$

   b $\Diamond p$ It is possibly the case that p
              $\exists w\,(p$ is true in w$)$

   $\sim\Box\sim p$ It is not necessarily the case that not p
              $\sim\forall w\,(\sim p$ is true in w$)$

   c $\Box\sim p$ It is necessarily the case that not p
              $\forall w\,(\sim p$ is true in w$)$

   $\sim\Diamond p$ It is not possibly the case that p
              $\sim\exists w(p$ is true in w$)$

d   ◇~p   It is possibly the case that not p
            ∃w (~p is true in w)
    ~□p   It is not necessarily the case that p
            ~∀w (p is true in w)

3.3   COUNTERFACTUALS

We saw in Chapter 2 that the implication connective → fits for some uses of English *if* ··· (*then*) but not all. The two most striking differences are that (i) English *if* ··· (*then*) statements commonly express a causal relationship, but any logical connective simply specifies combinations of truth values, and (ii) according to the truth table for →, when the antecedent is false the whole implication is true, no matter what the consequent is. Because of the second point, generally only the first two lines of the truth table give the expected results for *if*-sentences.

	p	q	p→q
line 1	T	T	T
line 2	T	F	F
line 3	F	T	T
line 4	F	F	T

The anomalousness of lines 3 and 4 is clearly illustrated with **counterfactual conditionals**, which are conditionals with false antecedents, like (22). (This example is from Lewis (1973).)

(22)a   If kangaroos had no tails they would topple over.

   b   If kangaroos had no tails they would not topple over.

Kangaroos have tails, so the antecedent shared by both (22a) and (22b) is false. According to the truth table for implication both (22a, b) are true, and yet they contradict each other. Plausibly, (22a) is true and (22b) false.

   Now to assign the value 'false' to the antecedent and work from there is to judge the statement according to the facts of reality. This is like responding to either statement with 'But they do have tails', and refusing to consider the matter further. A response like this misses the point, which is that a counterfactual makes a statement about hypothetical situations, not about how things really are.

   Two things are needed here. First, the counterfactual must be interpreted in a way that acknowledges its hypothetical character. Secondly, if (22a) is true and (22b) is false, which seems correct, the difference between them must depend on the consequent, because they have the same antecedent. Both these points can be taken into account if the interpretation is based on lines 1 and 2 of the truth table.

To bring lines 1 and 2 into play we make the antecedent true, which is simply a matter of moving to possible worlds in which kangaroos have no tails. So imagine those worlds with tailless kangaroos leaping about. If there are any worlds in which they don't topple over then 'If kangaroos had no tails they would topple over' is false. But if the tailless kangaroos in all those worlds do topple over then 'If kangaroos had no tails they would topple over' is true. In the appropriate worlds, the first two lines of the truth table give the right result.

If in considering the tailless kangaroo worlds you decided that they do topple over, you cooperated with the hypothesis in a number of important respects, by considering worlds which also contain other relevant features carried over from reality. But the range of tailless kangaroo worlds also includes these:

(23) w1 Kangaroos have no tails. Earth's gravity is less than that of the real moon and kangaroos leap over its surface without toppling over.

w2 As kangaroos evolved and their tails disappeared, they developed a walking gait, moving the feet alternately. They don't topple over.

w3 As kangaroos evolved and their tails disappeared, their forelegs became longer and stronger. They developed a four-footed bounding gait. They don't topple over.

w4 Kangaroos have no tails. When they are weaned they are issued with gas-powered jet thrusters mounted on a harness, connected to orientation sensors and a little computer. When a kangaroo leans too far from the vertical the jet thruster fires a burst to push it back upright. Kangaroos do not topple over.

These are worlds in which the conditional has a true antecedent and a false consequent. IF these worlds are included in the analysis, 'If Kangaroos had no tails they would topple over' is false. But surely that's unreasonable – if the counterfactual is to be given an appropriate interpretation, worlds like these must be excluded as irrelevant. The background worlds must include only those worlds which are <u>similar to the actual world in the relevant respects,</u> in this case including at least gravity, kangaroos' leaping gait and kangaroos' small forelegs.

Specifying the right similar worlds is quite complicated, and will be discussed further below. For now the chief points of the analysis are expressed in the truth condition in (24).

(24)   'If kangaroos had no tails they would topple over' is true if and only if
       for every possible world w such that
           'Kangaroos have no tails' is true in w and w is otherwise similar to
           the actual world,
       'Kangaroos topple over' is true in w.

Once the similar worlds are selected and all the others stripped away, the truth of the whole conditional depends on the consequent being necessarily true in relation to that set of worlds – the conditional is true if and only if the consequent is true in all selected worlds.

The possible worlds analysis has a number of advantages. It expresses the hypothetical nature of counterfactuals, in that possible worlds are hypothetical realms, and it excludes the troublesome lines 3 and 4 of the conditional truth table.

The analysis rests on identifying the right set of worlds in terms of being similar to reality. We can't get a good analysis for counterfactuals in general unless we can state in general how similarity works, but this can be quite complicated.

One way of excluding worlds with lower gravity or worlds with kangaroo jet boosters is to stipulate that the worlds we want are like the actual world in EVERY respect except for what the antecedent specifies. But this is too strict – without tails the kangaroos would leave different tracks, and there would be no kangaroo tail soup. So we have to let in all the differences that follow directly from the lack of kangaroo tails.

We want to select worlds which, though they differ from actuality in matters of detail, are like the actual world in more important and more general ways. For one thing, the counterfactual expresses a hypothesis about the mechanics of kangaroo locomotion and balance. Here we have a creature which is functionally two-legged – the forelegs are not much used for weight-bearing. Several factors help to balance a leaping kangaroo, including the large landing surfaces of the elongated hind feet, the strength of the hind legs and the heavy tail as a counterweight. The hypothesis is that the other balance factors would be insufficient without tails as counterweights. The possible worlds we want must obey the general laws which govern these facts – perhaps we could ensure that by saying that the similarity criteria for this counterfactual include the laws of nature.

Unfortunately, the kangaroos required to test the hypothesis are highly unnatural beasts. They have an extraordinary high-speed bounding gait, like a two-legged cheetah, and insufficient ways of keeping their balance. This scenario must presuppose very unusual patterns for the evolution of species. Given the laws of nature governing biology, a kangaroo like ours except for the tail would have evolved some way of not toppling over, by walking instead of leaping, or developing a four-footed gait, or some other dodge. The hypothetical kangaroo is a monster. Some laws of nature, but not others, are carried over to establish the similarity we want between the actual and hypothetical worlds.

Generally, the way we calculate what similarity requires depends on the understood nature of the hypothesis. For example, consider the range of tailless kangaroo worlds outlined in (25).

(25)   Kangaroos have no tails, and
    1   Kangaroos' tracks do not include a tail track.
    2   There is no kangaroo tail soup.
    3   Kangaroos have a genetic code different from the genetic code for actual kangaroos.
    4   Kangaroos topple over.
    5   Kangaroos walk instead of leaping.
    6   Kangaroos have longer stronger forelegs than in actuality.

As we have already seen, to judge the truth of 'If kangaroos had no tails they would topple over' we include worlds with features 1–4, but we exclude worlds with features 5–6, because the hypothesis implicitly assumes that kangaroos have not adapted to taillessness in either of these ways. But for 'If kangaroos had no tails there would be no kangaroo tail soup' or 'If kangaroos had no tails they would have a genetic code different from the actual code' the selected worlds could include all the features 1–6. On the other hand, 'If kangaroos had no tails they would walk instead of leaping' expresses a hypothesis about adaptive evolution, so to evaluate this conditional we would use worlds with features 1, 2, 3, 5 and maybe 6, but we would exclude worlds with feature 4 on the grounds that it doesn't observe normal patterns of evolution.

These examples show that the worlds at issue can't be chosen until we know the nature of the hypothesis, which generally requires consideration of both the antecedent and the consequent. The key issue in fixing the right kind of similarity for a particular counterfactual is the causal connection between the antecedent and consequent which is almost always understood in the way we use *if*-sentences, and particularly with counterfactuals. For example, taillessness in kangaroos will cause the kangaroos to topple over only if the laws of dynamics which participate in causing kangaroo-toppling are also present, but the normal patterns of evolution which would compensate for taillessness are absent.

To sum up, the logical analysis outlined here shows that logical implication can after all be used to analyse counterfactual conditionals. In addition to the logical basis of the analysis, we have seen that pragmatic considerations also play an important part – we use commonsense considerations about what we think the speaker intended, to adjust our calculation of similarity and to choose the most appropriate worlds to test the speaker's hypothesis.

EXERCISES

(A)   Basic Review

Write the truth definitions, using possible worlds, for the sentences below. If a sentence strikes you as ambiguous between different kinds of modality, write the definitions for the different readings.

(1)   Necessarily, a bachelor is unmarried.
(2)   A child could have invented the mousetrap.
(3)   If wishes were horses beggars would ride.
(4)   The lake is sure to freeze tonight
(5)   Villagers' goats may graze on the green.
(6)   Right-turning traffic must give way.

(B)   Modal Verbs: Discussion

Does *would* have the same kind of meaning in (1) and (2)?
Does *could* have the same kind of meaning in (3) and (4)?
(Hint: (1) and (3) are alike, and (2) and (4) are alike.)

(1)   If the weather had been better the truck <u>would</u> have arrived on time.
(2)   We knew the truck would arrive on time.

(3)   If she'd been taller she <u>could</u> have seen in the window.
(4)   I remember Stan <u>could</u> bench 450 pounds.

(C)   Necessary Truth: Discussion

Which of the statements below (if any) are necessarily true?

(1)   No statement can be true and false at the same time.
(2)   All men are mortal.
(3)   A solid body occupies space.
(4)   A dog is four-legged.
(5)   A dog is canine.
(6)   A dog is an animal.
(7)   Orange is the colour of oranges.
(8)   Oranges are orange-coloured.

(D)   Possible Worlds: Discussion

In possible worlds theory, the truth condition or meaning of a sentence is the set of possible worlds in which it is true. What can you conclude from this about the meanings (in this theory) of the sentences below?

(1)   Either God exists or God does not exist.
(2)   Every rose is a rose.
(3)   The sum of two and two is four.

(E)   Possible Worlds: Discussion

What are the truth definitions for the sentences below? Which, if either, is true?

(1)   If squares were circles then cubes would be spheres.
(2)   If squares were circles then cubes would be cylinders.

FURTHER READING

For modality and possible worlds, see Chapter 15 in Martin (1987) and Bach (1989). A more advanced introduction to modality is in McCawley (1993), Chapter 11.

   Kratzer (1977) discusses different kinds of modality, such as deontic, epistemic and logical modality.

   For more advanced discussions of conditionals see Sanford (1989), McCawley (1993), Chapter 15, and Nute (1984), especially sections 1–6.

4 Natural Language Quantifiers

4.1 NATURAL LANGUAGE QUANTIFIERS AND FIRST ORDER LOGIC

Quantificational determiners are words or expressions like those underlined in the examples in (1).

(1) <u>several</u> post offices, <u>at least three</u> hostages, <u>a few</u> flakes of paint, <u>most</u> vineyards in this area, <u>every</u> star in the sky

We have seen that first order logic analyses *every*, *each* and *all* as the universal quantifier $\forall$, and *some* and *a/an* as the existential quantifier $\exists$. However, not all natural language quantifiers can be analysed in first order logic. The clearest example of this is *most*.

As we saw in Chapter 2, quantified propositions in first order logic have a general format:

(2) All men are mortal.
     A dog barked

$\forall x$	$(\text{MAN}(x)$	$\rightarrow$	$\text{MORTAL}(x))$
$\exists x$	$(\text{DOG}(x)$	$\&$	$\text{BARK}(x))$
quantifier	NP predicate	connective	VP predicate

(The order of 'BARK(x)' and 'DOG(x)' can be reversed because conjunction isn't fixed in order.) The chief point here is that the NP predicate (that is, MAN or DOG) and the VP predicate form separate atomic propositions which must be joined by a connective to form a single proposition.

If we use the same general format for *most* there are four possibilities to choose from:

(3) Most dogs are domestic.
  a Most x (DOG (x) & DOMESTIC (x))
  b Most x (DOG (x) v DOMESTIC (x))
  c Most x (DOG (x) → DOMESTIC (x))
  d Most x (DOG (x) ↔ DOMESTIC (x))

Formula (3a) is interpreted according to the truth table for conjunction:

	DOG (x)	DOMESTIC (x)	DOG (x) & DOMESTIC (x)
line 1	T	T	T
line 2	T	F	F
line 3	F	T	F
line 4	F	F	F

(3a) is true only if line 1 is true for most things x. That is, (3a) is true if and only if for most things x, 'DOG(x)' is true and 'DOMESTIC(x)' is true – in short, x is a domestic dog. 'Most things are domestic dogs' is clearly not the same meaning as 'Most dogs are domestic.'

Formula (3b) is a disjunction:

	DOG (x)	DOMESTIC (x)	DOG (x) v DOMESTIC (x)
line 1	T	T	T
line 2	T	F	T
line 3	F	T	T
line 4	F	F	F

(3b) is true if for most things x, any of lines 1, 2 and 3 is true for x. So (3b) is true if and only if for most things x, x is a domestic dog (line 1), or x is a wild dog (line 2), or x is a domestic non-dog (line 3). Suppose that half of all things in existence are wild dogs, a quarter of all things are domestic cattle, and there are no domestic dogs. Then (3b) is true, but 'Most dogs are domestic' is false.

(3c) is an implication:

	DOG (x)	DOMESTIC (x)	DOG (x) → DOMESTIC (x)
line 1	T	T	T
line 2	T	F	F
line 3	F	T	T
line 4	F	F	T

According to lines 1, 3 and 4 of the truth table, (3c) is true if and only if for most things x, x is a domestic dog (line 1) or x is a domestic non-dog (line 3) or x is a wild non-dog (line 4). Suppose that 85 per cent of all things are domestic cattle and the rest are wild dogs. Then (3c) is true by line 3, even though all the dogs are wild. Suppose there exist three dogs (all wild), and a large number of wild seagulls. Then (3c) is true by line 4, but again there are no domestic dogs at all, and 'Most dogs are domestic' is false.

The final possibility is the biconditional:

	DOG (x)	DOMESTIC (x)	DOG (x) ↔ DOMESTIC (x)
line 1	T	T	T
line 2	T	F	F
line 3	F	T	F
line 4	F	F	T

(3d) is true if and only if for most things x, x is a domestic dog (line 1) or x is a wild non-dog (line 4). This formula is also true in the universe containing only three wild dogs and a lot of seagulls, where 'Most dogs are domestic' is false.

In short, none of the possible formulae gives the right truth condition for 'Most dogs are domestic', and *most* cannot be analysed in the same way as the universal and existential quantifiers.

The problem here is that quantified propositions in first order logic are completely general, in that every thing there is can be a value of the variable. The most basic kind of universal proposition is obviously completely general, as in (4).

(4)   God made everything $\forall x$ (MAKE (g, x))

A proposition like (5)

(5)   All men are mortal $\forall x$ (MAN (x) → MORTAL (x))

is also analysed as a completely general proposition, in that the bracketed open proposition 'MAN(x) → MORTAL(x)' is true of every entity there is, if the whole proposition is true, as it is in fact. Consider some objects as values for x:

(6)   Tom, a man
      Zeus, a god
      Charlotte, a spider

	MAN (x)	MORTAL (x)	MAN (x) → MORTAL (x)
line 1	T	T	T
line 2	T	F	F
line 3	F	T	T
line 4	F	F	T

Because Tom is a man, and mortal, both antecedent and consequent are true where x = Tom, and the whole implication is true of Tom (line 1). Because Zeus is a god, and immortal, both the antecedent and the consequent are false where x = Zeus, and the whole implication is true of Zeus (line 4). Because Charlotte is a spider, and mortal, the antecedent is false and the consequent is true where x = Charlotte, and the whole implication is true of Charlotte (line 3). So these three entities all satisfy the open proposition equally well, bearing out the full generality of quantification expressed by '∀x'.

But surely the proposition 'All men are mortal' is general only within limits. It is really about men, and the mortality or otherwise of everything which is not a man is simply irrelevant to the truth of the proposition – this is why the subject of the sentence is the noun phrase *all men*.

In fact the logical analysis of *all* does sort objects into relevant (that is, men) and irrelevant (that is, everything else), but the real work is done by the implication. For any value of x which is a man the antecedent is true and lines 1 and 2 come into play. On these lines, whether x is mortal or not determines the truth of the implication: it is the mortality or otherwise of men that is relevant. For any value of x which is not a man, the antecedent is false and lines 3 and 4 come into play. On these lines, the mortality or otherwise of x doesn't affect the outcome and the implication is true anyway: gods and spiders are irrelevant. So the antecedent of the implication sorts objects into men and everything else, but it can only do so on a yes/no or true/false basis. Sorting on a yes/no basis can only sort out the whole class of men, or all men, of which something can then be asserted, for instance, that they are mortal. The implication can serve as the sorter or restrictor ONLY for universal quantification.

What is needed, then, for *Most dogs are domestic* is quite different. Here, we want the whole class of dogs to be sorted out, or given at the outset so that *most* can then pick out a proportion – the greater part – of THAT set, not the greater part of everything there is. In other words, *most* can only be treated as a **restricted quantifier**, not as a fully general quantifier.

4.2 RESTRICTED QUANTIFIERS

To express *most* as a restricted quantifier in *Most dogs are domestic* we need a notation which combines *most* and *dogs* into a complex quantifier expression, to show that the quantification expressed by *most* (the majority or greater part) applies explicitly to dogs, not to objects in general. Only dogs can be values for the variable bound by *most* in *most dogs*. Such a notation also reflects the fact that quantifiers are syntactically expressed as NPs. The kind of NP we consider here consists of a determiner and an N′ ('N-bar'): N′ contains the rest of the NP.

(7) Most dogs are domestic
     [Most x: DOG (x)] DOMESTIC (x)

Information taken from N′ is now part of the quantifier which stands at the beginning of the whole proposition. The analysis does not form a complex proposition from 'DOG (x)' and 'DOMESTIC (x)', so the problem of finding an appropriate connective to do this does not arise.

The determiner identifies the type of quantification. All the information in N′ – the head noun and any modifiers, such as adjectives and relative clauses – restricts the range of the quantifier to the kind of thing to be considered. The restriction is placed after the colon. The restricted quantifier is the whole expression contained in square brackets, corresponding to the whole noun phrase.

(8) Restricted quantifier = [Determiner x: ...x...]
     For consistency, all quantifier determiners (including *all/every* and *a/some*) are represented the same way, for example:

(9) All men are mortal.   [All x: MAN (x)] MORTAL (x)
     Three leaves fell.   [Three x: LEAF (x)] FALL (x)
     John ate a peanut.   [A x: PEANUT (x)] EAT (j, x)

No is a negative determiner and is represented in the same way.

(10) No dogs barked.   [No x: DOG (x)] BARK (x)

Further examples are:

(11)a Several cars crashed
       [Several x: CAR (x)] CRASH (x)

   b   Mary read many books
       [Many x: BOOK (x)] READ (m, x)

   c   Marcia liked most plays written by Osborne
       [Most x: PLAY (x) & WRITE (o, x)] LIKE (m, x)

   d   Few books John owned were expensive
       [Few x: BOOK (x) & OWN (j, x)] EXPENSIVE (x)

   e   Many books John didn't own were expensive
       [Many x: BOOK (x) & ~OWN (j, x)] EXPENSIVE (x)

   f   Many books John owned weren't expensive
       [Many x: BOOK (x) & OWN (j, x] ~EXPENSIVE (x)

Example (10) above shows that negation expressed in the determiner is not analysed as the negation operator. The sequence *not many* is probably best analysed as a complex determiner, as in (12).

(12)   Not many books John owned were expensive
       [Not many x: BOOK (x) & OWN (j, x)] EXPENSIVE (x)

Using the form of noun phrases as a diagnostic, it looks as if *the* is a
quantificational determiner just like the others. If that is correct, then so-
called **definite descriptions** – noun phrases with *the* – would be represented in
the same way:

(13)a   John bathed the dog
        [The x: DOG (x)] BATH (j, x)

   b   The dog John bathed was howling
        [The x: DOG (x) & BATH (j, x)] HOWL (x)

But, on the other hand, the chief characteristic of quantifier noun phrases
which makes them quite different from names is that they don't refer to
anything in particular – that is why quantified propositions are general.
Noun phrases like *the dog* in the examples above, however, are used to
refer to a particular dog. Suppose on a particular occasion I see John kick
the dog that lives in his flat and I say 'John is in a bad mood – he kicked the
dog.' If I had remembered the dog's name at the time I might have said 'John
is in a bad mood – he kicked Ginger.' Wouldn't I have said the same thing?
In fact things are more complicated than this. The analysis of definite
descriptions will be discussed in the next chapter.

4.2.1   Scopal Ambiguity

As we saw in Section 2.4.3, when there are two or more quantifiers in a
sentence the sentence may be scopally ambiguous. Wide and narrow scope
readings are represented by the order of quantifiers in a logical representation. For example, the ambiguous sentence *Some man loves every woman* can
have the two readings represented in (14).

(14)   Some man loves every woman.
       a $\exists x (MAN(x) \& \forall y (WOMAN(y) \rightarrow LOVE(x, y)))$
           'There is a man such that he loves all women.'

       b $\forall x (WOMAN(x) \rightarrow \exists y (MAN(y) \& LOVE(y, x)))$
           'For every woman there is at least one man who loves her.'

The same strategy of ordering quantifiers in a formula is used with
restricted quantifier notation. The two readings for (14) are:

(15)a   [Some x: MAN (x)] [Every y: WOMAN (y)] LOVE (x, y)

   b   [Every y: WOMAN (y)] [Some x: MAN (x)] LOVE (x, y)

4.3 QUANTIFICATIONAL DETERMINERS IN GENERALIZED QUANTIFIER THEORY

We have seen that the traditional logical treatment of universal and existential quantification does not extend to all natural language quantifiers. Restricted quantifier notation provides a system of representing quantifier NPs, but we still need definitions for the quantifier determiners to provide truth conditions for statements with quantifiers. Current research in the semantics of natural language quantification uses definitions in terms of set theory, taken from a programme in mathematical logic called **Generalized Quantifier Theory**.

Simply, in Generalized Quantifier Theory a quantifier determiner expresses a relation between sets. For example, if *Most dogs are domestic* is true, the greater part of the set of dogs overlaps with (or intersects) the set of domestic things. In other words, the intersection of the set of dogs with the set of domestic things is greater than the remainder of the set of dogs.

4.3.1 Set Theoretic Definitions

The following basic terms from set theory are used. Capital letters represent sets.

Set Theory Terms

$A = B$	A and B are identical: they have exactly the same members.
$A \subset B$	A is a proper subset of B: all the members of A are also members of B, and B has at least one member which is not a member of A.
$A \subseteq B$	A is a subset of B: A is a proper subset of B or is identical to B.
$\lvert A \rvert$	The cardinality of A, which is the number of members in A.
$\lvert A \rvert = 9$	The cardinality of A is 9: A has 9 members.
$\lvert A \rvert > \lvert B \rvert$	The cardinality of A is greater than the cardinality of B: A has more members than B.
$\lvert A \rvert \geq \lvert B \rvert$	The cardinality of A is greater than or equal to the cardinality of B: A has at least as many members as B.
$\lvert A \rvert \geq 6$	The cardinality of A is greater than or equal to 6: A has at least 6 members.
$A \cap B$	The intersection of A and B, which is the set of entities which are members of A and also members of B.
$A - B$	The set of members of A which are not also members of B ('A minus B').

Definitions for Quantifiers

F = the set denoted by N′: this is the **restriction** on Det.
G = the set denoted by the main predicate/verb phrase (VP).

Group 1

All Fs are G   F ⊆ G
'The set of Fs is a subset of the set of Gs.'

Most Fs are G $|F \cap G| > |F - G|$
'The cardinality of the set of things which are both F and G is greater than the cardinality of the set of things which are F but not G.'
'Things which are both F and G outnumber things which are F but not G.'

Few Fs are G $|F - G| > |F \cap G|$
'The cardinality of the set of things which are F but not G is greater than the cardinality of the set of things which are both F and G.'
'Things which are F but not G outnumber things which are both F and G.'

Group 2

No F is G $|F \cap G| = 0$
'The cardinality of the set of things which are both F and G is zero.'
'There are no things which are both F and G.'

An F is G $|F \cap G| \geq 1$
'The cardinality of the set of things which are both F and G is greater than or equal to 1.'
'There is at least one thing which is both F and G.'

Some Fs are G $|F \cap G| \geq 2$
'The cardinality of the set of things which are both F and G is greater than or equal to 2.'
'There are at least two things which are both F and G.'

Four Fs are G $|F \cap G| = 4$
'The cardinality of the set of things which are both F and G is 4.'
'There are four things which are both F and G.'

Many Fs are G $|F \cap G| = $ many
'The cardinality of the set of things which are both F and G is many (or large).'
'There are many things which are both F and G.'

Several Fs are G $|F \cap G| = $ several
'The cardinality of the set of things which are both F and G is several.'
'There are several things which are both F and G.'

Few Fs are G $|F \cap G| = \text{few}$
'The cardinality of the set of things which are both F and G is few (or small).'
'There are few things which are both F and G.'

A few Fs are G $|F \cap G| = \text{a few}$
'The cardinality of the set of things which are both F and G is a few (or small).'
'There are a few things which are both F and G.'

With these definitions, quantifiers are analysed as relations between sets, or in other words, as two-place predicates taking sets as arguments. *Few* and *many* appear in both Group 1 and Group 2. The differences between the groups are discussed in the next section, and *few* and *many* are discussed in section 4.3.3.

4.3.2   Different Types of Quantifiers

Determiners in the first group express asymmetric relations, in that the order of the arguments is significant, and the sets have different roles in the relation, for example:

'All Fs are G' is not equivalent to 'All Gs are F'
'$F \subseteq G$' is not equivalent to '$G \subseteq F$'

'All (F, G)' is not equivalent to 'All (G, F)'
'All dogs bark' is not equivalent to 'All barkers are dogs.'

'Most Fs are G' is not equivalent to 'Most Gs are F'
'$|F \cap G| > |F - G|$' is not equivalent to '$|G \cap F| > |G - F|$'

'Most (F, G)' is not equivalent to 'Most (G, F)'
'Most leaves are green' is not equivalent to 'Most green things are leaves.'

Determiners in the second group give the cardinality of a set which is defined as the intersection of F and G, and because intersection is symmetric, the roles of the F set and the G set in the relation are not different in principle, for example:

'No F is G' is equivalent to 'No G is F'
$|F \cap G| = |G \cap F| = 0$
'No rose is black' is equivalent to 'No black thing is a rose.'

'An F is G' is equivalent to 'A G is F'
$|F \cap G| = |G \cap F| \geq 1$
'A spy is present' is equivalent to 'Someone present is a spy.'

'Some Fs are G' is equivalent to 'Some Gs are F'
$|F \cap G| = |G \cap F| \geq 2$
'Some plants are meateaters' is equivalent to 'Some meateaters are plants.'

'Four Fs are G' is equivalent to 'Four Gs are F'
$|F \cap G| = |G \cap F| = 4$

'Four clocks are in the hall' is equivalent to 'Four things in the hall are clocks.'

The first order quantifiers $\forall$ and $\exists$ also show this distinction. The universal quantifier belongs with Group 1. As we saw above, in the first-order analysis

All men are mortal $\forall x(\text{MAN}(x) \rightarrow \text{MORTAL}(x))$

the role of the predicate *men* as a sorter is captured by placing MAN in the antecedent of the implication, with MORTAL in the consequent. The implication, unlike the other truth-functional connectives, is asymmetric, and accordingly the predicates MAN and MORTAL have different roles in the proposition.

The existential quantifier belongs with Group 2 of the restricted quantifiers. The first order analysis contains the conjunction connective, which is symmetric, and the predicates DOG and BLACK in the example below are interchangeable without affecting the truth condition.

'Some dog is black' is equivalent to 'Some black thing is a dog.'
'$\exists x(\text{DOG}(x) \& \text{BLACK}(x))$' is equivalent to '$\exists x(\text{BLACK}(x) \& \text{DOG}(x))$.'

The differences reviewed above arise out of the special status of the restriction predicate with quantifiers in the first group. The quantifiers in the first group express a PROPORTION of the F set (or restriction set), and are sometimes called **proportional quantifiers**.

You need to know (roughly) the size of the whole F set to know how many Fs count as all Fs, most Fs or few Fs. For example, suppose that eight dogs were vaccinated for rabies. If there are thirty dogs altogether, it's true that few dogs were vaccinated; if there are eleven dogs altogether, it's true that most dogs were vaccinated; and if there are eight dogs altogether, it's true that all dogs were vaccinated.

Determiners which form proportional quantifiers are called **strong determiners**. Noun phrases formed with strong determiners are commonly called **strong noun phrases** or **strong NPs**.

The quantifiers in the second group express a quantity which is not a proportion. For example, for the truth of 'Several dogs were vaccinated' or 'Eight dogs were vaccinated', it matters only how many vaccinated dogs there are, and the number of dogs in total is irrelevant. These quantifiers give the cardinality of the F and G intersection, and are called **cardinal quanti-**

fiers. Determiners which form cardinal quantifiers are **weak determiners**. Noun phrases formed with weak determiners are **weak noun phrases** or **weak NPs**.

4.3.3 *Few* and *Many*

Few and *many* are often considered to be ambiguous between strong and weak readings. On their weak readings *few* and *many* denote a small number and a large number, respectively.

The strong reading of *few* is rather like the reading of the partitive construction, so *few fleas* on the strong reading means much the same as *few of the fleas*. This reading expresses a proportion of the group of fleas, and to know how many *few* indicates, we need to know roughly how many fleas there are altogether.

Suppose a new insecticide is being tested on flies, fleas and cockroaches. After the first trial exposure the survivors are tallied.

(16)   No flies and few fleas survived.

Here *few fleas* has the strong reading, expressing a small proportion, substantially less than half of the set of fleas used in the test. Say the trial used 1000 fleas and 89 survived – then *Few fleas survived* is true. But if the trial used 160 fleas and 89 survived then *Few fleas survived* is false.

The weak reading of *few* does not express a proportion, as in (17).

(17)   The house seemed clean and Lee found (very) few fleas.

This sentence just means that the number of fleas Lee found was small, and the fleas Lee found are not expressed as some proportion of a given set of fleas.

The strong/weak contrasts are less clear with *many*, and speakers differ more on whether or not *many* has a strong or proportional interpretation at all. For those speakers who consider *many* to have a proportional reading, *many* is like a weaker version of *most*: *many* denotes a proportion greater than half, and *most* a proportion which is substantially greater than half of the background set. For example, consider a class of 300 students voting on assessment methods.

(18)   Many students preferred assignments to tests.

For proportional-*many* speakers, this is true only if more than 150 students preferred assignments, while for some speakers (including the writer) 100 students is a sufficiently large number to count as many, even though it is only a third of the total number of students, and the sentence is true if 100 students preferred assignments.

These judgements are quite sensitive to the size of the background set. Suppose the class has 24 students and eight of them preferred assignments. In this instance it is not so clear that many students preferred assignments to tests, because eight is not a large number, even though it represents the same proportion of the total as 100 out of 300. With the class of 24 students as background, it is more likely that numbers which count as large will be the same as numbers which are greater than half, in which case cardinality and proportionality cannot be distinguished.

Suppose there are six students in the class and five prefer assignments. The assignment-preferrers are substantially more than half the class, and it is true that most students prefer assignments, but because five is an absolutely small number it seems that 'Many students prefer assignments' is an inappropriate and somewhat misleading way to describe the situation. Because no large numbers at all are involved, *many* does not apply.

In short, it may be that *many* is really cardinal in all uses and simply denotes a large number.

Large is a **gradable predicate**: that is, whether or not a thing counts as large depends on what kind of thing it is. A common example of this is that a small elephant is very much larger than a large butterfly. *Large* and *small* do not have absolute values. When we talk about small elephants and large butterflies we can set the scale for largeness or smallness in comparison with the typical size of elephants and butterflies, which will fall somewhere near the middle of a fixed range. There is a maximum size and a minimum size for elephants (although the cut-off points are fuzzy). An elephant counts as large if it is considerably larger than an average-sized or typical elephant, and small if it is considerably smaller than an average-sized or typical elephant.

The largeness of numbers cannot be judged so easily without a relevant context because there is no upper limit on numbers in general, and so no fixed range to determine the typical or average number. (Negative numbers are not used in everyday talk about quantities, so generally zero is the lower limit on the relevant range of numbers.) Which numbers count as large varies with the context. In the examples above the total class size provides a number (300, 24, 8) as a standard for comparison – the comparison standard sets the overall scale for judging numbers as large or not. With a comparison range like 1–300 the numbers which count as large may begin at around 80 or 90, which is less than half the comparison upper limit. Against a range of 1–24 the numbers which count as large will generally be the numbers which are larger than the average, or midpoint, of the range: then many and most will be the same quantities. But if the whole scale is confined to small numbers then perhaps no number on the scale can count as many, even if numbers near the top of the scale can count as most. The uses of *many* which seem to be proportional are the uses where *many* picks out a large number of members of a known 'medium-sized' background set. The background set provides a scale for judging what is a large number, and numbers which count as large coincide with numbers greater than half the background set.

4.3.4 *Few* and *A Few*

Cardinal *few* and *a few* both denote a small number, but they are not interchangeable. The difference between them seems to be pragmatic, rather than strictly semantic, as the choice of *few* or *a few* seems to depend on what is expected in the general context rather than on differences in truth conditions. This is illustrated in (19).

(19)a   Spring was late in coming, and few flowers were blooming.
   b ? Spring was late in coming, and a few flowers were blooming.
   c ? Winter was ending at last, and few flowers were blooming.
   d   Winter was ending at last, and a few flowers were blooming.

In (19a, b) the first clause *Spring was late in coming* suggests, or introduces an expectation that there may be no flowers in bloom, or that the number of flowers in bloom will be smaller than one might otherwise expect for the time of year. In other words, there are only a small number of flowers or at most a small number of flowers in bloom. With this 'at most, only (possibly none)' expectation, *few* is appropriate as in (19a) and *a few* is anomalous as in (19b).

In (19c, d), on the other hand, the clause *Winter was ending at last* introduces the expectation that flowers will be beginning to bloom. The small number of flowers in bloom is at least as many as one might have expected. Here *a few* is appropriate as in (19d) and *few* is anomalous as in (19c).

The 'only n flowers' expectation with 'Spring was late' in contrast with 'Winter was ending' is also illustrated in (20).

(20)a   Spring was late in coming, and only five tulips were blooming.
   b ? Winter was ending at last, and only five tulips were blooming.

The appropriate combinations in (19) are reversed, however, if the clauses are joined with *but*, which signals a clash in expectation between the two parts of the statement.

(21)a ? Spring was late in coming, but few flowers were blooming.
   b   Spring was late in coming, but a few flowers were blooming.
   c   Winter was ending at last, but few flowers were blooming.
   d ? Winter was ending at last, but a few flowers were blooming.

4.3.5 *Some* and *Several*

Plural *some* and *several* are both cardinal determiners of vague plurality, not specified as either large or small. *Some* is defined here as the existential quantifier with singularity or plurality marked on the N′, as in (22).

| (22) | Some dog is barking. | $\|D \cap B\| \geq 1$ | 'at least one' |
| | Some dogs are barking. | $\|D \cap B\| \geq 2$ | 'at least two' |

Several seems to differ from *some* in requiring a slightly larger number than two as the lower limit. In particular, if two dogs are barking then 'Some dogs are barking' is true but 'Several dogs are barking' is false.

4.4 PROPORTIONAL DETERMINERS AND DISCOURSE FAMILIARITY

The proportionality of strong determiners affects the way strong NPs function in a discourse. We know that strong determiners express a proportion of a total set, given by the restriction predicate, and that whether a proportion counts as all, few or most depends on the size of the whole set.

In fully general statements the whole set is the set of all things there are of the kind described. In the examples in (23) the proportions picked out are all of the men there are, most of the people there are, and few of the cars there are.

(23)a All men are mortal.
    b Most people are protective of children.
    c Few cars can exceed 180 m.p.h.

But the quantified statements we use day to day, as in (24), are usually far less general, and pick out a proportion of a smaller set.

(24)a All men must report before taking leave.
    b Most people voted for Continuance.
    c Few cars are expected to finish the trial.

Compared to the first group, these sentences strike us as being taken out of context, because a context is needed to provide the information of which men, which people and which cars are the relevant background: for example, men on a particular military base, people who voted in a particular referendum, and cars in a particular performance trial. The use of examples like (24) signals that the speaker or writer assumes, or presupposes, that the audience can identify the background set, either from general shared knowledge, or because the information has been given earlier in the discourse. If the background set is known to the audience by being previously mentioned in the discourse it has **discourse familiarity**.

But suppose that the background set hasn't been mentioned previously and isn't part of the audience's shared knowledge. Then the background set must be provided by including the information in N', as shown in the bracketed NPs below.

(25)a [All enlisted men now serving on this base] must report before taking leave.

b [Most people who voted in the October temperance referendum] voted for Continuance.

c [Few cars now competing in the Sunfuels trial] are expected to finish the trial.

If the description in N' contains enough information to identify a background set which was not already familiar, then the incompleteness effect we see in (24) disappears.

Cardinal quantifiers do not express a proportion and do not require a given background set. Accordingly, a weak NP can be used to introduce new entities into a discourse without seeming to be incomplete. The example used above for weak *few*, *The house seemed clean and Lee found very few fleas* makes the first mention of fleas in the discourse; *very few fleas* shows **discourse novelty**. In contrast, in *No flies and few fleas survived*, the example for strong *few*, the fleas mentioned are taken from the familiar set of fleas in the insecticide test.

Although weak NPs do not need to denote familiar individuals, they can pick out individuals from a previously mentioned group, as in (26).

(26) As I waited, a large school party entered the museum. Several children went to the Egyptian display and looked at the mummy.

Here the NP *several children* denotes children from the previously mentioned school party, but this effect is produced by mechanisms of discourse coherence, and not by the semantics of *several*, which is not proportional.

4.5 QUANTIFIERS AND *THERE BE* SENTENCES

NPs were classified as strong or weak by Milsark (1977), who pointed out that the NP position after *there BE* in sentences like *There is a fly in my soup* must be filled by a weak NP. Strong NPs in this position are anomalous.

(27)a   There was a dog in the garden.
b   There were several dogs in the garden.
c   There were many dogs in the garden.
d   There were four dogs in the garden.
e # There was every dog in the garden.
f # There were most guests in the garden.

The strong/weak classification of NPs includes referring NPs such as names, demonstratives and personal pronouns, which are all strong.

(28)a   # There was Terry in the garden.
    b   # There was that dog in the garden.
    c   # There were they/them in the garden.

Studies of the *there BE* construction and similar constructions in other languages have come up with a range of explanations for the resistance to strong NPs, generally along the following lines: the *there BE* construction <u>asserts</u> the existence of the denotation of NP. This clashes with the semantics of strong NPs, which <u>presuppose</u> the existence of the referent (for referential NPs) or presuppose the existence of a background set (for quantificational NPs).

Testing for the strong/weak distinction with *there BE* sentences can be confusing, as there seem to be at least four kinds of *there BE* sentences:

(i)   Basic existential *there BE*
(ii)   Presentational *there BE*, introducing a new entity or situation into the discourse.
(iii)   Task *there BE*, in the frame *there BE NP to VP*.
(iv)   List *there BE*.

These types sre reviewed below – only the first two types are diagnostic for strong NPs.

4.5.1   Basic Existential *There BE*

The main diagnostic *there be* sentences, and the easiest kind to recognize, are basic existential sentences like those in (29).

(29)a   There is a solution to this problem.
    b   There are no ghosts.
    c   There is no antidote to cyanide.
    d   There is a *roman-à-clef* about them but I forget the title.

These sentences simply assert the existence or non-existence of whatever the NP denotes. In these sentences the NP must be weak.

(30)   As for spontaneous combustion...
      a   There are several books on the subject.
      b   There are many books on the subject.
      c   There are four books on the subject.
      d   There are a few books on the subject.
      e   There are few books on the subject.
      f   There are some books on the subject.
      g   # There are the books on the subject.

h # There are all the books on the subject.
i # There are most books on the subject.
j # There is every book on the subject.

Existential *there BE* sentences are said without any stress on *there*, so that (30j), for example, sounds like 'Th'z every book...'. This is not the same as *there* indicating location, which is pronounced with more stress, as in (31).

(31) Here is the reading list, and there are all the books on the subject. (pointing)

Locative *there* with *be* can combine with any kind of NP, including strong NPs as in (32).

(32) There are most of the team now, over by the gate.

Suppose that *BE* in the *there BE* construction is 'existence' *BE*, in keeping with the view that *there BE* has existential force. Then the analysis of (30i), for example, is along the lines of (33).

(33) There are most books on the subject
$$|F \cap G| > |F - G|$$
where F = the set of all x such that x is a book on the subject
and G = the set of all x such that x exists

According to this definition the books on the subject which exist outnumber the books on the subject which don't exist. The trouble is that *most* requires the background set of all books on the subject, and this includes the assumption that all such books exist (in whatever mode of existence the discourse sets up). Given that all members of the background set of books on the subject exist, what can it mean to assert that the greater part of this same set exists? Such an assertion is redundant, at best, and such sentences are accordingly anomalous.

4.5.2 Presentational *There BE*

Presentational *there BE* introduces a new entity into the discourse, or an entity and situation combined, as illustrated in (34).

(34)a In the corner between the bus shelter and the school wall there were [a number of cigarette butts] and [a couple of muddy heel-prints].
   b There was [a small brown cat] sitting on top of the door.
   c They can't sneak in without a warrant – there are [some tenants] in the house.
   d There are [only three rooms] available.

    e   There are [five residents] sick.
    h   There's [someone] knocking on the back door.
    g   There's [a weta] in your curry.

By comparison with type (i), these sentences do not simply assert the existence of the entities described, but also give information about the state of affairs in which the entities are involved. This is particularly clear in (34d, e) where the availability of the rooms and the sickness of the residents are the main information conveyed. Sentences like these must have a weak NP. Examples with strong NPs are in (35).

(35)a   #   There were most fans screaming on the jetty.
    b   #   There were most of the fans screaming on the jetty.
    c   #   There was every customer demanding a refund.
    d   #   There were all the children playing in the garden.

Unlike the basic existentials, these sentences have a near-paraphrase without the *there BE* construction, as in (36).

(36)a   A number of cigarette butts and a couple of muddy heel prints were in the corner between the bus shelter and the school wall.
    b   A small brown cat was sitting on top of the door.
    c   Some tenants are in the house.
    d   Only three rooms are available.
    e   Five residents are sick.
    f   Someone is knocking on the back door.
    g   A weta is in your curry.

The other two kinds of *there BE* sentences allow strong NPs.

4.5.3   Task *There BE*

The task *there BE* construction takes the form *there BE NP to VP*, as illustrated in (37). Task *there BE* takes strong and weak NPs.

(37)a   There are most of the fruit trees still to prune and spray.
    b   There are many fruit trees still to prune and spray.
    c   There are Maria, Lee and Casey to notify.
    d   ?   If they try to block the road they'll find there's us to contend with.
    e   ?   The meeting could be delayed – there's that to consider.

This construction presents a task or action which lies ahead of someone; someone has to prune and spray the fruit trees, notify Maria, Lee and Casey, and so on. Although (37d, e) with pronouns sound a little odd, they sound more natural than a pronoun in either existential *there BE* (38a, b) or presentational *there BE* (38c, d).

(38)a # There is she / her.
   b # Forget Ayesha – there is no she / her.
   c # There's he / him needing a new muffler.
   d # There are they / them still expecting a reply.

The Task *there BE* construction is like an impersonal variant of a construction with *HAVE*, which includes the information of whose task it is.

(39)a The apprentices have most of the fruit trees to prune and spray.
   b I have Maria, Lee and Casey to notify.
   c They'll have us to contend with.
   d We have that to consider.

4.5.4 List *There BE*

The last kind of *there BE* construction gives the list reading, so called because list *there BE* typically introduces a list of NPs uttered with a characteristic 'list-reading' intonation. The listed NPs denote entities with a common property, which may be identified in a question. The list is the answer to the question, for example:

(40)a Who might have seen Lenny leaving the bar?
     – Well, there's the barman of course, Miss Radlett and her friend, everyone who was waiting to use the phone, . . .

   b Who's free to work on Saturday?
     – There's me for a start, Paula, Larry and Henry . . . is four enough?

   c What do you have under $100.00?
     – There's this one, this one, and that one over there. (*pointing*)
     – There's everything in this case here.
     – There's most of the Ragzic range – they're very popular.

Like task *there BE*, list *there BE* also takes strong NPs quite freely.

In summary, strong NPs clash with existential and presentational *there BE*, and these two constructions are good tests for NP strength, but it is important to avoid list and task *there BE*, both of which allow strong NPs.

4.6 QUANTIFIERS AND NEGATIVE POLARITY ITEMS

Negative Polarity Items (NPIs or **negpols** for short) are expressions which can only occur in special contexts, including contexts which are in some sense in the scope of negation. Idiomatic NPIs include *budge an inch* and *lift a finger*, as illustrated in (41). The negative expression is underlined.

(41) a   <u>Nobody</u> lifted a finger to stop him.
     b   #   Several people lifted a finger to stop him.
     c   I do<u>n't</u> suppose they'll lift a finger to help.
     d   #   I suppose they'll lift a finger to help.
     e   He wo<u>n't</u> budge an inch on this issue.
     f   #   He might budge an inch on this issue.
     g   For all their efforts the trailer <u>never</u> budged an inch.
     h   #   After all their efforts at last the trailer budged an inch.

The commonest NPIs are *any* (*anyone*, *anything*) and *ever*.

(42) a   Sue wo<u>n't</u> ever go there again.
     b   #   Sue will ever go there again.
     c   The office has<u>n't</u> notified anyone.
     d   #   The office has notified anyone.

Despite their name, NPIs are not actually confined to negative contexts, and occur with some quantifier determiners (in addition to *no*). As the examples in (43) with NPI *ever* show, the NPI may appear in N′ or in VP or in both.

(43)   <u>every</u>
     a   [Everyone who has ever been to Belltree Island] will want to go back.
     b   #   [Everyone who has been to Belltree Island] will ever want to go back.

     <u>no</u>
     c   [No one who has ever been to Belltree Island] will want to go back.
     d   [No one who has been to Belltree Island] will ever want to go back.

     <u>few</u> (weak *few*)
     e   [Few people who have ever been to Belltree Island] will want to go back.
     f   [Few people who have been to Belltree Island] will ever want to go back.

     <u>some</u>
     g   #   [Someone who has ever been to Belltree Island] will want to go back.
     h   #   [Someone who has been to Belltree Island] will ever want to go back.

four

i # [Four people who have ever been to Belltree Island] will want to go back.

j # [Four people who have been to Belltree Island] will ever want to go back.

These examples show that the NPI *ever* is licensed in N' with *every*, *no* and *few*, but not with *some* or *four*, and is licensed in VP with *no* and *few*, but not with *every*, *some* or *four*. The results are summarized in (44).

(44)

	ever in N'	*ever* in VP
every	yes	no
no	yes	yes
few	yes	yes
some	no	no
four	no	no

Ladusaw (1980) identified the contexts which license NPIs as **downward-entailing environments**. **Entailment** is a relation between propositions. When A entails B, if A is true then B must also be true – B is an entailment of A.

The entailing environments of interest in Ladusaw's analysis are N' and VP. In a sentence *Det Fs are G*, N' denotes the F set and VP denotes the G set. Whether an N' or VP is downward-entailing or upward entailing depends on the determiner.

The N' environment can be tested with the frames in (45).

(45)a If 'Det Fs are G' entails 'Det Es are G' and E$\subseteq$F, then F is downward-entailing.

b If 'Det Fs are G' entails 'Det Es are G' and F$\subseteq$E, then F is upward-entailing.

Given that the set of large dogs is a subset of the set of dogs, we can use the test sentences *Det dogs are white* and *Det large dogs are white*. Entailment from the *dogs* sentence to the *large dogs* sentence is entailment towards the subset, and is a downward entailment. Entailment from the *large dogs* sentence to the *dogs* sentence is an entailment towards the superset, and is an upward entailment.

The VP environment can be tested with the frames in (46).

(46)a If 'Det Fs are G' entails 'Det Fs are H' and H$\subseteq$G, then G is downward-entailing.

b If 'Det Fs are G' entails 'Det Fs are H' and G$\subseteq$H, then G is upward-entailing.

Given that the set of people whistling 'Dixie' is a subset of the set of people whistling, the VP test sentences can be *Det N is/are whistling* and *Det N is/are whistling 'Dixie'*. An entailment from the *whistling* sentence to the *whistling 'Dixie'* sentence is a downward entailment, and an entailment from the *whistling 'Dixie'* sentence to the *whistling* sentence is an upward entailment.

The tests for the different determiners are shown below.

N' with *Every*:   DOWNWARD
'Every dog is white' entails 'Every large dog is white'.
'Every large dog is white' does not entail 'Every dog is white'.

VP with *Every*:   UPWARD
'Everyone is whistling' does not entail 'Everyone is whistling "Dixie"'.
'Everyone is whistling "Dixie"' entails 'Everyone is whistling'.

N' with *No*:   DOWNWARD
'No dogs are white' entails 'No large dogs are white'.
'No large dogs are white' does not entail 'No dogs are white'.

VP with *No*:   DOWNWARD
'No one is whistling' entails 'No one is whistling "Dixie"'.
'No one is whistling "Dixie"' does not entail 'No one is whistling'.

N' with *Few*:   DOWNWARD
'Few dogs are white' entails 'Few large dogs are white'.
'Few large dogs are white' does not entail 'Few dogs are white'.

VP with *Few*:   DOWNWARD
'Few people are whistling' entails 'Few people are whistling "Dixie"'.
'Few people are whistling "Dixie"' does not entail 'Few people are whistling'.

N' with *Some*:   UPWARD
'Some dogs are white' does not entail 'Some large dogs are white'.
'Some large dogs are white' entails 'Some dogs are white'.

VP with *Some*:   UPWARD
'Someone is whistling' does not entail 'Someone is whistling "Dixie"'.
'Someone is whistling "Dixie"' entails 'Someone is whistling'.

N' with *Four*:   UPWARD
'Four dogs are white' does not entail 'Four large dogs are white'.
'Four large dogs are white' entails 'Four dogs are white'.

VP with *Four*:   UPWARD
'Four people are whistling' does not entail 'Four people are whistling "Dixie"'.
'Four people are whistling "Dixie"' entails 'Four people are whistling'.

The downward and upward entailments are summarized in (47).

(47)

	N'	VP
every	down	up
no	down	down
few	down	down
some	up	up
four	up	up

The environments which allow negative polarity items were listed in (44), repeated here in (48). As we see, the NPI licensing environments are exactly the downward-entailing environments, as predicted.

(48)

	ever in N'	ever in VP
every	yes	no
no	yes	yes
few	yes	yes
some	no	no
four	no	no

EXERCISES

(A)   Restricted Quantifier Notation: Basic Review

Using restricted quantifier notation, give the formulae for the sentences below.

Example:
  John photographed every model that Bill hired.
  [Every x: MODEL(x) & HIRE(b, x)] PHOTOGRAPH(j, x)

(1)   Anne has read most books on psychoanalysis.
(2)   Few who knew him supported Baxter.
(3)   Some students who heard both concerts were interviewed by Holmes.
(4)   Morris showed Jane every fingerprint he dusted.
(5)   Marcia peeled and quartered three apples.
(6)   Most travellers entering or leaving Australia visit Sydney.
(7)   Ramòn signs every sculpture he makes.
(8)   Marcia and Clive ate four apples each.
(9)   Jones restored and sold several valuable paintings.
(10) Most bulbs will not grow if they are dry.

(B)   Two Quantifiers: Scopal Ambiguity

Using restricted quantifier notation, give the two representations for each sentence below and indicate their meanings.

(1)   Everyone in this room speaks two languages.
(2)   Three investigators described a new technique.
(3)   John gave all his students a book on Derrida.

(C)   Quantifier Definitions

All of the underlined sequences below can be analysed as quantifiers. Give the set theoretic definitions for these sentences, using the symbols given in the chapter.

Example: More than four ants are black. $|A \cap B| > 4$

(1)   <u>The ten</u> apples are bruised.
(2)   <u>Neither</u> artist is Bulgarian.
(3)   <u>Just two of the ten</u> arrows are broken.
(4)   <u>Between five and ten</u> airlines are bankrupt.
(5)   <u>Both</u> avenues are broad.
(6)   <u>Fewer</u> than five aubergines are baked.

The discontinuous determiners in the next examples relate three sets, two in a complex N$'$ and one in the VP.

(7)   <u>More</u> architects <u>than</u> bricklayers are cricketers.
(8)   <u>Exactly as many</u> almond fingers <u>as</u> brownies are cooked.
(9)   <u>Fewer</u> autobiographers <u>than</u> biographers are candid.

(D)   Restricted Quantifier Notation

Using restricted quantifier notation, give the formulae for the sentences below.

(1)   The witch picked a leaf from every tree in the forest.
(2)   A few people from each town lost everything they owned.
(3)   Three dogs and several cats killed two or three rats each.
(4)   Every dog that chased a cat that chased Mickey got a bone.

(E)   *All*, *Every* and *Each*: Discussion

The first order formula:

$$\forall x(F(x) \rightarrow G(x))$$

analyses universal quantification in terms of individual propositions: if a, b, c, d, ... are names of individuals, the propositions below, formed by substituting a name for x, are true if the universal proposition is true.

$$F(a) \rightarrow G(a)$$
$$F(b) \rightarrow G(b)$$
$$F(c) \rightarrow G(c)$$
$$F(d) \rightarrow G(d)$$

The set theory definitions for *all* and *every* are also based on individuals, given that the sets used are sets of individuals, that is:

All Fs are G $F \subseteq G$
where $F =$ the set of all x such that $F(x)$
and $G =$ the set of all x such that $G(x)$.

Now consider the sentences below. (Some of these sentences are anomalous.) It seems that *all* and *every* are not interchangeable. What is the difference between them, and how does the difference bear on the analysis of universal quantification used here?

(1)   All ravens are black.
(2)   Every raven is black.
(3)   All raven is black.
(4)   Every ravens are black.

(5)   All these pieces fit together to make a picture.
(6)   Every piece here fits together to make a picture.

(7)   The price of all these pieces is $20.00.
(8)   The price of every piece here is $20.00.

What about *each*? Can you identify what makes *each* different from *all* and *every*?

(9)   John checked that all the delegates were registered.
(10)   John checked that every delegate was registered.
(11)   John checked that each delegate was registered.

(12)   The park is open to all local residents.
(13)   The park is open to every local resident.
(14)   The park is open to each local resident.

(15)   The committee met every day.
(16)   The committee met each day.
(17)   The committee met every single day.
(18)   The committee met each single day.
(19)   The committee met every second day.
(20)   The committee met each second day.

(F)   Negative Polarity Items: Discussion

Section 4.6 outlines Ladusaw's proposal that negative polarity items (NPIs) are licensed in downward-entailing environments, and shows how this applies with quantifiers. NPIs also occur in other environments such as those illustrated in the sentences below – the NPI here is *anyone*. Can all these environments be described as downward-entailing?

(1)	Mary didn't see anyone.
(2)	# Anyone didn't see Mary.

(3)	Did Mary see anyone?
(4)	Did anyone see Mary?

(5)	If Mary saw anyone she'll tell us.
(6)	If anyone saw Mary she'll tell us.

(7)	Had Mary seen anyone she would have told us.
(8)	Had anyone seen Mary she would have told us.

(9)	I doubt that Mary saw anyone.
(10)	I doubt that anyone saw Mary.
(11)	# I suspect that Mary saw anyone.
(12)	# I suspect that anyone saw Mary.
(13)	Mary forgot that she saw anyone.
(14)	Mary forgot that anyone saw her.
(15)	# Mary remembered that she saw anyone.
(16)	# Mary remembered that anyone saw her.

(17)	Mary denied that she saw anyone.
(18)	Mary denied that anyone saw her.
(19)	# Mary confirmed that she saw anyone.
(20)	# Mary confirmed that anyone saw her.

(21)	Only Mary saw anyone.
(22)	# Anyone saw only Mary.

Further Reading

On generalized quantifiers, see Section 2.5, pp. 38–47, 'Quantifiers in Natural Language' in Neale (1990), and Keenan (1996).

On the weak / strong distinction, see Section 8.4.2, pp. 286–94, in Larson and Segal (1996), papers in Reuland and ter Meulen (1987), especially the editors' introduction, and Milsark (1977).

On negative polarity items, see Section 8.4.1, pp. 281–6, in Larson and Segal (1996), and Ladusaw (1996).

5 Definite Descriptions

Traditionally, definite NPs pick out definite or particular objects that the hearer can identify. Definite NPs include names, possessive NPs such as *John's jacket*, demonstrative NPs such as *that boulder*, *those tablets*, and referring pronouns. But generally, discussion of definite descriptions concentrates on NPs beginning with the definite article *the*, like the examples below.

(1) *singular*:
the earth, the moon, the president of Venezuela, the director of 'Eraserhead', the pie Clive had for breakfast

plural:
the days of our lives, the books on that shelf, the leaders of fashion.

Singular definite descriptions seem to bridge the divide between quantifier NPs and names. On the one hand, a description like *the director of 'Eraserhead'* is structured like a quantifier NP, consisting of a determiner and an N′ with descriptive content, parallel to *some fans of Rosemary Clooney* or *every yacht in the marina*. On the other hand, this NP picks out a particular individual, and seems to refer to him just as the name *David Lynch* refers to him. A number of issues concerning the meaning of *the* arise out of the apparent dual nature of singular descriptions.

Our starting point for discussion of *the* is the classic analysis of Bertrand Russell, reviewed in the next section.

5.1 RUSSELL'S THEORY OF DESCRIPTIONS

Russell held that the reference of names is simple and direct. The semantic value of a name is simply the object it refers to, and accordingly the proposition expressed by a sentence containing a name contains that object as a component: such propositions are therefore said to be object-dependent. For example, the proposition expressed by the sentence *Mt. Cook is high* contains the mountain itself as a constituent. Consequently, a sentence containing a name which has no referent fails to express any proposition at all.

On this point, names and singular descriptions are different. The difference can be illustrated with the examples below.

(2)a Brogdasa is becoming larger.
  b The volcano near Paris is becoming larger.

Assuming that the name *Brogdasa* doesn't refer to anything, sentence (2a) doesn't express a proposition. If it did, we should be able to tell what kind of state of affairs would constitute the truth condition for such a proposition. Depending on what Brogdasa is (if the name has a referent) the situation might be a living creature growing, a cyclone building, or a town spreading. In fact the meaninglessness of the empty name leaves us in the dark. In contrast, sentence (2b) is meaningful, despite the fact that there is no volcano near Paris, and it is clear what kind of state of affairs would hold if the sentence were true. There would be one volcano near Paris and that volcano would be becoming larger.

Accordingly, Russell proposed that a sentence with a non-denoting definite description is meaningful – it does express a proposition, and the proposition is false.

Generally, as Russell observed, a correct use of a definite description to denote an individual has two requirements: there must be an individual accurately described by the description, and there must be only one. These two requirements, commonly called **existential commitment** (there is such a thing) and the **uniqueness requirement** (there is only one), are built into the meaning of *the* in Russell's analysis, as shown below.

(3)   The King of France is bald:

$\exists x$ (KING OF FRANCE(x) & $\forall y$ (KING OF FRANCE(y) $\rightarrow$ y = x) & BALD(x))
'There is an x such that x is a King of France, and any y which is a King of France is the same object as x, and x is bald'.

   a   'There is a King of France' (existential commitment)
   b   'There is no King of France other than x or there is only one King of France' (uniqueness requirement)
   c   'He is bald.'

Here, to assert *The King of France is bald* is to assert three conjoined propositions, shown in (3a–c) above. If any of these is false the whole proposition is false. Given that France is a republic, the description *the King of France* doesn't denote anything, and so *The King of France is bald* expresses a false proposition because clause (3a), the first conjunct, is false.

The main enduring feature of Russell's theory is that *the* is analysed as a quantifier (for Russell, the existential quantifier with the uniqueness qualification). If this is correct, a definite description should show the characteristics of quantifiers outlined in Chapter 4.

5.2   *THE* AS A GENERALIZED QUANTIFIER

Russell's main focus was the different referential properties of names and singular definite descriptions. Concentrating on singular definite descriptions, Russell built the uniqueness requirement into the meaning of *the*. This implies that the definite article in plural descriptions must be analysed as a different word, because the meaning of a plural description such as *the books on that shelf* obviously is not compatible with the claim that there is only one such book. But surely the word *the* in *the book on that shelf* and *the books on that shelf* is the same word, and the analysis should separate out the uniqueness requirement so that it only applies to the singular NPs. Ideally, there is some constant meaning for *the* which is found in both singular and plural NPs.

What kind of quantificational meaning might *the* have in plural NPs? Consider the underlined NPs below.

(4) Bob bought some livestock, sheep and cows, at the sale. Jenny vaccinated <u>the cows</u> the following week, and Bob dipped <u>the sheep</u>.

Here, Jenny vaccinated all of the cows that Bob bought, not just some of them, and Bob dipped all of the sheep he bought, not just some of them. So plural *the* seems to be a universal quantifier, meaning 'all'. The difference between singular and plural NPs is only marked on the noun, just as it is in NPs with *some*.

(5) Some dog ripped open the rubbish.
Some dogs ripped open the rubbish.

The number distinction with *some* was analysed in Chapter 4 like this:

(6) Some Fs are G $|F \cap G| \geq 2$
'At least two things are both F and G'
Some F is G $|F \cap G| \geq 1$
'At least one thing is both F and G'

Both of these definitions define *some* as giving the cardinality of the intersection of two sets. The extra information, 'at least two' or 'at least one', must come from the form of the noun.

The same strategy can apply to *the*. Assuming that *the* is a universal quantifier, the definition for it contains the definition clause given in Chapter 4 for *all* and *every*.

(7) All Fs are G $F \subseteq G$

Now add the information about number derived from the singular or plural form of the noun.

(8) The Fs are G $F \subseteq G$ & $|F| \geq 2$
'All Fs are G and there are at least two Fs'

The F is G $F \subseteq G$ & $|F| = 1$
'All Fs are G and there is exactly one F'

Existential commitment is coded in both the cardinality statements, '$|F| \geq 2$' and '$|F| = 1$', because both statements guarantee that at least one such thing exists. The uniqueness requirement is coded in '$|F| = 1$', and only applies to singular descriptions, as required.

5.3   DEFINITE DESCRIPTIONS AS STRONG NPS

To analyse *the* as a universal quantifier determiner is to class definite descriptions with strong NPs, and we would expect to see the familiarity effects reviewed in Section 4.4 and the *there BE* effects reviewed in Section 4.5. This expectation is fulfilled. In fact, both these phenomena were first noticed with definite descriptions and have been traditionally identified as characteristic of definite descriptions. The realization that strong NPs in general share these effects came later.

5.3.1   Familiarity Effects

In traditional grammars, before Russell's logical analysis, the meaning of *the* was explained in terms of a contrast between the two articles, *the* and *a/an*, as illustrated below.

(9)   An old man came down the road leading a donkey. The donkey carried
      a load of produce for market, and now and then the old man adjusted
      the load more securely.

Here *a* signals a novel referent, used for the first mention of something, as in *an old man* and *a donkey*. *The* signals a familiar referent, so *the donkey* must refer to the donkey introduced by *a donkey*, and so on.

   Earlier, this was not considered to be a quantificational phenomenon – the difference between *the* and *a/an* was described in terms of their use in the context of a discourse, and accordingly classed as pragmatic rather than semantic. More recently, formal versions of what is called the familiarity theory of definiteness were developed by Irene Heim (1982) and Hans Kamp (1981).

   In fact, the quantificational analysis of *the* can be shown to predict the familiarity effect. Recall that strong quantifiers express a proportion of a set. To understand a proposition with a strong quantifier, the hearer must be able to identify the background set. For example, the quantifier in *Most people voted for Continuance* takes as a background set the set of people who voted in a particular referendum, and the hearer must know this to understand the proposition. Commonly, the relevant set is made known to the hearer by being previously mentioned in the discourse, in which case it has discourse familiarity.

According to the definition above, the NP *the donkey* in (9) expresses a universal quantification over a background set of donkeys with just one member. In identifying this set, the hearer also identifies the individual which is its only member. Because of the singularity component, a singular definite description provides not only a familiar SET, but, more saliently, a familiar INDIVIDUAL, and in this regard singular definites are unlike other quantificational NPs. The familiarity of an individual is more striking than the familiarity of a background set, which is probably why the familiarity effect was first identified as a characteristic of *the*.

We saw in Section 4.4 that a strong quantifier NP does not need to take a familiar background set if the NP itself contains an adequate description of the background set. The examples in (10), repeated from Chapter 4, are **incomplete descriptions**.

(10)a [All men] must report before taking leave.
   b [Most people] voted for Continuance.
   c [Few cars] are expected to finish the trial.

When the sentences stand alone, as they do here, they seem to be taken out of context – the NPs are incomplete in that they don't give enough information for us to know which men, which people and which cars are mentioned. In an appropriate context these NPs would show a familiarity effect. The relevant groups of men, people and cars would count as familiar in being already known to the audience, commonly by being previously mentioned in the same text or discourse.

The examples in (11) contain more informative descriptions, where the background set of men, people or cars would not need to be familiar because it is identified in the NP.

(11)a [All enlisted men now serving on this base] must report before taking leave.
   b [Most people who voted in the October temperance referendum] voted for Continuance.
   c [Few cars now competing in the Sunfuels trial] are expected to finish the trial.

Strictly speaking, the NPs in (11) are still incomplete, because we still need a context to identify, for example, the time *now* refers to, the base that *this base* refers to, and to identify exactly the October temperance referendum and the Sunfuels trial in question. So the sentences in (11) would still need to be used in a context which provides this information. To make the NPs in

(11) complete, we would need to spell out all the information which depends on a context. For example, (11a) might be

(12)   [All enlisted men serving on the RNZAF base at Wigram on 24th December 1969] must report before taking leave.

The bracketed description in (12) is a **complete description** because it can be fully interpreted independently of any particular context of use. An incomplete description is a description which is partly dependent on a particular context, such as the bracketed NPs in (10) and (11).

The same kind of contrast is found with definite descriptions. Although incomplete descriptions are used more often in everyday talk, earlier discussions of definite descriptions focused on complete descriptions like those in (13).

(13)a   The author of *Waverley*
     b   The king of France in 1770
     c   The director of *Eraserhead*

These descriptions are complete because they pick out a unique individual regardless of any particular context. There aren't any particular contexts (in the actual world) which would provide alternative sets of authors of *Waverley*, or kings of France in 1770, or directors of *Eraserhead*. As things are, there is only one set of authors of *Waverley* with any members in it, and that is the set containing Sir Walter Scott as its only member. Similarly, the set containing Louis XV as its only member is the only non-empty set of kings of France in 1770, and the set containing David Lynch as its only member is the only non-empty set of directors of *Eraserhead*.

Descriptions like these (that is, complete singular definite descriptions) give the strongest support to Russell's claim that singular definite descriptions have a uniqueness requirement, because these descriptions fit absolutely only one individual: in other words, there is absolutely only one thing of the kind described. When we turn to incomplete descriptions we see that the uniqueness requirement must work in tandem with information supplied from the context. An incomplete description does not fit absolutely only one individual – there may be many individuals the description fits. But in a particular context there may be only one such individual, and the uniqueness requirement is relative to that context. For example, the description *the donkey* fits thousands of individuals, assuming that there are thousands of donkeys in the world, but in the context provided by the narrative in (9) there is only one donkey. To interpret *the donkey*, we find the appropriate context with just one donkey in it – here, the context of the narrative. This amounts to fixing the background so that there is just one set of donkeys in the background, and that set has only one member.

So far the universal quantifier analysis of *the* predicts that plural definites have roughly the same meaning as NPs with *all* or *every*, except (possibly) for existential commitment. If this is so we would expect the universal quantifiers to be interchangeable, but in some contexts they are not.

(14)a   All men are mortal.
   b   Every man is mortal.
   c ? The men are mortal.

It seems that (14c) is odd because plural *the* cannot be completely independent of a particular context, and must take some contextual subset. (14c) suggests that the men in some particular group, not men in general, are mortal. Even though *the* is interpreted as a kind of universal quantifier, unlike *all* and *every*, *the* is marked for use relativized to a context.

5.3.2   *There BE* Contexts

The peculiar effect of strong NPs in *there BE* contexts was also first noticed with definite descriptions, and is traditionally called the **definiteness effect** for this reason. (Now that definiteness effects are known to hold for strong NPs generally, some writers apply the term *definite NP* to all strong NPs.)

(15)   # There was the dog in the garden.
      # There is the antidote to cobra venom.

5.4 SCOPAL AMBIGUITY

The does not show all the quantifier characteristics as clearly as other quantifiers: in particular, it has been claimed that scopal ambiguities do not arise between *the* and another quantifier in the same sentence. This may not be quite true, as the examples below indicate.

(16)   Rex has been buying vintage cars in a remote country district, and was delighted with his purchases. *Several cars had not left the garage in 30 years.*
      [Several x: CAR(x)] [The y: GARAGE(y)] $\sim$ LEAVE(x, y)

(17)   When the car-hire firm was wound up, *several cars had not left the garage in 30 years.*
      [The x: GARAGE(x)] [Several y: CAR(y)] $\sim$ LEAVE(y, x)

In (16), each car introduces a subdomain in which there is a unique garage, and the quantifier is interpreted as picking out the unique garage for each

car. In (17), *the garage* is interpreted from the context or the preceding
discourse, and the sentence is interpreted as being about the car-hire firm's
large commercial garage. As the formulae show, the difference can be
represented as a difference in scope of the two quantifier determiners, *the*
and *several*.

Take a second example:

(18)   The way to prepare all solutions for this lab is in the Lab Manual.

    a   [The x: PREPARATION METHOD(x) & [All y: SOLUTION FOR
       THIS LAB(y)] FOR(x, y)] x is in the Lab Manual
    b   [All x: SOLUTION FOR THIS LAB(x)] [The y: PREPARATION
       METHOD(y) & FOR(y, x)] y is in the Lab Manual

According to (18a), there is some standard method of preparing solutions in
this lab, and it is in the manual. In (18b), every solution has a different
preparation method or recipe, and the recipes are in the manual. Again, the
difference is represented in the formulae as a difference in scope between *the*
and *all*.

The most important types of scopal ambiguity with *the* do not involve
another quantifier, like the examples here. They involve interactions between
definite descriptions and modal expressions or certain kinds of verbs, as
reviewed in the next section.

5.5   OPACITY: DESCRIPTIONS, MODALITY AND PROPOSITIONAL ATTITUDES

At the beginning of this chapter I said that singular definite descriptions
seem to bridge the gap between quantifiers and names. They are like quantifiers in their form, having a determiner and a meaningful descriptive N'. As
we have seen, definite descriptions are also like quantifiers in showing scopal
interactions with other quantifiers, and like other strong quantifiers in
showing familiarity effects and definiteness effects.

On the other hand, definite descriptions seem to be namelike in their
common use to pick out particular individuals. An example of this I used
earlier was that the description *the director of 'Eraserhead'* and the name
David Lynch both seem to pick out, or refer to, the same individual in the
same way.

Treating definite descriptions as referring expressions (like names) leads to
an intriguing phenomenon which the philosopher Quine called 'referential
opacity'. To set up the problem as Quine identified it, we must adopt the
assumption that singular definite descriptions really are referring expressions, and therefore are grouped with names rather than with quantifiers

where reference is concerned. As we shall see, this choice is crucial to the problem. The discussion below draws on Quine's outline of the problem and on Kripke's response.

5.5.1 Referential Opacity

To understand Quine's point, in addition to classing definite descriptions as referring expressions, we also need a couple of basic logical principles. The first is Leibniz's Law, also known as the Indiscernibility of Identicals.

Leibniz's Law (the Indiscernibility of Identicals)
If A and B are identical, anything which is true of A is also true of B, and vice versa.

Remember that the word *identical* here means 'having the same identity', and does not mean 'having the same appearance' as it does when we speak of identical twins. So *A and B are identical* means that A and B are one and the same thing. In this use *Mohammed Ali and Cassius Clay are identical* means 'Mohammed Ali and Cassius Clay are one and the same person.'

It appears to follow from Leibniz's Law that if A = B, anything you can truly say about A can also be truly said about B: after all, whatever you say is said about exactly the same thing under another name. This assumption gives us an important rule of inference called the Principle of Substitutivity.

Principle of Substitutivity
IF

(1) 'a' refers to a and 'b' refers to b, and
(2) 'a = b' is a true identity statement, and
(3) S1 is a statement containing the expression 'a', and
(4) S2 is a statement identical to S1 EXCEPT that the expression 'b' appears instead of 'a',

THEN S1 and S2 have the same truth value.

According to this principle, two NPs which refer to the same thing can be substituted one for the other in a sentence without changing the truth value of the sentence, which seems reasonable.

Take an example:

(19)a   Mohammed Ali = Cassius Clay   true
   b   <u>Mohammed Ali</u> was a boxer   true
   c   <u>Cassius Clay</u> was a boxer   true

The two names refer to the same person, so the identity statement (19a) is true. (19b) is true. If we take (19b) and substitute one name for the other

name which refers to the same person, the sentence which results from this is
(19c). According to the Principle of Substitutivity (19c) must also be true,
which is correct. In other words, given that (19a) is true, (19b) and (19c)
must have the same truth value, whatever it is.

Example (19) involves the substitution of names. Recall that we are
assuming for now that singular definite descriptions are also referring
expressions, like names, so the same substitutivity should apply to them.
(That is, if definite descriptions are referring expressions they can be values
for 'a' and 'b' in the Principle of Substitutivity.)

Take some further examples:

(20)a Earth = the third rock from the sun.   true
    b <u>Earth</u> is inhabited by humans.   true
    c <u>The third rock from the sun</u> is inhabited by humans.   true

(21)a The director of *Eraserhead* = the director of *Blue Velvet*.   true
    b <u>The director of *Eraserhead*</u> is tall.   true
    c <u>The director of *Blue Velvet*</u> is tall.   true

(22)a John and Cleo have two children: a daughter, Marcia,
       and a son, Damien.   true
    b Clive met <u>Marcia</u> in town.   false
    c Clive met <u>Cleo's daughter</u> in town.   false
    d Clive met <u>John's daughter</u> in town.   false
    e Clive met <u>the daughter of John and Cleo</u> in town.   false
    f Clive met <u>Damien's sister</u> in town.   false

In all of these examples, if two NPs refer to the same thing, you can
substitute one for the other in a sentence, preserving the truth value, whether
true or false.

Quine identified two main kinds of contexts in which the Principle of
Substitutivity apparently fails, and described these contexts as **opaque contexts**. Contexts where the Principle of Substitutivity works are **transparent
contexts**.

The first kind of opaque context is a modal context, as shown in the
examples below.

(23)a Yuri Gagarin = the first man in space   true
    b Yuri Gagarin might not have been <u>the first man in space</u>. true
    c Yuri Gagarin might not have been <u>Yuri Gagarin</u>.   false

Sentences (23b) and (23c) are modal contexts because of the modal expression *might*. According to the possible worlds analysis of modality in Chapter
3, (23b) says that there is at least one possible world or state of affairs in

which Gagarin is not the first man in space, which is true. An alternative possible world which didn't actually eventuate is the possible world in which the American astronaut Alan Shephard is the first man in space.

Example (23c) says that there is at least one possible world in which Yuri Gagarin is not Yuri Gagarin. This is not to say that Gagarin exists in that world under another name. The sentence says that Gagarin exists in that world but isn't the same person as himself. That is, a man exists in another possible world who isn't Gagarin – that is certainly so, but in that case the sentence isn't about this man, because he isn't Gagarin, and the sentence refers to Gagarin by name. Wherever you locate Gagarin in an alternative possible world, he IS Gagarin, and a sentence that says about him that he isn't Gagarin is false. (23c) is false, and the substitution of the underlined NPs in (23) produces a change in truth value.

Here is an example of a necessity context, taken from Quine.

(24)a The number of planets = nine   true
   b   Necessarily, <u>nine</u> is nine.   true
   c   Necessarily, <u>the number of planets</u> is nine.   false

Example (24b) says that the number nine is the same number as nine in every possible world. It's important here to remember that we must stick to the language used in the example, which is Earth Modern English. There are certainly possible worlds in which people use the wordform *nine*, pronounced and spelt as we pronounce and spell it, to refer to a different number. This is irrelevant to (24b), because (24b) is a sentence in our language about other worlds, not a sentence in some other possible language. So (24b) is true. (24c) says that the number of planets is nine in every possible world, which is clearly false. There are possible worlds in which the number of planets (in our solar system) is five, or twelve, or thirty.

To sum up, we see that modal sentences are opaque contexts, because substituting NPs which refer to the same thing (*Yuri Gagarin* and *the first man in space*, *the number of planets* and *nine*) can produce a change in truth value.

The second kind of opaque context is found with verbs such as *know*, *believe*, *think* and *hope*. In Chapter 2 we saw that propositions themselves can be arguments to predicates, in sentences like (25a) and (25b), represented as (25c) and (25d).

(25)a John thinks [that Maria is Polish].
   b   Bella hopes [that Carol will ring Matt].
   c   THINK(j, POLISH(m))
   d   HOPE(b, RING(c,m))

Here *think* is analysed as expressing a relation between John and the proposition expressed by *Maria is Polish*, and *hope* is analysed as expressing a relation between Bella and the proposition expressed by *Carol will ring Matt*. This relation could be described as an attitude held by the thinker or hoper towards the proposition, and these verbs are commonly called **propositional attitude** verbs. The holder of a propositional attitude holds a proposition in mind as a thought of a certain kind, such as a hope, belief or desire. The chief point for our purposes, which we will return to, is that the bracketed parts in (25a) and (25b) describe some sort of mental contents of John and Bella respectively, rather than describing some situation out in the world.

Now consider an example from Quine. Quine sets the scene as follows:

> There is a certain man in a brown hat whom Ralph has glimpsed several times under questionable circumstances on which we need not enter here; suffice it to say that Ralph suspects he is a spy. Also there is a grey-haired man, vaguely known to Ralph as rather a pillar of the community, whom Ralph is not aware of having seen except once at the beach. Now Ralph docs not know it, but the men are one and the same.
>
> (Quine, 1976, p. 187)

Quine also tells us that Ralph knows the man seen at the beach by name, as Bernard J. Ortcutt. According to Ralph, the pillar of the community whom he once saw at the beach is no spy. Therefore:

(26)a   Bernard J. Ortcutt = the man seen at the beach = the
        man in the brown hat.   true
   b   Ralph believes [that <u>Ortcutt</u> is a spy].   false
   c   Ralph believes [that <u>the man in the brown hat</u> is a spy].   true
   d   Ralph believes [that <u>the man seen at the beach</u> is a spy]. false

Here we see that the embedded sentence after *believes* is an opaque context.

To sum up: If we assume that names and singular definite descriptions alike are referring expressions, we must also assume that the Principle of Substitutivity applies to singular definite descriptions as well as to names. In fact, Substitutivity apparently fails in a modal context (a sentence modified by *might, possibly, necessarily*, etc.) or a propositional attitude context (after a verb like *believe*, the expression which describes the content of a belief) and these contexts are called opaque contexts. Transparent contexts are all the others, where Substitutivity works as it should. The examples (19)–(22) at the beginning of this section illustrate transparent contexts.

Now the Principle of Substitutivity, as a logical law, should have no exceptions. In the discussion above I said that in certain cases Substitutivity apparently fails, but if in fact the Principle never fails, the examples above should tell us something about the way the Principle is being applied.

The Principle itself states that one NP can be exchanged for another, preserving the truth value of the sentence, where both NPs are referring expressions and refer to the same thing. So if we have an apparent failure of Substitutivity, this must be a signal that it actually does not apply to these cases: presumably our two NPs don't refer to the same thing, perhaps because at least one of them is not really a referring expression.

As we have seen in the earlier part of this chapter, there are good grounds for treating definite descriptions as quantifiers, and quantifiers are not referring expressions. Singular definite descriptions are unique among quantifiers because of their particular combination of familiarity and singularity. A singular definite description directs the hearer to a known background set which has only one member, and in effect this directs the hearer to the actual individual. In other words, a singular definite description can be used to direct the hearer's attention to a definite individual, but semantically it is not a simple referring expression.

In short, the Principle of Substitutivity provides extra support for the quantificational analysis of definite descriptions. If descriptions are quantifiers, Substitutivity does not apply to them.

In the next two sections we will compare descriptions (analysed as quantifiers) and names in the two kinds of special context. As we shall see, modal contexts are not really opaque, so long as we don't try to substitute quantifiers. Propositional attitudes are more complicated.

5.5.2 Modality, Descriptions and Names

In this section we look at modal contexts in a little more detail, starting with names in modal contexts. Take the sentence *Mozart might not have died young*, with the representation below.

(27)a Mozart might not have died young.
   b $\Diamond \sim$ DIE YOUNG(m)

Working from left to right, we read this formula as

$\Diamond$

'There is at least one possible world w such that...'

$\sim$ DIE YOUNG(m)

'"Mozart did not die young" is true in w'.

The first point here is that the rest of the proposition after '$\Diamond$' is interpreted as describing a state of affairs in another possible world, not in the actual world. The whole sentence is true: there is at least one possible world in which Mozart lived to a seasoned maturity. Choose one of these worlds and consider it.

The second point is that the aged Mozart in that world is Mozart himself, that same person who in our world was a child prodigy and musical genius. The sentence is not about some quite different hypothetical individual who had the same name, or looked like Mozart, or had a similar musical career. The sentence describes a hypothetical situation in which the man himself lived on past his youth. In particular, the name *Mozart* (in Earth Modern English) refers to the same person in our world as it does in any hypothetical world where he appears.

Technically, names are **rigid designators**. A name designates the same individual in all possible worlds where that individual occurs, rigidly or inflexibly. A modal operator cannot alter the reference of a name.

Given that names are rigid designators and cannot be affected by modal contexts, they can be substituted without changing the truth value.

(28)a   Mohammed Ali = Cassius Clay   true
   b   Mohammed Ali might never have won the world title.   true
   c   Cassius Clay might never have won the world title.   true

Any possible world in which Mohammed Ali exists and never won the world title is a world in which Cassius Clay exists and did not win the world title – (28b) and (28c) cannot differ in truth value. So according to Quine's definition, modal contexts are not opaque where the substitution of same-referring names is concerned.

Now consider definite descriptions – if we analyse them as quantifiers, does modality affect their interpretation? Take the Gagarin example again.

(29)   Yuri Gagarin might not have been [the first man in space].

To construct the formula, first move the quantifier to the beginning and leave a variable in its place:

[The x: FIRST MAN IN SPACE(x)] Yuri Gagarin might not have been x

Now move the modal operator to the beginning:

◇ [The x: FIRST MAN IN SPACE(x)] Yuri Gagarin not have been x

The last step is to represent *Yuri Gagarin not have been x* using negation and identity:

◇ [The x: FIRST MAN IN SPACE(x)] ~ g = x

To read off the formula, start at the beginning:

◇
'There is at least one possible world w such that ...'

[The x: FIRST MAN IN SPACE(x)]
'There is exactly one thing (in w) which is the first man in space, and "x" refers to him'

Suppose we have chosen a world in which the Russians launched the first human into space, but the astronaut was a man called Popov. Then x refers to Popov. Now for the rest of the formula:

$\sim g = x$
Gagarin is not the same person as x (in w)

So far so good: this gives the expected reading for *Yuri Gagarin might not have been the first man in space*, which could be paraphrased as 'Some astronaut other than Gagarin might have been launched into space first' – this is true.

There is also another much less plausible reading for sentence (29). Indeed, given that there are two scopal expressions (not counting negation) in the sentence, we would expect it to be scopally ambiguous, having another reading with the modal and quantifier in the opposite order, as in (30).

(30)   [The x: FIRST MAN IN SPACE(x)] ◇ $\sim g = x$

Starting again at the beginning of the formula, we read as follows:

[The x: FIRST MAN IN SPACE(x)]
'There is exactly one thing which is the first man in space, and "x" refers to him ...'

At this stage we have not reached ◇, which switches us into another possible world, so this quantifier is interpreted in the actual world. There is in fact exactly one first man in space, and that is Gagarin, so x refers to Gagarin in this formula. Proceed:

◇
'There is at least one possible world w such that ...'

$\sim g = x$
'Gagarin is not the same person as x (in w).'

We have just established that x refers to Gagarin in this formula, so the formula is false, just as (23c) *Yuri Gagarin might not have been Yuri Gagarin* is false.

To sum up the substitutions in the examples repeated below:

(31)a   Yuri Gagarin might not have been Yuri Gagarin.
    b $\Diamond \sim g = g$
    c   Yuri Gagarin might not have been the first man in space.
    d $\Diamond$ [The x: FIRST MAN IN SPACE(x)] $\sim g = x$
    e   [The x: FIRST MAN IN SPACE(x)] $\Diamond \sim g = x$

Because names are rigid designators, the two occurrences of the name *Yuri Gagarin* in (31a) must refer to the same individual. In any possible world, if Gagarin exists at all he is the same person as himself, so (31a) = (31b) is false.

Descriptions, as quantifiers, are not rigid designators. Which individual is picked out by a description depends on where the description is interpreted. If the modal operator $\Diamond$ has scope over a description, then the description takes another possible world as background, and picks out an individual from that world (if any) according to the descriptive content. Accordingly, in a modal context a name and a 'co-referring' description may refer to, or pick out, different individuals, and so cannot be exchanged. (31c) interpreted as (31d) does not have the same truth value as (31a), but (31c) interpreted as (31e) does have the same truth value as (31a).

5.5.3   Propositional Attitudes and Descriptions

In the previous section we saw that names and descriptions are not inter-changeable in modal contexts because descriptions, unlike names, are affected by being in the scope of a modal operator. Descriptions with wide scope and descriptions with narrow scope can pick out different individuals, because they are interpreted against different possible worlds.

The scopal variation found with descriptions is also at play in proposi-tional attitude contexts. To illustrate this, take a selection of examples repeated from (26).

(32)a   The man in the brown hat = the man seen at the beach.   true
    b   Ralph believes [that <u>the man in the brown hat</u> is a spy].   true
    c   Ralph believes [that <u>the man seen at the beach</u> is a spy].   false

Remember that Ralph knows he has seen Ortcutt, a respectable citizen, at the beach, but he does not know that Ortcutt is also the man in the brown hat. The judgements above, that (32b) is true and (32c) is false, are com-monly supported by reasoning that Ralph is the most reliable witness concerning his own beliefs. So if we were to present him with the bracketed sentences alone, and ask him to indicate agreement or disagreement, we would expect him to respond:

(33)a   The man in the brown hat is a spy.
        'Yes, so I believe.'
   b   The man seen at the beach is a spy.
        'Good gracious! Certainly not!'

Now suppose that Ralph tells a friend about his observations of the man in the brown hat and his suspicions of espionage. Ralph's friend knows that Ortcutt wears an old brown hat to meet up with old college buddies to drink some liquor and shoot a little pool. Ralph's friend knows that Ralph is talking about Ortcutt. To tease Ralph, his friend says to someone else, 'Have you heard the latest? Ralph here thinks old Ortcutt is a spy!' Ralph protests bitterly, but when the facts are revealed he must admit that in a sense he DID have the spy-belief about Ortcutt, without realizing it. That is, the person he had the spy-belief about is actually Ortcutt, also known to Ralph as the man seen at the beach.

This reveals two different ways of reporting someone else's belief about a person. The first way is to describe the person in terms that the believer himself might use. In this case, the description or information used to identify the person is plausibly part of the believer's thought.

This is termed a **de dicto belief**, from the Latin meaning roughly 'about the words'. The believer has a thought about a person or thing as described or identified in a particular way.

Given that a de dicto belief includes the description as part of its content, we can say that the description is in the scope of the belief predicate – the description has narrow scope.

de dicto – description has narrow scope

(34)a   Ralph believes that the man in the brown hat is a spy.
   b   BELIEVE(r, [The x: MAN IN THE BROWN HAT(x)] SPY(x))
   c   Ralph believes that the man seen at the beach is a spy.
   d   BELIEVE(r, [The x: MAN SEEN AT THE BEACH(x)] SPY(x))

As we have seen, on the de dicto reading (34a) is true, because Ralph's spy-belief is connected in his thoughts only with Ortcutt-identified-as-the-man-in-the-brown-hat, and not recognized by Ralph as simply Ortcutt. (34d) is false, because the way of identifying Ortcutt as the man seen at the beach is not combined with the spy-belief in Ralph's thoughts.

The other way of reporting a belief is for the speaker to identify the person the thought is about in the speaker's own terms, which may or may not be how the believer would identify the person. The belief is reported as being held directly about the person or thing in question, and is called **de re belief**, from the Latin 'about the thing'.

Suppose Sally, a retired Olympic gymnast, and her friend Kay are watching a group of nine-year-olds practising at the local gym. One child is unusually talented, and Sally says about her:

(35)   That kid could be a contender.

Kay knows that the talented child lives next door to her sister-in-law Ann. That night Kay remarks to her husband:

(36)   Sally thinks the kid who lives next door to Ann could be a top gymnast.

Kay reports what Sally said in words which make more sense to her husband, who would have no idea what she was talking about if she said 'Sally thinks that kid could be a contender.' Sally would not immediately agree with the statement *The kid who lives next door to Ann could be a top gymnast*, because that statement would not give Sally enough information to identify the child in question: the description *the kid who lives next door to Ann* would not identify the child for Sally. Nevertheless, it is clear that (36), what Kay said, is true. In (36) Kay reports Sally's assessment as a de re belief.

Given that the description is not part of the belief content in reporting a de re belief, the quantifier takes wider scope than the belief predicate in the representation. (36) can be represented as in (37) with certain details simplified.

de re belief – description has wide scope

(37)   [The x: KID WHO LIVES NEXT DOOR TO ANN(x)] THINK(s, ◇ (TOP GYMNAST(x)))

The speaker, Kay in this case, uses the description to identify a particular child, because this description can be fully understood by her husband. Suppose the little girl is called Marama. Then x in the formula refers to Marama. The rest of the formula

THINK(s, (TOP GYMNAST(x)))

can be read as 'Sally thinks she could be a top gymnast', where *she* refers to Marama. The information that the little girl lives next door to Ann is not included in the representation of Sally's thought.

Returning to the examples about Ralph, we now see that (38a) below (=(34c) repeated) is ambiguous between the de dicto belief in (38b) (= (34d) repeated) and the de re belief in (38c).

(38)a Ralph believes that the man seen at the beach is a spy.
   b   BELIEVE(r, [The x: MAN SEEN AT THE BEACH(x)] SPY(x))
   c   [The x: MAN SEEN AT THE BEACH(x)] BELIEVE(r, SPY(x))

This explains why (38a) is false in one sense but true in another. Interpreted as the de dicto belief in (38b), it is false, but interpreted as the de re belief in (38c), it is true.

The sentence (39a) (=(34a) repeated) is also ambiguous, but the difference is more subtle because both readings are true.

(39)a Ralph believes that the man in the brown hat is a spy.
   b   BELIEVE(r, [The x: MAN IN THE BROWN HAT(x)] SPY(x))
   c   [The x: MAN IN THE BROWN HAT(x)] BELIEVE(r, SPY(x))

As we have seen, (39b) is true because Ralph has his spy-belief about an individual whom he identifies to himself as the man in the brown hat, so that information can be part of his belief. (39c) is also true: here the individual, who happens to be Ortcutt, is identified (perhaps for an audience) as the man in the brown hat. Given this individual, (39c) continues 'Ralph believes he is a spy', where *he* refers to the man just identified. And Ralph's belief is indeed about that man.

5.5.4 Summary: Descriptions and Scope

As soon as we recognize that singular definite descriptions are not referring expressions but quantifiers, we see that the phenomenon of substitution is complicated by scopal ambiguity. Each of our test sentences presents two readings:

(40) $\diamond$ [The x]...x...   narrow scope
   [The x] $\diamond$ ...x...   wide scope
   BELIEVE(a, [The x]...x...)   narrow scope: de dicto
   [The x] BELIEVE(a,...x...)   wide scope: de re

A modal operator or propositional attitude predicate affects the interpretation of a description in its scope. Accordingly, substitution of NPs can produce a change in truth value <u>if the narrow scope reading for the NP is chosen</u>.

(41)a Yuri Gagarin might not have been Yuri Gagarin.   false
   b   Yuri Gagarin might not have been the first man in
       space.   ambiguous

substitution with narrow scope reading: change

c	$\Diamond \sim g = g$	false
d	$\Diamond$ [The x: FIRST MAN IN SPACE(x)] $\sim g = x$	true

substitution with wide scope reading: no change

c	$\Diamond \sim g = g$	false
e	[The x: FIRST MAN IN SPACE(x)] $\Diamond \sim g = x$	false

(42)a Ralph believes that the man seen at the beach is a
spy.   ambiguous
  b Ralph believes that the man in the brown hat is a
spy.   ambiguous

substitution with narrow scope reading: change

c	BELIEVE(r, [The x: MAN SEEN AT THE BEACH(x)] SPY(x))	false
d	BELIEVE(r, [The x: MAN IN THE BROWN HAT(x)] SPY(x))	true

substitution with wide scope reading: no change

e	[The x: MAN SEEN AT THE BEACH(x)] BELIEVE(r, SPY(x))	true
f	[The x: MAN IN THE BROWN HAT(x)] BELIEVE (r, SPY(x))	true

This explanation of the data in terms of scopal ambiguity is available only if we analyse definite descriptions as quantifiers. Moreover, if descriptions are quantifiers rather than referring expressions then the truth value changes demonstrated here violate no logical law, because the Principle of Substitutivity does not apply to descriptions. If the Principle of Substitutivity does not apply to descriptions in any case, none of the data reviewed so far demonstrate the existence of opacity, so long as opacity is strictly defined in terms of the substitution of real referring expressions, such as names. Genuinely opaque contexts, if any, must involve the substitution of same-referring names.

We have seen that same-referring names such as *Mohammed Ali* and *Cassius Clay* can be exchanged in a modal context without affecting the truth value, so modal contexts are not opaque. What about propositional attitudes?

5.5.5   Propositional Attitudes and Names

Ralph's embarrassment in the Ortcutt affair ('Ralph thinks old Ortcutt is a spy') came about because he failed to recognize the man he saw in the brown hat as Ortcutt, whom he already knew from different circumstances. Consequently, he formed two different concepts of Ortcutt, each associated with a different complex of information drawn from his different encounters with Ortcutt.

(43) Ortcutt-concept-1
type: man
name: unknown
general: seen in suspicious circumstances, wearing a brown hat, drinking in a bar in a rough part of town near the college campus in November, a spy.

Ortcutt-concept-2
type: man
name: *Bernard J. Ortcutt*
general: pillar of the community, local Boosters Club president, seen at the beach with wife and family in July, wearing a brightly coloured silk shirt and a panama hat.

Ralph thinks about Ortcutt in two ways, depending on which of these concepts is involved in his thought. A de dicto report of Ralph's thoughts about Ortcutt takes into account the particular way in which Ralph is thinking about Ortcutt at the time, and is expressed in terms that Ralph will recognize and agree with. What Ralph himself cannot do, or assent to, is to combine information from concept 1 with information from concept 2.

A de re report takes a wider view. Ralph's thoughts connect with the world to the extent that the things and events he thinks about are real, not imaginary. Ralph's error lies in separating his rather mistaken concept 1 from his more accurate concept 2, but nevertheless concept 1 is of a real person. When either concept 1 or concept 2 is activated, Ralph is thinking about the man Ortcutt, although only concept 2 is linked to his name. This 'bottom line' evaluation of Ralph's thought is a de re evaluation.

We can't test the substitution of same-referring names with Ralph's two concepts, because only one of them has a name. But if we add different names to distinct concepts which actually represent the same person, we find that the substitution of same-referring names can change the truth value.

The Roman statesman Marcus Tullius Cicero is generally known to us these days as Cicero, but previously he was also commonly referred to as Tully, using an anglicization of *Tullius*. Lydia, a classics student, has prepared for an exam with an essay about Cicero in mind. As she leaves for the exam her elderly neighbour says to her:

(44) Classics today, Lyddie? Off to write about Tully then?

Lydia knows that Tully was a Roman politician around the first century BC – he was alive at the time Julius Caesar was assassinated. She doesn't know he's the same person as Cicero. She answers:

(45)   I hope not! If the essay's about Tully I'm sunk!

Fortunately, the essay question contains the magic word *Cicero* – Lydia writes a long essay about Tully without knowing it.

As Lydia is on her way to the exam, the statements below would seem to have the indicated truth values.

(46)a   Lydia hopes there will be an essay question about Tully.   false
    b   Lydia hopes there will be an essay question about Cicero.   true

So it seems that unlike modal environments, propositional attitude environments do not allow the exchange of same-referring names with a constant truth value.

The judgements in (46) accord with the standard expectation that the thinker or hoper is the best witness on what exactly is thought or hoped. Lydia rejected Tully as a good essay topic, so (46a) is false. But on the other hand, surely it is also true to say that Lydia wrote the essay she hoped to write, and it was about Tully – she wrote about that man. So in another sense (46a) is true.

Lydia's problem with Marcus Tullius Cicero can be seen as a matter of vocabulary, rather than a lack of knowledge about the man himself. Basically, she doesn't know who the name *Tully* refers to – she doesn't know what the word *Tully* means.

Whether or not the thinker knows certain words can affect the apparent accuracy of propositional attitude reports even where no names are involved. Consider Liam, aged two. He can count one, two or three objects accurately, and he knows how to march 'one, two, one, two'. He knows that people walk 'one, two, one, two' and so does a duck, but the cat doesn't walk 'one, two, one, two' because 'she got lots of legs'.

(47)a   Liam knows that a duck has two legs.
    b   Liam knows that a duck is two-legged.
    c   Liam knows that a duck is bipedal.

Although (47a) and (47b) are easily judged as true, (47c) can be judged as false. On the reading judged to be false, (47c) is understood to mean partly that Liam could apply the word *bipedal* to ducks, which seems unlikely: that would be comparable to a de dicto reading. But common sense indicates that Liam has a good concept of bipedality and applies that concept to ducks, so (47c) is true if understood in that way.

In these sorts of examples there is no question of reference and the issue is not confined to the Principle of Substitutivity. The general point is that a propositional attitude report may be intended and understood as reporting both (i) the thinker holds this proposition AND (ii) the thinker could associate the concepts in his or her mental representation of the proposition with the words used in the statement.

These phenomena raise extremely difficult problems for semantic analysis, chiefly because the logical representations used for propositions do not seem to be appropriate for either kind of reported thought. If the reports are understood narrowly, so that the word which is chosen, such as *Tully/Cicero* or *two-legged/bipedal* is important, it seems that some stipulation about the required words should be added to the logical representation. For example, Lydia wants what is represented in (48a) but not (48b).

(48)a   [An x: ESSAY(x) & ABOUT(x,m)] WRITE(l,x)
           where m = Marcus Tullius Cicero and *Cicero* refers to m
    b   [An x: ESSAY(x) & ABOUT (x,m)] WRITE(l,x)
           where m = Marcus Tullius Cicero and *Tully* refers to m

Introducing words in this fashion is not a simple matter, particularly as we can truthfully report the thoughts of people who do not speak the same language. For example, (49a) is true, but Galileo would not have assented to (49b) because he spoke medieval Italian, and popular tradition has it that what he said (when before the Inquisition) was (49c).

(49)a   Galileo insisted that the earth moves round the sun.
    b   The earth moves round the sun.
    c   Eppur, si muove!

Broad interpretations (including de re readings) are also puzzling. There's a true reading of *Lydia wants an essay question about Tully*: a third party talking to Lydia's elderly neighbour might truthfully describe Lydia's hopes to him in these words. And as we saw earlier, there's a true reading of what Ralph's friend said to tease Ralph:

(50)a   Ralph thinks Ortcutt is a spy.
    b   THINK(r, SPY(o))

The intuition that *Ralph thinks Ortcutt is a spy* is true (on the appropriate reading) seems to lead us to say that Ralph 'thinks' the proposition represented by 'SPY(o)', but doesn't mentally represent it, whatever THAT means.

That is, there is a proposition expressed by 'SPY(o)' which Ralph has a propositional attitude towards, but 'SPY(o)' isn't exactly the content of Ralph's thought. Rather, Ralph has a mental representation involving his Ortcutt-concept 1 which is accurate or faulty according to the same circumstances in which 'SPY(o)' is true or false, respectively. Ralph's actual mental content and the proposition expressed by 'SPY(o)' have some kind of parallelism, but the precise relationship between them is not clear.

In summary, propositional attitude reports contain embedded sentences which denote mental contents. Our system of semantic representation, on the other hand, uses symbols which denote things and situations in reality and possible realities, not conceptual representations in a thinker's mind. Any reality-denoting representational system seems to be the wrong sort of system in principle for representing mental contents.

To the extent that we seem to successfully report the thoughts of others, we must assume that (i) humans generally share a basic conceptual representation system, in which for the most part they represent reality and possible realities in sufficiently similar ways, and (ii) the language we speak in reporting the thoughts of others is translatable into the conceptual representational system (shared by the thinker). This also applies for false beliefs: for example, the sentence *John believes that the earth is flat* is true if in fact John does NOT represent reality to himself as it really is, but is interpretable as intended only if the words *the earth* can be mapped to John's mental representation of the earth, however inaccurate, and if the word *flat* can be mapped to John's representation of flatness. That is, we assume that his erroneous complex representation of a flat earth situation is made up of cognitive components we can speak of, because to some extent we all share them.

Even this kind of assumption is uncertain when we report the thoughts of thinkers unlike us, such as small children, whose developing cognitive structures are known to be different. If we say of a young child *She thinks clouds are alive*, what exactly are we reporting? It could be that the child hasn't mastered the use of the word *alive* and applies it to all sorts of moving objects, generally to objects which are alive. It could be that the child thinks that clouds move under their own motive power and identifies that property as the property of being alive. Or it could be that she thinks clouds are animate.

A number of strategies have been proposed for analysing propositional attitude reports, but none is particularly successful. This book does not introduce any special notations for attitude reports, but remember that any expression which appears in the scope of a propositional attitude predicate may be interpreted in a way which is quite different from its denotational semantics. The details may differ from case to case.

EXERCISES

(A)   Scope and Modality: Basic Review

The following sentence is ambiguous, with one true reading and one false reading. Give the formulae for both readings and indicate which is which.

(i)   Elizabeth Windsor might not have been the richest woman in Britain.

(B) Scope and Propositional Attitudes: Basic Review

The following sentence is ambiguous. Give the formulae for both readings, and sketch a context in which the two readings differ in truth value.

(i) Clive wants to read the book that June is reading.

(C) Traditional Referential Opacity: Basic Review

According to the <u>traditional</u> view outlined in section 5.5.1, which of the underlined NPs below is in an opaque context? (Sketch a context and show a substitution of NPs which does or does not preserve the truth value to support your case.)

Example:
(i) Clive ate <u>the last cake</u>.

Suppose that the last cake = the thing I had my eye on.
Substituting the NPs gives:

(ii) Clive ate <u>the thing I had my eye on</u>.

If (i) is true then (ii) must also be true, and vice versa. So long as the last cake IS the thing I had my eye on (the test assumes that this is so) then these two sentences must have the same truth value. Substituting a different NP referring to the same thing can NOT change the truth value here so the context *Clive ate . . .* is not opaque.

(1) Marcia hopes that <u>the winner of the competition</u> will talk to her.
(2) My neighbour knows <u>the Director of MI5</u> quite well.
(3) Clive says that <u>the guy sitting over there</u> is a millionaire.
(4) Then Bob said '<u>Your husband</u> has had an accident.'
(5) They needed a signature from <u>Clive's wife</u>.
(6) Obviously they needed a signature from <u>Clive's wife</u>.
(7) Clive told <u>my brother</u> to shove off.
(8) The getaway car was driven by <u>the former bank manager</u>.

(D) Opacity and the Fourth Estate

The extract below, taken from a news report on the trial of O. J. Simpson, sounds odd (and strictly speaking, false) because of a referring expression which appears in an opaque context. What is the referring expression in question, and what creates the opaque effect?

(i) Then came the cliffhanger: with most of the lawyers caught by surprise and absent from the courtroom, Judge Lance Ito said he would seal the verdict and wait to announce it in open court at 6 am New Zealand time today. That left the former football star, his lawyers, prosecutors and trial buffs around the world in the dark on whether he has been found guilty or not guilty of the murders of his former wife, Nicole Brown Simpson, and her friend, Ron Goldman.

(*Christchurch Press*, 4 October 1995)

(E) Propositional Attitudes and Existence

Ralph thinks that the man who lives upstairs from him is a spy. Ralph is a little paranoid – the flat upstairs is empty, and the noises Ralph hears on the stairs are merely a poltergeist. Does the sentence below encounter problems through the existential commitment of *the*?

(i)   Ralph thinks that the man who lives upstairs is a spy.

(F) Modality and Quantifiers

Paraphrase all the readings you can detect for the following sentence, and give the formula for each reading.

(i)   Everyone in the village might have been rich.

(G) Sense and Reference Again: Discussion

Compare:

(a)   Cicero is Tully.
(b)   Tully is Tully.
(c)   Hesperus is Phosphorus.
(d)   Hesperus is Hesperus.

(1)   Do the words *Cicero* and *Tully* have different meanings?
(2)   Do the words *Hesperus* and *Phosphorus* have different meanings?
(3)   Are (b) and (d) true in all possible worlds? (That is, in all possible worlds where referents of the names occur – in worlds where they don't occur, (b) and (d) do not express propositions, and the issue of truth or falsity does not arise.)
(4)   Are (a) and (c) true in all possible worlds where the referents occur?
(5)   Is the difference between (c) and (d), if any, a truth conditional difference?

(H)   A Little Problem from Russell: Discussion

First man: I thought your boat was longer than it is.
Second man: No, my boat is not longer than it is.

Can you figure out what the problem is in this dialogue?
  (i)   What did the first man mean?
 (ii)   What did the second man suggest that the first man meant?
(iii)   If the first man had meant what the second man implies he meant, what would he have said?

(I)   Propositional Attitudes: Discussion

Can you substitute the words *bipedal* and *two-legged* in the sentences below, preserving the truth value? Do (1) and (2) mean the same thing? (Can you describe possible circumstances in which one would be true and the other one false?)

(1)   Liam knows what *bipedal* means.
(2)   Liam knows that bipedal creatures are two-legged.

FURTHER READING

For a recent Russellian analysis of descriptions see Neale (1990), especially Chapters 1 and 4.

See dictionary and encyclopaedia entries for *descriptions, reference, opacity, belief contexts, intensionality, propositional attitudes,* and *sense and reference.*

Berg (1988) discusses pragmatic effects on the substitution of NPs in belief contexts.

The discussion of opacity is based on Quine (1956) and Kripke (1980). Kripke (1980) is a classic discussion of a number of interrelated issues, including the reference of names and descriptions. The notion of names as rigid designators is presented in this monograph.

In a number of papers, Partee discusses the relationship between formal and psychological approaches to semantics, with particular reference to the problem of analysing belief-sentences. The 'clouds are alive' example above is from 'Semantics – mathematics or psychology?' (1996). Also recommended is Partee's 'Belief-sentences and the limits of semantics' (1982). Johnson-Laird (1982) on the same problem covers a wide range of issues and is particularly recommended.

6 Indefinite Descriptions, Plurals, Generics and Mass NPs

This chapter reviews several further issues in the interpretation of NPs. In Section 6.1 we review a phenomenon closely allied to opacity, discussed in Chapter 5. The two following sections discuss the special properties of NPs which denote groups and substances, rather than the kind of ordinary individuals we have considered so far, and the way they combine with predicates. We then review the interesting properties of plural NPs without determiners, and finally look at NPs with generic reference.

6.1 INDEFINITE DESCRIPTIONS AND SPECIFICITY

We saw in Chapter 5 that modal and propositional attitude contexts can affect the reference of NPs they contain. In particular, definite descriptions and names which otherwise pick out the same individual do not always have the same interpretation in these contexts.

Specificity and **nonspecificity** are properties of indefinite noun phrases in certain kinds of ambiguous sentences, including propositional attitude and modal contexts. In these contexts, specificity and nonspecificity are closely related to the transparent and opaque readings of definite NPs. Specificity and nonspecificity in a propositional attitude context are illustrated in (1).

(1) propositional attitude, specific
    a Mary wants to buy a Norton – she is negotiating with the owner.

    propositional attitude, nonspecific
    b Mary wants to buy a Norton – she will look for one at the Biker Meet.

In (1a) *a Norton* is specific because it refers to a specific or particular bike which Mary wants to buy. In (1b) Mary has no particular bike in mind and here *a Norton* is nonspecific. Another example of this ambiguity is *John wants to marry a Frenchwoman*, with the two readings 'John wants to marry a particular woman who is French' (specific) and 'John wants to have a French wife' (nonspecific).

The specific/nonspecific ambiguity in propositional attitude contexts is very like the de re/de dicto distinction applied to definites. A specific or de re reading appears where a reported thought is directed towards a particular individual the speaker refers to. A nonspecific reading appears where a reported thought is directed towards a class of objects or to any individual fitting the description contained in the NP, and no particular individual is referred to. This is like a de dicto reading, in which a reported thought is directed towards an individual as identified or described in a particular way.

As the comparison with opacity suggests, specific and nonspecific readings are generally analysed as instances of scopal variation. The different readings in (1) can be represented as in (2).

(2)   propositional attitude, specific
    a Mary wants to buy a Norton (she is negotiating with the owner.)
        [A x: NORTON(x)] WANT(m, BUY(m, x))

    propositional attitude, nonspecific
    b Mary wants to buy a Norton (she will look for one at the Biker Meet.)
        WANT(m,[A x: NORTON(x)] BUY(m, x))

As with opacity, specific and nonspecific ambiguities also appear in modal contexts, as illustrated in (3). Again, the ambiguities are analysed as instances of scopal variation.

(3)   modal context, specific
    a John might have visited a friend – Amy Ho, do you know her?
        [A x: FRIEND(x, j)] $\diamond$ VISIT(j, x)

    modal context, nonspecific
    b John might have visited a friend – I really don't know where he went.
        $\diamond$ [A x: FRIEND(x, j)] VISIT(j, x)

The specific reading of *a friend* in (3a) refers to a particular person, while the nonspecific reading in (3b) does not refer to anyone in particular.

Indefinite NPs also show specificity contrasts in combination with negation. Again, these ambiguities are analysed as instances of variations in scope, as illustrated in (4).

(4)   specific
    a George didn't see a car coming round the bend – it nearly hit him.
        [A x: CAR(x)] $\sim$ SEE(g, x)

    nonspecific
    b George didn't see a car coming round the bend – but he wasn't really watching the road, so he's not sure whether any cars passed or not.
        $\sim$[A x: CAR(x)] SEE(g,x)

The terms *specific* and *nonspecific* characterize the contrast in interpretation as the presence or absence of reference to a specific individual. Note that although there must be a particular individual referred to by a specific NP, because the NP is indefinite, unlike a definite NP, it does not signal the hearer that he or she can identify the individual referred to.

The specificity contrast can also be described in terms of existential commitment. On the specific readings of *a Norton*, *a friend* or *a car* in the examples above, such an individual must exist in actuality. On the nonspecific readings, a Norton figures in Mary's thought, a friend figures in a hypothetical situation involving John, and a car figures in a nonrealized situation involving George, but in fact there may be no such entity. Only the specific readings are committed to the existence of at least one Norton bike, friend of John or car on the road.

The fourth kind of specificity ambiguity arises with scopal interactions between an indefinite description and another quantifier, as discussed in Chapter 4. This kind of ambiguity involves only the question of whether or not a particular individual is referred to, and does not show variation in existential commitment.

(5)   Every student prepared a paper by Quine.
      specific
      a   [A x: PAPER BY QUINE (x)] [Every y: STUDENT (y)]
          PREPARE (y, x)

      nonspecific
      b   [Every y: STUDENT (y)] [A x: PAPER BY QUINE (x)]
          PREPARE (y, x)

On the specific reading of *a paper by Quine* there is a particular paper which every student prepared – for example, every student prepared for a seminar to discuss 'On Mental Entities'. On the nonspecific reading every student prepared a paper and all the prepared papers were by Quine, but they may have all been different papers. As before, the two readings are easily represented as scopal differences.

The term *specificity* is rather like the term *definiteness*, in that both terms in traditional grammar applied to rather vague referential properties of NPs. The analysis presented here, that specific NPs have wider scope than another scopal expression in the sentence, gives a plausible analysis for the traditional examples of specificity contrasts. In this analysis specificity is not a single unitary semantic property. With modality, propositional attitude verbs and negation, a specific interpretation (that is, the indefinite NP has wide scope) expresses particular reference and existential commitment. On the nonspecific interpretation, where the indefinite NP has narrow scope, particular reference and existential commitment are both lacking. Scopal variation between an indefinite NP and another quantifier, on the other hand, only affects particular reference, and both the specific and nonspecific readings entail the existence of what the indefinite NP denotes.

6.2 PLURAL NPs AND GROUPS

In this section and the next we review certain kinds of NP which do not denote ordinary individuals. The nonindividual interpretations of these NPs arc signalled by the different ways they combine with their predicates.

The quantificational analysis used so far for NPs such as *three cups* is **distributive**: the quantificational expressions are analysed in terms of individual variables, and the predication is distributed to the individuals that the variables represent. This is shown in (6).

(6) Three cups broke.
     [Three x: CUP(x)] BREAK(x)

 a, b, c are cups
  a broke
  b broke
  c broke

Here the predicate *broke* is distributed across the cups a, b and c, and applies to each of them individually, so that if 'Three cups broke' is true, then 'a broke', 'b broke' and 'c broke' are all true.

The two readings of (5) above also illustrate distributivity with both NPs on both readings, as in (7).

(7)a [A x: PAPER BY QUINE (x)] [Every y: STUDENT (y)]
      PREPARE (y, x)
      a = a paper by Quine

   1, 2, 3, 4, ··· are students
    1 prepared a
    2 prepared a
    3 prepared a
    4 prepared a, etc.

  b [Every y: STUDENT (y)] [A x: PAPER BY QUINE (x)]
     PREPARE (y,x)

   a, b, c, d,... are papers by Quine
   1, 2, 3, 4,... are students
   one possible set of combinations is:
    1 prepared c
    2 prepared a

3 prepared c
4 prepared b
5 prepared d, etc.

In both readings the situation described involves pairs of individuals, each consisting of a single student preparing a single paper. Even if two or more students prepare the same paper, as in reading (a) or students 1 and 3 in reading (b), the analysis presents the student-paper pairs separately.

Not all predication is individually distributive. Predication which is not distributive is collective – the next section reviews collective predication.

6.2.1   Collective Predication

Predications with NPs denoting more than one entity are not always distributive, as shown in (8).

(8)a   <u>Sally and Harry</u> met for lunch.
  b   <u>Sally, Harry, Jeff and Buzz</u> met for lunch.
  c   <u>Harry, Jeff and Buzz</u> surrounded Charles.
  d   <u>The gang</u> met for lunch.
  e   <u>The forest</u> surrounded the castle.

All the underlined NPs refer to groups or collections of individuals which participate in the described action or situation as a group. It isn't possible to make the same predication of one of the individuals composing the group.

(9)a   # Sally met for lunch.
  b   # Buzz surrounded Charles.
  c   # A pine tree surrounded the castle.

Predicates which apply to groups are **collective** predicates. Two kinds of collective predicate are illustrated here. Section 6.2.2 reviews cumulative predication, which is a third kind of collective predication.

The first kind, which I shall call **group collectives**, describes some kind of interaction or relationship among individual members of a group, as illustrated in (10).

(10)a   Several leaders agreed on a plan.
   b   The seven houses on this spur are alike.
   c   The leaders debated a compensation proposal.

The predications in (10) cannot be applied to a single individual alone. They can be applied to groups, as shown here. Some of the predicates, or closely related predicates, can take a singular subject, so long as at least one other participant is mentioned in the sentence to allow for the interaction reading. This is illustrated in (11).

(11)a Hogan agreed on a plan with Burgo.
  b This house is like that house.
  c Atkinson's lawyer debated a compensation proposal with Boot's lawyer.

The second kind of collective predicate, including *surround, disperse* and *gather,* applies primarily to a substance, as in (12a, b). I shall call these predicates **substance collectives**. Predicates like these can also apply to the kind of subjects illustrated in (12c–f).

(12)a The floodwater dispersed slowly.
  b Sand gathered in the corners of the courtyard.
  c A lawn surrounded the pavilion.
  d Grass surrounded the pavilion.
  e The forest surrounded the castle.
  f The crowd dispersed slowly.

In each sentence in (12) the subject denotes a substance or a vague amount of a substance. Floodwater, sand and grass are substances and a lawn is an area of grass. Substances are often formed of separable individual parts, such as the grains in sugar or the flakes in confetti – a forest could be described as an amount of the substance formed of trees, and a crowd could be described as an amount of the substance formed by people. Generally, a vague collection or plurality of entities can be seen as forming a kind of substance – this point is raised again in Chapter 9.

The NPs in (12) appear with predicates like *disperse* because they have substance-like denotations, although substances are most typically denoted by mass NPs, reviewed in the next section.

To recap, group collective predicates like *meet* and *be alike* apply to collections of individuals which interact or are interrelated in some way. Substance collective predicates like *surround, disperse* and *gather* apply mainly to substances, and also to individuals which are composed of a substance or of a substance-like agglomeration of individuals. Neither of these kinds of collective predicate can apply directly to an ordinary individual, or to an isolated individual taken from the larger grouping.

In what follows, the differences between group collectives and substance collectives will not be represented. These differences would be expressed in more detailed definitions for predicates which are represented here simply as SURROUND, GATHER, DISPERSE, and so on. The chief point at issue here is the representation of the collection which a collective predicate applies to.

If a collection is denoted by a singular NP such as *the forest* or *the crowd*, then the analysis of quantified NPs we have used so far will work, because the individual variable used in the analysis stands for the collective large individual, not for its members: for example, the variable x in (13) stands for a whole forest, not for an individual tree.

(13)   A forest surrounded the castle.
       [A x: FOREST(x)] [The y: CASTLE (y)] SURROUND(x, y)

A more complex analysis is needed for collective predicates with quantified plural NPs like *several leaders* or *a thousand trees*, because the analysis for NPs like these that we have used so far always gives a distributive reading, as shown in (14). According to (14), each individual tree surrounds the castle.

(14)   A thousand trees surrounded the castle.
       [A thousand (x): TREE(x)] [The y: CASTLE(y)] SURROUND(x, y)
       'For 1000 things x, such that x is a tree, x surrounded the castle.'

For plural NPs with collective predicates we need to introduce into the logical form a variable which stands for the collection or group as a whole, and also find a way to represent the quantity expressed by the quantificational determiner. One way to do this is to use set theory notation, with uppercase variables for sets, as a group is a kind of set. Then (14), for example, can be analysed as in (15).

(15)   [A X:|X| = 1,000 & $\forall$y (y $\in$ X $\rightarrow$ TREE(y))] [The z: CASTLE(z)]
       SURROUND (X, z)
       'For some thing X, such that X has 1000 members and every member of X is a tree, X surrounded the castle.'

Although some predicates are always collective, many predicates can be interpreted either collectively or distributively, in which case the choice of reading may be pragmatic, and in principle both readings are available semantically.

(16)a   The apples in this barrel weigh at least six ounces.
    b   The apples in this barrel weigh at least 100 pounds.

Common sense chooses a distributive reading for (16a) and a collective reading for (16b), but the general predicate *weigh at least* ... is not fixed either way. (The predication in (16b) is a kind of cumulative predication. Cumulative predication is reviewed in the next section.)

The difference between collective and distributive predication is the key to different uses of quantifier determiners which appear to express the same quantification. Examples from exercise E, Chapter 4 repeated below, illustrate differences between *every* and *all*. *Every*, unlike *all*, is syntactically singular, as shown in (17a-d). The group collective predicate *fit together* combines with *all*, as in (17e), but not with *every*, as in (17f). This shows that *every* is semantically distributive, as it cannot appear with a collective predicate. *All* can be either collective or distributive, as shown by the ambiguity of (17g) in contrast to (17h), which can only have a distributive reading.

(17)a   All ravens are black.
   b   *   All raven is black.
   c   Every raven is black.
   d   *   Every ravens are black.
   e   All these pieces fit together to make a picture.
   f   #   Every piece here fits together to make a picture.
   g   The price of all these pieces is $20.00.
   h   The price of every piece here is $20.00.

Given that many predicates may be either distributive or collective, the possible ambiguities for sentences with plural NPs are multiplied, as illustrated in (18). The now familiar distributive readings are (18a, b).

(18)   Two men lifted a rock.

    a   [Two x: MAN(x)] [A y: ROCK(y)] LIFT(x, y)
       a, b are men
       1,2 are rocks
         a lifted 1
         b lifted 2

    b   [A y: ROCK(y)] [Two x: MAN (x)] LIFT(x, y)
       a, b are men
       1 is a rock
         a lifted 1
         b lifted 1

    c $[A \, X: |X| = 2 \, \& \, \forall x \, (x \in X \rightarrow MAN(x))] [A \, y: ROCK(y)] LIFT(X, y)$
       'For an X such that X has two members and every member of X is a man, there is a rock y such that X lifted y'.
         A is a group of two men
         1 is a rock
         A lifted 1

The group reading in (18c) is a particular kind of group collective predication, denoting individuals performing in unison an action which can also be performed by a single individual – this is a kind of 'team' reading.

6.2.2   Cumulative Predication

Sentences with plural NPs can also have **cumulative** predication. Cumulative predication is the most natural interpretation for sentences like (19).

(19)   Ten architects submitted seventeen designs to the competition for the new Art Gallery.

On the cumulative reading, architects submitted designs to a competition: ten architects in all were involved and seventeen designs in all were submitted. The cumulative reading is neutral among particular pairings of architects to designs. Possibly nine architects submitted one design each and the tenth architect submitted eight, or three architects submitted one each and the others each submitted two designs, and so on.

Cumulative readings express *overall summaries* over individual predications. A collective interpretation like the interpretation of *two men* in (18c) is wrong for (19), as the architects and designs do not function as groups – for one thing, we assume that the architects are competing against each other. The 'overall summary' character of cumulative predication is particularly sharp in examples like (20).

(20)   Four separate research units produced three tentative solutions by the end of the year.
'A total of four separate research units produced a total of three tentative solutions.'

Here (assuming that no two units produced the same solution), the predication 'produced x, where x is a tentative solution' does not apply at all to at least one of the research units.

6.3   MASS NPs

Many English nouns, perhaps most nouns, can be used in both count and mass NPs, as illustrated below.

(21)   *count NPs*
       a   Tigger caught <u>seven rats</u> under the shed.
       b   We had a choice of <u>three paints</u>.
       c   <u>Two sculptures</u> stood at the entrance.

       mass NPs
       d   Tigger's mouth was full of <u>rat</u>.
       e   We need more <u>paint</u>.
       f   Larissa decided to go in for <u>sculpture</u>.

Mass NPs as discussed in this section are NPs used in a mass sense, denoting stuff or matter, possibly abstract stuff like fortitude or information, rather than countable individuals like cups, dogs and screwdrivers.

6.3.1   Mass NPs and their Predicates

Words like *gold*, *water* and *sand* can be used as NPs to refer, as in (22a–d), and also as predicates, as in (22e–g).

(22)a   <u>Water</u> is a liquid.
   b   <u>Gold</u> is a precious metal.
   c   <u>Water</u> is wet.
   d   <u>Gold</u> is yellow.

   e   That puddle on the floor is <u>water</u>.
   f   This ring is <u>gold</u>.
   g   The <u>gold</u> ring is missing.

Mass predicates like *gold* and *water* are interpreted as 'made of gold/water, consisting of gold/water', so both the NP and its related predicate have the same denotation – both the NP and the predicate denote the substance, gold or water. Ideally, an analysis of mass terms should show this relationship between the NP and predicate forms.

6.3.2   The Homogeneity of Mass Terms

One of the key properties of mass terms (both NPs and predicates) is the **homogeneity** of their denotation. A **homogeneous** predicate is both distributive and cumulative.

We have already seen that basic quantification is distributive to individuals, as in *Three cups broke*, repeated below.

(23)   Three cups broke.
       [Three x: CUP(x)] BREAK(x)

   a, b, c are cups
       a broke
       b broke
       c broke

The predicate *broke* is distributed to each of the three cups, rather than applying to the group of three as a whole.

With mass predicates, the predication is distributed throughout every part of the subject. For example, 'That ring is gold' entails that every portion of matter composing the ring is gold, and 'That puddle is water' entails that every portion of matter composing the puddle is water. Strictly speaking, a gold ring or a puddle of water are likely to contain impurities, so the predicates *gold* and *water* do not distribute to absolutely every portion of matter they contain, but in a general manner of speaking, distributivity holds. Distributivity is clearly shown by contrast with a nondistributive predicate such as *is circular*. 'That ring is circular' does not entail that every portion of matter contained in the ring is circular.

A cumulative predicate (see also Section 6.2.2) applies to sums, fusions or combinations of its subjects. For example, suppose I take two glasses of water. What is in the first glass is water, and what is in the second glass is water. If I pour them both into a jug, what is in the jug is also water, and accordingly *water* is a cumulative predicate.

(24)   This is water   (glass 1)
        This is water   (glass 2)
        This is water   (glass 1 + glass 2)

By way of contrast, a predicate such as *has two horns* is not cumulative. Ferdinand has two horns and Big Business has two horns, but it isn't the case that the combination of Ferdinand and Big Business has two horns.

To sum up, in analysing words like *gold* and *water*, we want to account for (i) the fact that mass terms denote substances rather than countable individuals, and (ii) the fact that both NP uses and predicate uses denote substances. We also want to show that, because the substances denoted by mass terms are homogeneous, their predicates are both distributive and cumulative.

6.3.3   Definitions for Mass Terms

As we saw in Chapter 1, predication on countable individuals is analysed in terms of membership in sets. So, for example, *Midge is a dog* is analysed as 'Midge is a member of the set of dogs.' But amorphous matter does not form sets of things, so we need a different analysis for mass terms.

In parallel to sets and the individuals x which are their members to model individual predication, we need to include amounts of substances and the smaller portions of those substances which make up the total amount. The total amount of a certain substance is called the **sum**, and a smaller portion which is included in the sum is **part of** the sum. The comparison with set structure is shown in (25).

(25)   countable individuals: sets and members
        a   F = the set of Fs; that is, the set of all x such that F(x)
        b   b ∈ the set of Fs
            'an individual b is a member of the set of Fs'

mass substances: sums and parts
c   G = the G sum (that is, the sum of all the stuff there is that is G)
d   M ≤ the G sum
    'a portion of matter M is part of or identical to the G sum'

Note that the symbol '≤' is read as 'is part of or identical to', although as a relationship between numbers or quantities it is read as 'is less than or equal to'. A model which is built on the 'part of' relation is called a **mereology**, from Greek *meros*, meaning 'part, fraction'. Recall that a meronym denotes a part: *palm* and *finger* are meronyms of *hand*.

Using *gold* as an illustration, we can now define mass terms in a little more detail. First, consider all the actual gold there is. We can define an entity which is the total sum of all the actual gold, called the gold sum. Every actual amount of gold is part of the gold sum.

(26)a   Sum(gold) = the sum entity for gold
    b   ∀M(M ≤ Sum(gold) iff M instantiates gold)
        'For every portion of matter M, M is part of or identical to the sum entity for gold if and only if M is an instance of gold.'

The homogeneity of gold is defined in (26b). Consider first distributivity. Suppose we take a portion M which is part of the gold sum. Now divide M into smaller portions M1 and M2, assuming that if they are part of M, which is part of the gold sum, then they are also part of the gold sum. According to the definition, M1 and M2 are parts of the gold sum if and only if they are instances of gold. So if M1 and M2 are not gold, then the definition does not fit them, M1 and M2 are not gold and nor is M. But if M *is* gold, then its goldness extends to M1 and M2 – that is, the goldness of M extends to every part of M.

To show cumulativity, take M1 and M2 which are parts of the gold sum, and are therefore instances of gold. Combine M1 and M2 into M3, assuming that M3 is also part of the gold sum, because it is formed of M1 and M2. Again, according to the definition, M3 is part of the gold sum if and only if it is an instance of gold. If M3 is not gold and the definition does not fit, then M1 and M2 are not gold either. But if M1 and M2 ARE gold, then M3 is also gold.

So according to the definitions in (26), the gold sum is a homogeneous entity comprising the sum of all instances of gold.

Now the predicate form of *gold* (that is, 'GOLD') can be defined in terms of the gold sum, as in (27), using M as before as a variable over portions of matter.

(27)   GOLD(M) iff M ≤ Sum(gold)
       'A portion of matter M is gold if and only if M is part of or identical to the gold sum.'

So to say 'That matter is gold' is to say 'That matter is part of the gold sum', which amounts to saying 'That is made of gold' or 'That consists of gold'.

Predicate *gold* is also illustrated in (28) below. The basic representation for (28a) is (28b). The definition for predicate GOLD in (27) states that the predicate applies to matter M if and only if M is part of the gold sum, so (28b) entails (28c).

(28)a The stuff Jake saw was gold.
    b [The M: SEE(j, M)] GOLD(M)
    c [The M: SEE(j, M)] M $\leq$ Sum (gold)

Quantifier *the* in (28a) is interpreted as a kind of universal quantifier which denotes a total sum, in this case the total sum of gold that Jake saw. (Although universal quantification with mass substances can be analysed in terms of sums, other quantifiers are more complex.)

A definite NP with the noun *gold* is illustrated in (29). Here *the gold* refers to the whole of a definite portion of gold identified from the context.

(29) Shelley passed the gold to Leo.
    [The M: GOLD(M)] PASS(s, M, l)

In *The stuff Jake saw was gold* and *Shelley passed the gold to Leo*, the predicate GOLD applies directly to a portion of matter M in 'GOLD(M)'. But if the matter to be identified is presented as made up into a particular individual, such as gold made up into a ring, we need to account for the difference between the ring and the stuff it is made of. After all, a Schiaparelli gown is not at all the same thing as six yards of cloth and a few buttons. Accordingly, *The ring is gold* can be analysed as in (30).

(30)a The ring is gold.
    b [$\exists$M: [The x: RING(x)] CONSTITUTE(M, x)] GOLD(M)
       'For some portion of matter M such that M constitutes the ring, M is gold.'

So far we have analysed the uses of mass terms like *gold* used in NPs and also used as predicates. The homogeneity of predicate *gold* is analysed in two steps: (i) we define the gold sum as a homogeneous entity, and (ii) we define predicate GOLD in terms of the gold sum, so that anything that predicate GOLD applies to is homogeneously gold.

There are many other predicates which, in contrast to predicate *gold* and predicate *water*, are not basically terms for substances, but do apply homogeneously to mass substances. For example, *yellow* in *Custard is yellow* applies homogeneously to custard. To analyse the homogeneity of a predicate like *yellow* along the same lines as the homogeneity of predicate *gold*, we can define a sum entity called the yellow sum, comprising the sum of all that is homogeneously yellow.

(31) ∀M (M ≤ Sum (yellow) iff YELLOW(M))
      'For all portions of matter M, M is part of or identical to the yellow sum if and only if M is yellow.'

Because of the homogeneity requirement expressed in the definition, the yellow sum only contains matter which is homogeneously yellow, such as gold, yellow paint and custard. It does not contain lemons or canaries, because they are not yellow throughout. A sum individual can be defined for any predicate which can apply homogeneously to substances, including *yellow, liquid, alkaline, hot* and so on.

Now we can analyse *Custard is yellow* as in (32), using the yellow sum and the custard sum.

(32) Custard is yellow.
      Sum (custard) ≤ Sum (yellow)
      'The custard sum is part of (or equal to) the yellow sum.'

Here we take *Custard is yellow* to mean that custard in general or all actual custard is yellow, and *custard* in (32) refers to the custard sum, as shown. Note that if the custard sum is part of the yellow sum, then the custard sum is a value for M in (31), the definition for the yellow sum. The definition ensures that any M which is part of the yellow sum is homogeneously yellow, so it follows from (32) that custard is homogeneously yellow.

6.4   BARE PLURAL NPs

Bare plurals are plural NPs without a determiner, such as *people, trees, suggestions, mechanisms*, and so on. These NPs do not appear to fall into any of the kinds of NP discussed so far: they are not names or pronouns, they are not mass terms, and although they are marked as plural, they do not have quantificational determiners. As we shall see in this section, bare plural NPs seem to be unquantified descriptions which combine with quantificational meaning drawn from elsewhere in the sentence.

6.4.1   Generic and Existential Readings

The sentences in (33) contain bare plural subjects with two kinds of predicates. The predicates in (33a–d) denote properties or actions which hold at a particular point in time, and are temporary, while the predicates in (33e–h) denote permanent or enduring properties of the subject.

(33)　temporary property
　　　a　Firemen are available.
　　　b　Teachers are on duty.
　　　c　Lilies are blooming in the field.
　　　d　Cups and saucers are in the cupboard.

　　　enduring property
　　　e　Firemen are altruistic.
　　　f　Teachers are white-collar workers.
　　　g　Lilies are elegant.
　　　h　Cups and saucers are breakable.

These two kinds of predicate combine with different quantificational readings of the bare plural subjects. Temporary situation predicates evoke an **existential reading** while enduring attribute predicates evoke a **generic reading**, as paraphrased in (34). As the paraphrases show, a statement with a generic NP makes a generalization about things of the kind the noun denotes.

(34)　temporary property: existential NP
　　　a　Firemen are available.
　　　　　There are some firemen available.
　　　　　Some firemen are available.
　　　　　For at least two x such that x is a fireman, x is available.

　　　b　Teachers are on duty.
　　　　　There are some teachers on duty.
　　　　　Some teachers are on duty.
　　　　　For at least two x such that x is a teacher, x is on duty.

　　　c　Lilies are blooming in the field.
　　　　　There are some lilies blooming in the field.
　　　　　Some lilies are blooming in the field.
　　　　　For at least two x such that x is a lily, x is blooming in the field.

　　　d　Cups and saucers are in the cupboard.
　　　　　There are some cups and saucers in the cupboard.
　　　　　Some cups and saucers are in the cupboard.
　　　　　For at least two x such that x is a cup and at least two y such that y is a saucer, x is in the cupboard and y is in the cupboard.

　　　enduring property: generic NP
　　　e　Firemen are altruistic.
　　　　　Firemen in general are altruistic.
　　　　　Firemen as a class are altruistic.
　　　　　Generally for x such that x is a fireman, x is altruistic.

f   Teachers are white-collar workers.
  Teachers in general are white-collar workers.
  Teachers as a class are white-collar workers.
  Generally for x such that x is a teacher, x is a white-collar worker.

g   Lilies are elegant.
  Lilies in general are elegant.
  Lilies as a class are elegant.
  Generally for x such that x is a lily, x is elegant.

h   Cups and saucers are breakable.
  Cups and saucers in general are breakable.
  Cups and saucers as a class of object are breakable.
  Generally for x such that x is a cup and generally for y such that y
    is a saucer, x is breakable and y is breakable.

Using the symbol *Gen* to represent generic quantification, the different readings for the examples above can be represented as in (35).

(35)a   [∃x: FIREMAN(x)] AVAILABLE(x)
  b   [∃x: TEACHER(x)] ON DUTY(x)
  c   [∃x: LILY(x)] BLOOMING IN THE FIELD(x)
  d   [∃x: CUP(x)] [∃y: SAUCER(y)] IN THE CUPBOARD(x) & IN THE
    CUPBOARD(y)

  e   [Gen x: FIREMAN(x)] ALTRUISTIC(x)
  f   [Gen x: TEACHER(x)] WHITE-COLLAR WORKER(x)
  g   [Gen x: LILY(x)] ELEGANT(x)
  h   [Gen x: CUP(x)] [Gen y: SAUCER(y)] BREAKABLE(x) &
    BREAKABLE(y)

Note that bare plural NPs are not the only NPs with generic readings. Singular NPs with *a* and *the* can also have generic readings, as is shown by the apparent equivalence of the sentences in (36).

(36)a   Lilies are true bulbs.
  b   The lily is a true bulb.
  c   A lily is a true bulb.

Generic readings of different NPs are discussed further in section 6.5.

The analysis of the existential readings in (34a-d) introduces an existential quantifier, so that *Firemen are available* is given the same truth condition as *Some firemen are available*. One way to arrive at this analysis is to say that the bare plural in sentences like these actually contains existential quantification as part of the NP, and that *firemen* and *some firemen*, for example, are just two forms for the same meaning.

Another way to understand the analysis is to say that the bare plural really is a free description introducing an unbound variable. So *firemen*, for example, is analysed as 'FIREMAN(x)' and the existential quantification is added from some other source. The sentences considered so far do not give a clear choice between these two options, but as we shall see in the next section, the facts concerning quantificational adverbs indicate that bare plurals are not in themselves existentially quantified NPs, but descriptions with a free variable.

6.4.2   Bare Plurals and Quantificational Adverbs

On their basic readings, quantificational adverbs quantify over occasions or times of occurrence, as illustrated in (37).

(37)   Liam never / seldom / occasionally / sometimes / often / usually / always has breakfast.

The adverbs express a quantity of occasions or times at which Liam has breakfast. The whole set of times that the quantifiers apply to is not all the times there are, but rather the times at which Liam would have breakfast – say, shortly after getting up in the morning. This is clear from *Liam always has breakfast*, which is true if Liam eats breakfast every morning and does not state that every time is a time at which Liam is eating breakfast. Thinking in terms of counting the mornings on which Liam eats breakfast, it is clear that the quantificational adverbs express the same quantifications as the quantificational determiners, as in (38).

(38)   never   no mornings
       seldom   few mornings
       occasionally   a few mornings
       sometimes   some mornings
       often   many mornings
       usually   most mornings
       always   every morning

Quantificational adverbs are not restricted to quantifying over times, and can also bind variables introduced by bare plural NPs, as in (39).

(39)a   Dogs are often noisy.
   b   Encyclopaedias are usually expensive.
   c   Patients with this disorder seldom recover.

Each of these sentences is ambiguous. On one reading the adverb quantifies over times and the bare plural subject has a generic reading, as in (40).

(40c) is somewhat odd on this interpretation, as a patient does not usually have a series of recoveries.

(40)a Dogs in general are noisy on many occasions / much of the time.
    b Encyclopaedias in general are expensive most of the time (though there are special price offers occasionally).
    c Patients with this disorder in general make a recovery on few occasions.

On the more likely readings for (39) the quantificational adverb binds the variable introduced by the bare plural subject, as shown in (41).

(41)a Dogs are often noisy.
      [Many x: DOG(x)] NOISY(x)
      'Many dogs are noisy'

    b Encyclopedias are usually expensive.
      [Most x: ENCYCLOPAEDIA(x)] EXPENSIVE(x)
      'Most encyclopaedias are expensive'

    c Patients with this disorder seldom recover.
      [Few x: PATIENT WITH THIS DISORDER(x)] RECOVER(x)
      'Few patients with this disorder recover'

The readings in (41), in which the quantificational adverb binds the variable associated with the bare plural NP, indicate that the variable must be free in the NP and therefore available to be bound from outside. This supports the view that a bare plural NP has no implicit quantification: for example the NP *firemen* has the semantics 'FIREMAN(x)' and not [∃x: FIREMAN(x)]'. So in (41a), the NP *dogs* contributes just 'DOG(x)' and the adverb *often* contributes 'Many'. *Often* and *dogs* combine to form the whole restricted quantifier.

6.5 GENERIC NPs AND REFERENCE TO KINDS

A central puzzle with generic NPs is illustrated in (42).

(42)a Lilies are true bulbs.
    b A lily is a true bulb.
    c The lily is a true bulb.

Despite the different forms of the NP subjects, the sentences in (42) appear to be roughly synonymous. The question then arises whether the NPs have the same interpretation in these sentences, and if not, what are the differences among them. Some of the identified differences are discussed below.

One kind of generic reference is reference to what is called a **natural kind**, which is a kind of substance or individual given by nature. Mass substances such as gold, water, sand and coal, and animal and plant kinds such as tigers and conifers are natural kinds. A natural kind can be referred to as a single abstract individual. The clearest instances of individual kind reference are references to natural kinds such as plant and animal species by name or by a singular definite description, as in (43).

(43)a   *Canis familiaris* is a popular pet in Western society.
   b   *Pinus radiata* is evergreen.
   c   The dog is a popular pet in Western society.
   d   The white pine is evergreen.

A kind individual is also indicated by a few predicates which apply to a kind as a whole, rather than to individual members of the kind, as in (44). The underlined NPs refer to kinds.

(44)a   The dodo is extinct.
   b   The panda may die out.
   c   *Ailuropoda melanoleuca* may die out.

Unlike the predicates in (44), most predicates which can combine with a kind name or with a definite kind NP denote properties of individual members of the kind, as in (45).

(45)a   The African grey parrot has a strong curved beak.
   b   The kiwi lays enormous eggs.
   c   The lion has a handsome mane.
   d   *Panthera leo* has a handsome mane.

Given the difference between the predicates in (44), applying to the kind as an abstract entity and (45), applying to the individual members of a kind, we need to decide whether or not the NPs must be given different interpretations. In particular, we must decide whether or not the NPs in (45) should be interpreted as referring to groups of individuals, with the predicate distributed to the individuals.

There are several reasons for not interpreting the NPs in (45) as group references.

First, the apparently distributive readings in (45) can be accounted for without interpreting the NPs as denoting groups of individuals. A kind as an abstract entity is always 'abstracted' from the individuals that make it up, and all the properties of the kind ultimately depend on properties of individual members. For example, the predicate *be extinct* applies to kinds, not to basic individuals, but the kind property of being extinct depends on all the members of the kind being dead. The predicates in (45) can be interpreted as kind properties in a similar way – properties of individuals can be attributed to the kind itself, if the kind is characterized by those properties of its members. Conversely, the members have those (characteristic) properties because they are members of the kind.

Secondly, to analyse the NPs in (45) as denoting groups of individuals with distributive predication would require some commitment as to how many members of the kind (some? all? most?) have the described property. The examples show that this can vary considerably. All African grey parrots have a strong curved beak except only for those, if any, with deformities or mutilations, but only a minority of kiwis lay enormous eggs, as males and unfertilized females lay no eggs at all. Similar uncertainties arise with examples like *The hedgehog is affected by ringworm*: being affected by ringworm (that is, not immune to it as a species) is characteristic of the hedgehog kind but it isn't possible to fix how many actual hedgehogs, if any, must have ringworm for the sentence to be true. These difficulties are avoided if properties are attributed to kinds directly, rather than to selected individual members of the kind.

A third point concerns a contrast in the possible interpretations of different NPs which are classed as generic. It can be shown that although some generic NPs do have group or plurality readings, generic singular definite NPs like *the lion* cannot have clear group readings in typical contexts.

Recall that bare plural NPs have both generic and existential readings, as in (46).

(46)a   Teachers are white-collar workers.
   b   Teachers are on duty.

Accordingly, *teachers* in (46a) is one type of generic NP. *Teachers* in (46a) was analysed above as a vague general quantification over teachers, with the quantification providing distributive predication as in (47).

(47)   [Gen x: TEACHER(x)] WHITE-COLLAR WORKER(x)
   'Generally for x such that x is a teacher, x is a white-collar worker'.

Bare plurals on a generic interpretation can also have collective readings when they combine with collective predicates, which must apply to groups, as in (48).

(48)   Teachers gather in the staffroom for coffee.

Combining the generic interpretation 'teachers in general' with the group interpretation required for *gather*, (48) can be analysed as in (49).

(49)   [Gen X: $\forall$x (x $\in$ X $\rightarrow$ TEACHER(x))] GATHER IN THE STAFF-
       ROOM(X)
       'Generally for a group X such that every member of X is a teacher, X
       gathers in the staffroom.'

As examples (46)–(49) show, a bare plural NP like *teachers* with a generic
reading can combine with either a distributive predicate, such as *is a white-
collar worker*, or with a collective predicate, such as *gather in the staffroom*.
So these examples show that *teachers* on a generic reading can be interpreted
as a plurality of individual teachers, rather than as one abstract individual,
the teacher kind.
    The question at hand is whether generic singular NPs, like *the lion*, should
be interpreted as referring to the members of a kind as a plurality or group of
individual real lions, rather than referring to the kind as a single abstract
individual. The question arises because of examples like *The lion has a
handsome mane* where having a handsome mane is a property of individual
real lions.
    Suppose that *the lion* on a generic reading is to be interpreted like generic
lions, denoting a plurality of members of the lion kind. Then we would
expect that *the lion* should appear with collective predicates just as *lions*
does, but this is not the case, as shown in (50).

(50)a   Lions gather at the water-hole in the evening.
    b   Teachers gather in the staffroom.
    c   Hired demonstrators disperse at the first sign of trouble.
    d   Teachers meet regularly to discuss school affairs.
    e # The lion gathers at the water-hole in the evening.
    f # The teacher gathers in the staffroom.
    g # The hired demonstrator disperses at the first sign of trouble.
    h # The teacher meets regularly to discuss school affairs.

The problem in (50e–h) is not purely a syntactic clash between a singular
subject and a collective predicate which is semantically plural. A singular NP
which does denote a group, such as *committee* or *family*, can take a collective
predicate such as *meet* or *gather*, with either singular or plural marking on
the verb, as in (51).

(51)a   The committee meets regularly.
    b   The committee meet regularly.
    c   The family gathers for meals.
    d   The family gather for meals.

A predicate which takes a (semantically) plural subject, such as *support
each other*, can also appear with a singular collective NP (with a plural verb)

as in (52a), or with a generic bare plural as in (52b), but not with a definite singular kind NP as in (52c,d).

(52)a The family support each other.
  b Teachers support each other.
  c #The teacher support each other.
  d #The teacher supports each other.

These examples show that in contrast to generic *teachers*, the singular generic NP *the teacher* cannot denote the teacher kind as a plurality of its members, but must be interpreted as some kind of single individual. This is why generic *the teacher* cannot take a collective predicate.

A fourth point arises with cumulative predicates. Generic bare plurals (*bulls*) contrast with generic singular definites (*the bull*) in combination with cumulative predication.

(53)a Bulls have horns.
  b Unicorns have horns.
  c The bull has horns.
  d The unicorn has horns.

Examples (53a,b) have cumulative predications, expressing a sort of summary – a plurality of bulls or unicorns has a plurality of horns. The summarizing reading allows (53b) to be true. Unlike (53b), (53d) is false. *The unicorn* cannot be given a cumulative plural reading to harmonize with *horns*, so (53d) attributes at least two horns to the unicorn kind, from which it follows that an actual individual unicorn will have at least two horns. In fact the unicorn kind is characterized by having one horn, which can only be expressed as *The unicorn has a horn*.

In short, definite singular generic NPs are best interpreted as denoting a kind of abstract single individual. This abstract individual has properties which depend on properties of the actual members of the kind. The sentence *The bull has horns* expresses a property of the abstract individual bull-kind, and this property depends on the fact that actual bulls have actual horns. But *The bull has horns* and *Bulls have horns* do not mean exactly the same thing.

The fifth and final point concerns what counts as a kind. It has been observed that definite singular NPs sound odd if used generically for classes of objects that are not well established in some sense as abstract kinds, for example:

(54)a The Coke bottle has a narrow neck.
  b A Coke bottle has a narrow neck.
  c Coke bottles have narrow necks.
  d # The green bottle has a narrow neck.

e   A green bottle has a narrow neck.
f   Green bottles have narrow necks.

The oddness of (54d) is that it seems to presuppose that a green bottle is a particular kind of bottle in the same way as a Coke bottle is a particular kind of bottle, which isn't the case.

The same contrast shows up in (55), where *the white cat* purports to refer to an established kind, although white cats do not constitute a clear kind, in contrast to the breed known as Manx cats.

(55)a   # The white cat is deaf.
    b   A white cat is deaf.
    c   White cats are deaf.
    d   The Manx cat is tailless.
    e   A Manx cat is tailless.
    f   Manx cats are tailless.

In summary, there are at least two kinds of generically interpreted NP. Definite singular NPs apparently denote abstract kind individuals. The generic interpretation of indefinite NPs (such as *teachers* and *a teacher*) is more difficult to analyse. The examples reviewed above indicate that indefinite generic NPs, both singular NPs and bare plurals, are used to make generalizations about individuals fitting a given description, although they may not form an established kind.

To interpret generic *teachers* as making a generalization over individual teachers is consistent with the analysis outlined in section 6.4, using the generic quantifier *Gen*.

We saw in Section 6.4 that bare plural NPs have two main characteristics: (i) bare plurals have generic readings with predicates denoting enduring properties, and existential readings with predicates denoting temporary properties or episodes, and (ii) a bare plural can be interpreted as the restriction on a quantificational adverb.

Indefinite singular NPs also have both these properties, as shown below.

(56)   temporary property, existential reading
       a   A fireman is available.
       b   A teacher is on duty.
       c   A lily is blooming in the field.

       enduring property, generic reading
       d   A fireman is altruistic.
       e   A teacher is a white-collar worker.
       f   A lily is a true bulb.

Examples like these suggest that the generic quantifier *Gen* may also bind singular indefinites.

Singular indefinite NPs interpreted as the restrictions on quantificational adverbs are illustrated in (57).

(57)a A dog is often noisy.
    'Many dogs are noisy'
    [Many x: DOG(x)] NOISY(x)

b An encyclopaedia is usually expensive.
    'Most encyclopaedias are expensive'
    [Most x: ENCYCLOPEDIA(x)] EXPENSIVE(x)

c A patient with this disorder seldom recovers.
    'Few patients with this disorder recover'
    [Few x: PATIENT WITH THIS DISORDER(x)] RECOVER(x)

It was suggested in Section 6.4 that a bare plural NP has no quantifier of its own, so that the variable it introduces can be bound by a quantifier from some other part of the sentence. This might be *Gen*, a quantificational adverb such as *often* or *never*, or existential quantification. The same analysis has been proposed, for example by Heim (1982), for singular indefinite NPs with *a/an*, partly because of the evidence here that singular indefinite NPs are bound by quantifiers outside the NP. If this is correct, then *a/an* is not a quantificational determiner as defined in Chapter 4. For simplicity, we will use the quantificational analysis for *a/an* in this book, with the proviso that *a/an* doesn't always behave like a quantificational determiner.

EXERCISES

(A) Basic Review: Specificity

According to the scopal analysis of specificity in Section 6.1, each sentence below is structurally ambiguous. The underlined NP can be either specific or nonspecific in interpretation. Give both formulae for each sentence and indicate which is which.

(1) Karen wants to shoot a lion.
(2) Eric didn't meet a reporter.
(3) Clive might buy a painting.
(4) Every flautist played a sonata.

(B) Nonspecificity and Opacity

In the passage below the NP *an unnamed Democrat* in the first and last sentences is intended to be nonspecific. (Presumably respondents were asked to choose between voting for Bush (Republican) and voting Democrat.)

Does the nonspecific reading of the NP seem equally natural in both sentences? If not, what differences in the sentence contexts might be responsible for this difference in the NPs? Does this support the scopal analysis of specificity?

Bush's Popularity Slips in Poll

United States President George Bush was in a near dead-heat with an unnamed Democrat in a national poll that showed another drop in the President's approval rating and clear dissatisfaction with the nation's direction. The monthly survey provided fresh evidence of a dramatic shift in the US political landscape causes by persistent economic worries.

The latest survey, conducted between October 31 and November 10, found that 55 per cent of respondents approved of 'the way George Bush is handling his job as President' – down six points from a Times Mirror survey completed a month ago.

Asked whether they would prefer Mr Bush or an unnamed Democrat to win the 1992 presidential election, 43 per cent said they preferred a Democrat; 41 per cent Mr Bush.

(*Christchurch Press*, 13 November 91)

(C)   The Scopal Analysis of Specificity: Discussion

Janet Dean Fodor pointed out the example below, which is at least five ways ambiguous. The scopal analysis of specificity can only show three of those readings.

John wants to have a coat like Bill's.

(1)   What are the five readings of the sentence? (Set the circumstances and fill the gap in 'John thinks to himself, "I want — " '.)
(2)   Give the three formulae that the scopal analysis provides. Which readings do they express?
(3)   Why can't the other two readings be represented in this system?

(D)   Collective and Distributive Predication: Discussion

What kind of predication is expressed in the sentences below?

(1)   Several actors performed a skit.
(2)   Boxes filled the garage.
(3)   Boxes lay on the floor.
(4)   The collection was in large crates.
(5)   Wooden boxes held the collection.

(E)   Bare Plurals: Discussion

Bare Plural NPs can be interpreted either generically or existentially. Section 6.4.1 shows that the choice partly depends on whether the predicate describes a temporary state of affairs or an enduring property, as in

Firemen are available	temporary, existential
Firemen are altruistic	enduring, generic

(1)   In the examples below, all the predicates are habitual, therefore enduring. How are the existential and generic readings for bare plurals fixed here?

(a)   Beavers build dams.
(b)   Dams are built by beavers.
(c)   Toxic liquids are produced in landfills.
(d)   Landfills produce toxic liquids.

(2)   Say the sentences below with the main stress on the marked syllable. How does this affect the reading of *tornadoes*?

(a)   TorNADoes arise in Kansas.
(b)   Tornadoes arise in KANsas.

(3)   The bare plurals in the sentences below seem to be in exactly similar contexts. Do they have the same kind of interpretation?

(a)   Shoes must be worn.   (sign outside café)
(b)   Dogs must be carried   (sign by escalator)

(4)   Is the underlined NP below existential or generic? Is the predication distributive, collective or cumulative?

Native plants grow well in moist and shady to semi-shady areas and in full, blazing sun where the soil is dry and exposed to the elements.

(5)   Bare plurals can be usefully vague. What quantification (existential or generic) is expressed in these examples?

(a)   People don't support the health reforms.
(b)   Families are under increasing pressure these days.
(c)   Dentists recommend fluoride tablets.

(6)   Using ∀, ∃ and □ for deontic *must*, write representations for (3a,b) repeated below. For simplicity, treat the passive predicates *be worn* and *be carried* as 1–place predicates BE WORN, BE CARRIED.

(a)   Shoes must be worn.

(b)   Dogs must be carried.

(Examples in (3)–(6) are from Halliday (1970).)

(F)   Mass and Count NPs: Basic Review

Allan (1980) reviews four syntactic tests for the countability of NPs:

I.   Count nouns appear with determiner *a/an*.
       Adam ate *an apple*.
II.   Count nouns appear with 'fuzzy' count quantifiers *many*, *few* and
       several.
       Several apples had gone rotten.
III.   Count nouns appear in plural NPs with plural agreement on the verb.
       These apples are floury.
IV.   Count nouns do NOT appear in the frame *all N* with a singular verb.
       * *All apple* is delicious. (cf. All wine is delicious.)

Score the countability of the following nouns on these tests. How many
count classes do you find?

  *water, furniture, man, cattle, lightning, mist, scissors, measles, fish, non-
  sense, mischief, cedar, pleasure*

(G)   Generic NPs: Discussion

Given the apparent synonymy of the sentences repeated below, the NPs
lilies, a lily, and *the lily* have been considered to have the same interpretation
in these sentences. Section 6.5 argued that *the lily* refers to a kind, but the
indefinite NPs are interpreted as quantified by the vague quantifier *Gen*
'generally'.

(a)   A lily is a true bulb.
(b)   Lilies are true bulbs.
(c)   The lily is a true bulb.

Do the examples below support the distinction between singular definite
generics and indefinite generics? Can you find any difference between singular indefinite and plural indefinite generics?

(1)   (a)   A chimney should be swept regularly.
      (b)   Chimneys should be swept regularly.
      (c)   The chimney should be swept regularly.

(2)   (a)   A dog bites.
      (b)   Dogs bite.
      (c)   The dog bites.

(3) (a) A red sunrise means rain.
    (b) Red sunrises mean rain.
    (c) The red sunrise means rain.

(4) (a) A redhead is impulsive.
    (b) Redheads are impulsive.
    (c) The redhead is impulsive.

(5) (a) A child likes sweets.
    (b) Children like sweets.
    (c) The child likes sweets.

(6) (a) A nudge is as good as a wink.
    (b) Nudges are as good as winks.
    (c) The nudge is as good as the wink.

(H) Mass NPs and Mass Predicates: Review

Write representations for the sentences below. See Section 6.3 for relevant discussion.

(a) Snow is white.
(b) There's gold in Otago.
(c) The gold in this ring is soft.
(d) Every shirt Simon bought was silk.

FURTHER READING

Ioup (1977) gives a useful short review of specificity. Partee (1974) discusses specificity and opacity as the same phenomenon.

For a discussion of a number of phenomena found with indefinite NPs see Ludlow and Neale (1991).

See Fodor and Sag (1982) for discussion of indefinites, and arguments that some indefinites must be analysed as referential rather than quantificational.

On plurals, see Landman (1996).

On generics, see Chapter 1 in Carlson and Pelletier (1995).

For count and mass nouns, see Allan (1980).

The discussion of mass NPs in Section 6.3 is partly based on Higginbotham (1995).

Vendler's discussion of different universal quantifiers is in Vendler (1967).

Ojeda (1993) uses a mereological model for NP denotations, with an accessible introduction to mereologies.

7 Tense and Aspect

Both tense and aspect convey information about the time of a described event or state of affairs. Tense locates the whole event or situation on the timeline, in the past, present or future. Aspect does not locate an event in time, but concerns the internal temporal structure of the event itself.

The terms *tense* and *aspect* are used for both syntactic and semantic classifications, which overlap but do not match up entirely. (I use the terms *syntactic tense* and *syntactic aspect* to include morphological tense forms, such as *brings/brought* and *looks/looked*, and verb groups which express tense and aspect such as *is bringing*, *will bring*, and *has brought*.) For example, a verb form such as *left* in *He left early* is a syntactic past tense form and is also a semantic past tense because it denotes a past time, but there are uses of the syntactic past tense which do not convey semantic tense, just as there are ways of speaking of the past without using past tense verb forms. As we shall see, a similar mismatch arises with the English auxiliary verb *have*, which is commonly classified as an aspectual auxiliary but also has tense readings.

As a preliminary to the discussion of semantic tense and aspect, the next section reviews the range of syntactic tense and aspect forms in English verb groups.

7.1 THE ENGLISH VERB GROUP

The English verb group always contains the main verb, and may also contain a modal auxiliary and forms of the auxiliary verbs *have* and *be*. A verb group containing all these elements together is illustrated in (1).

(1) On the original timetable for this project, by this time the reports *would have been being printed*.

This example shows the order in which the different verbs always appear, and also illustrates how auxiliary *have* and both auxiliary verbs *be* determine the form of the verb immediately following.

(2)	WOULD	HAVE	BEEN	BEING	PRINTED
	Modal	perfective	progressive	passive	main verb
	will +	*have*	*be* + *-en*	*be* + *-ing*	*print* + *-en*
	past tense	(+ *-en* →)	(+ *-ing* →)	(+ *-en* →)	

The verb following a modal verb is in the stem form. The verb following perfective *have* is the past participle, which is the *-en* form of the verb. Although *-en* is the symbol for all past participle forms, the actual forms may vary, as illustrated in (3).

(3) *be + en*   we have <u>been</u>
     go + en   we have <u>gone</u>
     look + en   we have <u>looked</u>
     break + en   day has <u>broken</u>
     sing + en   we have <u>sung</u>

The verb following progressive *be* is always the *-ing* form, which is the present participle.

English verbs have only two morphological tenses: past tense (*looked, brought, sang*) and present tense (*looks, brings, sings*). The semantic future in English is not a true morphological tense as there is no form of the main verb marked for future. The semantic future is generally expressed by the auxiliary *will* as in *He will leave.*

In any verb group, syntactic tense is marked only once, and always appears on the first verb in the sequence. In (2) the modal verb *would* is the past tense form of *will*, and none of the other verbs has a tense marking.

The different components of the verb group can appear singly or in various combinations, as illustrated below.

(4) **Main verb** alone
     present tense   *June laughs*
     past tense   *June laughed*

     Passive voice
     present tense   *The dogs are fed every day*
     past tense   *The dogs were fed every day*

     Progressive aspect
     present tense   *June is laughing*
     past tense   *June was laughing*

     Perfect aspect
     present tense   *June has laughed*
     past tense   *June had laughed*

     Modal + main verb
     present tense   *June will laugh*
     past tense   *June would laugh*

The passive voice, marked by passive *be* and the past participle, contrasts with the active voice, which is the more basic form of the sentence:

(5) active: Barry feeds the dogs every day.
                  Barry fed the dogs every day.

   passive: The dogs are fed every day (by Barry).
                  The dogs were fed every day (by Barry).

In the passive voice, the NP which is the subject of the corresponding active sentence either is missing or appears in an optional *by*-phrase, and the NP which is the object of the corresponding active sentence appears in the subject position. Voice is quite distinct from tense and aspect – voice affects the syntactic argument structure of the verb and has no time-related interpretation.

   The morphological tenses marked on forms of the modal verbs commonly do not correlate with semantic tense readings. Other tense forms of the modals are shown in (6).

(6) **Present**   **Past**
    will   would
    can   could
    shall   should
    may   might
    must

The interpretation of modal verbs was discussed in Chapter 3, and the passive concerns argument structure, which was covered in Chapter 2. The matters to be discussed in this chapter are tense, the interpretation of the progressive and the interpretations of perfective *have*.

7.2   INTERPRETATIONS OF PRESENT AND PAST TENSE FORMS

7.2.1   The Present Tense

The interpretation of present tense forms varies according to the classification of the eventuality that the verb form describes. **Eventualities**, which are different kinds of events, actions and states of affairs, are discussed in more detail in Chapter 9. Here we need only the distinction between events and states.

States include psychological states such as believing and knowing, physical locations, permanent characteristics, and some perceptual states such as seeing and hearing. With verbs describing states the present tense has a present time reading.

(7)a   I <u>see</u> the trucks coming.
   b   Listen! I <u>hear</u> voices.

c   He <u>believes</u> this rubbish.
d   She <u>knows</u> where we are.
e   All those cupboards <u>contain</u> expensive equipment.
f   The house <u>stands</u> on a bluff overlooking the upper harbour.
g   Koalas <u>live</u> on eucalyptus shoots and leaves.

The present time reading of the present tense is vague in itself, and depends on the particular verb to give a 'right now' reading, as in (7a, b), or a more long-term reading including the time of speaking, as in (7e, f). Sentences like (7g) are classed as generic and are also sometimes considered to be semantically timeless.

Events are all the kinds of happenings which are not states, including actions. Event verbs in the present tense are most commonly interpreted as habitual. The **habitual** reading denotes not only habits, but any activity which is repeated from time to time or regularly, as illustrated in (8).

(8)a   Heath <u>bikes</u> to work.
  b   Barry <u>feeds</u> the dogs.
  c   She <u>writes</u> with a fountain pen.
  d   She <u>eats</u> peas but she won't eat silver beet.

The present habitual does not describe an event occurring at the time of speaking – for example, (8a) does not mean that Heath is on his bike at the time of speaking.

For certain kinds of predetermined event the simple present tense can also have a future time reading, as in (9).

(9)   The sun <u>sets</u> tomorrow at 6.03.
      I <u>leave</u> for Wellington this afternoon.

It isn't quite clear what fixes this use of the present tense, but it seems that the event must be either the result of some definite arrangement or fixed as a natural event.

Being certain that the event will take place isn't sufficient to allow the use of the future reading of the present tense. For example, suppose a chess championship is in progress, and there have been a number of cancellations in the preliminary matches. The weakest player has gone forward to the semi-final without any matches and tomorrow will play Sonja, the champion of the previous five years. It seems certain that Sonja will win tomorrow, but a present tense statement cannot be used to predict this.

(10)a   Sonja wins tomorrow.
   b   Sonja will win tomorrow.

Sonja's certain win can be predicted with (10b), but (10a) suggests that the match has been rigged.

The present tense with action verbs has a present event reading in commentaries such as sports commentaries or the commentary on a cooking programme.

(11)a   Pitama <u>passes</u> to Haggerdoorn, Haggerdoorn to Jones, and he nearly <u>misses</u> –
   b   Now I just <u>add</u> a few drops of water and <u>beat</u> the eggs...

These uses of the simple present tense may be somehow related to the habitual interpretation, as the present tense sounds awkward in the commentary context if it is used to describe something which isn't a normal part of the routine, such as the game or recipe, as in (12). The underlined verbs in (12a, b) would sound more natural in the progressive forms as in (12c, d).

(12)a   ...now the crowd <u>moves</u> onto the field...
   b   ...and I stir the sauce continually while it thickens, and it <u>sticks</u> a little so I <u>take</u> it off the heat for a minute...
   c   ...now the crowd is moving onto the field...
   d   ...it's sticking a little so I'm taking it off the heat...

The present tense also has a use called the narrative or historic present, with a past time interpretation, as in (13).

(13)   So just last week <u>I'm going</u> down Cashel St and this guy <u>comes</u> up to me...

7.2.2   The Past Tense

The basic use of the past tense is to indicate past time, as in (14).

(14)a   Barry <u>fed</u> the dogs (yesterday).
   b   In those days I <u>could</u> eat anything.
       (cf. These days I can eat anything.)

The past tense form is also used to show conditionality, as in (15). In a conditional sentence the past tense may be used of future times.

(15)   About next week – if we <u>left</u> early we <u>could</u> see the movie.

The contrast between present tense *may* and past tense *might* is also used to mark different kinds of modality, as noted in Section 3.1, although over the last few years this distinction seems to be weakening. The contrast is illustrated in the examples in (16).

(16)a She may have fallen down the cliff – we're still waiting for the rescue team's report.

   b She might have fallen down the cliff – thank goodness the safety harness held.

The verb forms in (17) are other common ways of expressing semantic tense, as marked. The modal *will* in (17d) is the main way of expressing semantic future.

(17)a She is leaving tomorrow.
   present progressive form of *leave*: future interpretation

   b She is going to leave
   present progressive form of *go* with infinitive *leave*: future interpretation

   c He used to live here
   idiom *used to*: past habitual interpretation

   d She will leave tomorrow
   present tense form of *will*: future interpretation

To sum up so far, the present and past tenses are not simply interpreted as their corresponding semantic tenses. The past tense frequently has past time meaning but it also conveys conditionality. The present tense has a range of interpretations and is compatible in different uses with past, present and future times.

7.2.3 Finiteness

One function common to all tensed forms is to code finiteness. **Finiteness** is the syntactic property of a simple declarative sentence which allows it to stand alone and express a proposition. Not all clauses are finite, for example:

(18)a I heard [Marcia playing jazz]
   b He wanted [Marcia to give Peter a piano lesson]
   c Don't let [that cat scratch the furniture]

The three bracketed sequences are embedded nonfinite clauses. In traditional logical terms each of these can be described as containing all the components for an atomic proposition because each clause contains a predicate combined with its arguments:

(19)a PLAY (m, j)
   b GIVE (m, a piano lesson, p)
   c SCRATCH(that cat, the furniture)

A proposition is also described as whatever is (or could be) a bearer of a truth value, but as the examples show, these two ways of defining propositions are not equivalent. All the bracketed clauses in (18) express complete predicate-argument complexes but none of them expresses a truth-value bearer. Only finite clauses, as in (20), can really express propositions.

(20)a Marcia is playing jazz.
   b Marcia gave Peter a piano lesson.
   c The cat scratched the furniture.

Semantic assertability, or the property of being a potential truth-value bearer, is coded syntactically as what we call finiteness, which is realized as tense in English.

7.3 THE FORMAL REPRESENTATION OF SIMPLE TENSES

In formal representations tense, like modality, can be analysed as an operator, as shown in (21).

(21)a Clive loves Marcia   Pres LOVE (c,m)
   b Fido bit Benny   Past BITE (f,b)
   c Benny will kick Fido   Fut KICK (b,f)

The operator symbols are defined in terms of reference to times, which are represented by variables t.

(22)a 'Pres LOVE (c, m)' is true at t^* iff
       'LOVE (c, m)' is true at t^*

   b 'Past BITE (f, b)' is true at t^* iff
       $\exists t\, (t < t^*$ & 'BITE (f, b)' is true at t)

   c 'Fut KICK (b, f)' is true at t^* iff
       $\exists t\, (t^* < t$ & 'KICK (b, f)' is true at t)

The marked variable t^* ('t star') represents a kind of reference point or anchor time, which is generally the time of speaking, or Now. The symbol '<' is read as 'is earlier than'. Then the definitions in (22) read in full as in (23).

(23)a 'Pres LOVE (c, m)' is true at Now if and only if 'LOVE (c, m)' is true at Now.

b 'Past BITE (f, b)' is true at Now if and only if there is a time t such that t is earlier than Now and 'BITE (f, b)' is true at t.

c 'Fut KICK (b, f)' is true at Now if and only if there is a time t such that Now is earlier than t and 'KICK (b, f)' is true at t.

Simply, the analysis says that 'Fido bit Benny' is true if and only if 'Fido bite Benny' is true at some past time.

Recall that finiteness and tense are expressed together. When past tense is removed from 'Fido bit Benny', the remaining sequence 'Fido bite Benny' is nonfinite and tenseless: it is a predicate-argument complex but not a proposition, and is not true or false at any time. If 'BITE (f,b)' corresponds to 'Fido bite Benny' (and not to 'Fido bites Benny'), this is a problem for the traditional analysis, because it doesn't make sense to say that 'Fido bite Benny' is true at some time t.

An alternative is to say that 'BITE (f, b) at t' is interpreted as 'an event of Fido's biting Benny occurs at time t'. This move avoids attributing truth or falsity to the sequence 'BITE (f, b)', and also introduces events into the semantics. The semantics of events is discussed in Chapters 8 and 9. For the present we will assume that the tense operators *Past*, *Pres* and *Fut* have event-based truth conditions as represented in (24).

(24)a Pres LOVE (c, m) iff
LOVE (c, m) at t^*
'A state of affairs of Clive loving Marcia holds at t^*'.

b Past BITE (f, b) iff
$\exists t (t<t^* \ \& \ BITE (f, b)$ at t)
'There is a time t earlier than t^* such that an event of Fido biting Benny occurs at t.'

c Fut KICK (b, f) iff
$\exists t (t^*<t \ \& \ KICK(b, f)$ at t)
'There is a time t such that t^* is earlier than t and an event of Benny kicking Fido occurs at t.'

The analysis here introduces times as individuals to be referred to and represented by variables. The definitions for *Past* and *Fut* also quantify over times, binding the t variable with the existential quantifier. Other kinds of quantification over times are considered in Exercise G at the end of this chapter. The analysis of tense is also discussed further in Sections 7.8 and 7.9.

7.4 ASPECT

The English progressive and perfective *have* are both commonly classed as aspects. The progressive is clearly aspectual in its semantics, but as we shall see, perfective *have* appears to have a dual nature, being aspectual in some uses but a kind of past tense in others.

The discussion of tense and aspect in this chapter draws a distinction between predicates of states, such as *be tall*, and predicates of events, such as *fall over*. The classes of states and events that different verb phrases describe are set up according to the internal temporal structure of states and events, and thus the classification system is aspectual. The aspectual classification of events is covered in Chapter 9.

7.5 THE PROGRESSIVE

The canonical reading of the progressive was described by Jespersen (1932: 178–80) as a temporal frame: the progressive reports the time of an event or situation as a temporal frame containing another time. Another way of describing the reading is to say that the progressive takes us inside the duration of a reported event to where the event is in progress. The examples in (25) show the progressive forms for each tense contrasted with the nonprogressive forms.

(25)a Alice <u>reads</u> the *Mail*.
   b Alice <u>is reading</u> the *Mail*.

   c When you arrive John <u>will make</u> coffee.
   d When you arrive John <u>will be making</u> coffee.

   e When Alice arrived John <u>made</u> coffee.
   f When Alice arrived John <u>was making</u> coffee.

Example (25a) has the habitual reading as in (8) above. The progressive in (25b) has the 'right now' reading – the time of reading the paper is a frame around the time of speech. In (25d, f) the progressive form of *make coffee* presents the time of the coffee-making event as a frame for the time of arrival, or in other words, the progressive takes us inside the coffee-making event to where it is in progress. In contrast, (25c, e) are interpreted as reporting a sequence of events in which the coffee-making follows the arrival.

The temporal frame reading is typical of the progressive with event verbs. State verbs generally have a temporal frame reading in the nonprogressive form, as illustrated in (26).

(26)a Generally when Lucas arrives home it <u>is dark</u>.
   b When Lucas opened the door the light <u>was on</u>.

On a normal interpretation, the state of darkness surrounds the time of Lucas's arrival in (26a), and it is already dark before he arrives. The state of the light's being on surrounds the time of opening the door in (26b) in the same way. If these sentences were interpreted in the same way as (25c, e), they would mean 'When Lucas arrives it will get dark' and 'When Lucas opened the door the light went on.'

Some state verbs do not take the progressive at all, as shown in (27). (This point is also raised in Chapter 9.)

(27)a # Tina is having long legs.
  b # A row of hills is bordering the plain.
  c # Jones is owning an old Jaguar.

With a number of state verbs, however, the progressive form suggests a shortened duration for the state, or suggests temporariness, for example:

(28)a We live in London.
  b We are living in London.
  c The statue stands in the south quadrangle.
  d The statue is standing in the south quadrangle.
  e John's house sits at the top of a hill.
  f John's house is sitting at the top of a hill.

In contrast with (28a), (28b) suggests that our living in London may be a temporary arrangement, and the same contrast is found in (28c, d). (28f) sounds odd because the location of a house is generally not temporary, but it sounds quite normal in a context where John's house is being relocated and has temporarily halted.

The temporary reading also applies to the progressive of event predicates interpreted as habituals, which are classed as states:

(29)a John was working when we arrived.
  b John was working at Woolworths.
  c John worked at Woolworths.

The basic frame reading for a single event is in (29a). Both (29b,c) have habitual readings, but the progressive in (29b) suggests a more temporary state of affairs.

Formal definitions for the progressive, which tend to be rather complex, will not be covered here. Some of the complications arise from the different interpretations the progressive has with predicates for different kinds of eventuality such as the events and states illustrated here. Further points concerning the progressive will be raised in Chapter 9.

7.6 PERFECTIVE *HAVE*

The perfect forms to be discussed in this section are illustrated in (30).

(30) **present perfect**
Pedro <u>has finished</u> his masterpiece.

past perfect
Pedro <u>had finished</u> his masterpiece.

future perfect
Pedro <u>will have finished</u> his masterpiece.

English perfective *have* is perhaps the most semantically complex of the English verb forms. It has two distinct readings, an embedded past tense reading and an aspectual reading. All tenses of the perfect have aspectual readings, but only the past and future perfects have tense readings. Because the present perfect has only aspectual readings it is used in the next section to illustrate the characteristics of aspectual perfects. The tense perfect is outlined in Section 7.8, and the aspectual readings of past and future perfects are discussed in Sections 7.8 and 7.9.

7.7 THE ASPECTUAL PERFECT

A number of components of the semantics of the present perfect have been identified, falling under two main points. First, the present perfect combines both pastness and presentness, and is said to describe a past event from a present point of view, or as being currently relevant, or as occurring in the past and continuing up to the present. Second, the present perfect describes a past event as occurring at an indefinite or unidentified time. Various phenomena related to these observations are illustrated below, beginning with the combination of past and present.

7.7.1 The Present Perfect: Reference to Past and Present

As we shall see, the difference between state and event predicates is significant with readings of the aspectual perfect. We begin the discussion with predicates for events.

Even though the present perfect with an event predicate describes an event which is in the past, it requires time adverbials which denote times or intervals that include the present, so it is incompatible with adverbials like *yesterday* which denote a completely past time. This is illustrated in (31), where *today*, *this week* and *since Wednesday* identify an interval containing both the reported event and the time of utterance.

(31)a   Have you read the paper today/this week?
   b   # Have you read the paper yesterday/last week?
   c   Did you read the paper yesterday/last week?

   d   Jones has sold three condos since Wednesday.
   e   # Jones has sold three condos last week.
   f   Jones sold three condos last week.

   g   # The mail has arrived an hour ago.
   h   The mail arrived an hour ago.

The interval spanning past and present is also evident in the so-called **result state reading** with event predicates, where the perfect is used to report a past event resulting in a state of affairs which still holds, as illustrated in (32). This is the chief instance of 'present relevance' conveyed by the present perfect: a past event is currently relevant because its consequences are still in force. In these examples the state of affairs resulting from the reported event is more pertinent than the event itself.

(32)a   Jill won't need that checkout job, she's won the lottery.
        (Jill is now rich.)

   b   Henry can't dance the pas seul, he's pulled a tendon.
       (Henry is now injured.)

   c   Kane has broken into our files, so we'll have to whack him.
       (Kane now knows our secrets.)

With typical examples of the result state reading like those in (32), the causing event is understood to be recent, but further examples show that the recency of the event is partly pragmatic. The resulting state for a result state reading can be identified in completely general terms as the state of an event of the kind described having occurred. So in (32b), for example, the result state is the state of an event of Henry's pulling a tendon having occurred. This state will hold indefinitely into the future. From the general state of Henry's having pulled a tendon holding, we can infer other consequences at different times. Given the context suggested in the example, we infer that the injury is still unhealed and therefore that the event is recent, and that we are in the early part of the state of the event's having occurred. But from a state of Henry's having pulled a tendon holding, we can also infer that Henry knows what the pain of a pulled tendon is like, and this consequence, unlike the injury itself, holds indefinitely. So if we say 'Henry has pulled a tendon, he knows what it feels like', the recent event inference is missing.

The same effect is found with utterances of *I have seen your dog*. For example, if the owner is looking for a dog which has wandered off, someone who says 'I have seen your dog' implies that he or she knows roughly where the dog is. Here the inference is that the sighting is very recent. But if the owner is trying to describe the appearance of the dog, a rare breed, the speaker implies that he or she knows what the dog looks like, and for this a sighting at any past time is relevant. In both cases, the state of the dog's having been seen by the speaker is the same state, although its consequences vary at different times. (The kinds of inferences mentioned here are discussed further in Chapter 11.)

The so-called 'hot news' perfect also shows a recent event effect, as in (33).

(33)a   Russia has invaded Poland.
    b   Krakatoa has blown up.

    c   Jones has had an accident.
    d   The big tree has fallen over.

The hot news perfect is described as appropriate for reporting what is recent news and somehow currently relevant. In comparison to (33c, d), which are normally interpreted as reporting recent events, the examples in (33a,b) are odd from a current perspective because they report distant historical events. Given that the hot news effect is simply a recent event effect, it may not be distinct from the recent event effect with result state readings. Plausibly, the hot news effect in (33a) is tied to the inference that Poland is still occupied by Russian troops, and (33b) suggests that the immediate physical aftermath of a volcanic eruption is still unfolding.

   In the light of the examples so far, we could say that the perfect states a relationship between two times: the time of utterance is in the 'aftertime' of the reported event, the aftertime being simply the ongoing time after the event concludes. Placing the present time in the aftertime of the reported event is one way of accounting for the relevance of the past event to the present circumstances.

   If there is a temporal adverbial such as *since June*, *today* or *this week*, the adverbial must identify an interval spanning a past time and the present, containing the reported event. The reported event sets up a result state which still holds at the present time. The times and intervals are diagrammed in (34).

(34)   Jones has sold a condo since Wednesday.

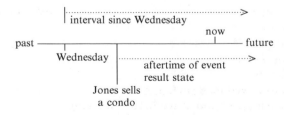

In this diagram we see that the event itself is a complete and fully past entity contained within the interval denoted by *since Wednesday*.

Predicates for states can have quite a different reading, as shown by the examples in (35), which describe a state of affairs beginning in the past and continuing up to the present. (The habitual reading of *work* in (35b) is a kind of state.) This is the **continuing state reading**.

(35)a I have stayed in today.
  (I am still in.)

   b Sheila has worked in the library since December.
  (Sheila still works in the library.)

   c The door has been open for ten minutes.
  (The door is still open.)

Here we see that the state denoted by a state predicate fills up the interval denoted by *today* or *since December*, as shown in (36).

(36) Sheila has worked in the library since December.

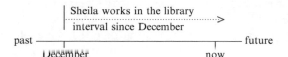

This difference between event and state predicates in the present perfect, combined with an interval adverbial, can be described in terms of the similarity between events and countable individuals, on the one hand, and the similarity between states and amorphous substances, on the other. This comparison between verbal predicates and count and mass NPs is explored in more detail in Chapter 9.

Briefly, the interval denoted by an adverbial such as *since December* is like a container – say, a bucket. A soft substance like water or sand, which has no inherent shape or quantity of its own, will spread out to fill a bucket it is poured into, taking the shape of the bucket. A bucket of sand is comparable to an interval filled by a state of affairs. But a countable individual such as a coffee mug has its own particular mass and shape, so if you place a coffee mug in a bucket it retains its own form, sitting within the bucket with room to spare. A coffee mug in a bucket is comparable to an event contained within an interval.

Note that the continuing state reading for a state predicate depends on the presence of an interval adverbial, as shown in (37).

(37)a They have lived here since 1985.
  Donna has had a job at Romero's this year.

b   They have lived here.
    Donna has had a job at Romero's.
c   They have lived here since 1985, but not recently.
    Donna has had a job at Romero's this year, but not recently.
d   Since 1985 they have lived here.
    This year Donna has had a job at Romero's.

The continuing state reading is the most salient reading for (37a), but not the only reading. If the adverbial is omitted as in (37b), the continuing state reading is not found and the state of affairs is understood to be completely in the past, and possibly not even recent. In fact, the completely past reading is also possible in (37a), which can be interpreted as reporting a completely past episode, a reading which is emphasized by adding *but not recently in* (37c). If the *since* adverbial is at the beginning of the sentence it is commonly considered to have only the continuing state reading, as in (37d).

The completely past reading for a state perfect is like the result state reading for an event perfect. With an event perfect like *Jones has read 'Erewhon'*, the result state of Jones' having read *Erewhon* holds at the time of speaking, and the reading event is completely in the past. Similarly, on the completely past reading of a state perfect like *Donna has had a job at Romero's*, the result state of Donna's having had a job at Romero's holds at the time of speaking, but the state of affairs of Donna's having the job is past.

The difference between a state filling the interval denoted by an adverbial and an event or state partly occupying the interval can be analysed in terms of universal and existential quantification over the times in the interval, as outlined in the next section.

7.7.2   Universal and Existential Readings

On the continuing state reading, a state of affairs fills the interval denoted by an adverbial, or holds at every time point in that interval, so the continuing state reading corresponds to universal quantification over the times in the interval. A completely past event or state, on the other hand, occupies some of the times in the interval denoted by an adverbial, so the completely past reading corresponds to existential quantification over the times in the interval. This is illustrated in (38). Times in general include both time points and intervals, so t variables can represent both.

(38)   They have lived here since the war.

    a   existential: completely past: result state
        [The t: SINCE THE WAR(t)] [$\exists t'$: IN(t',t)] they live here at t'
        The formula is read as follows:

For some time t′, such that t′ is in the interval t which is since the war, they live here at t′.

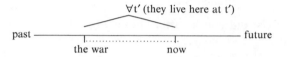

b <u>universal</u>: continuing state
[The t: SINCE THE WAR(t)] [∀t′: IN(t′,t)] they live here at t′
The formula is read as follows:
For all times t′, such that t′ is in the interval t which is since the war, they live here at t′.

∀t′ (they live here at t′)

past ——————————⌢——————————— future
            ├························┤
         the war   now

To sum up so far: we have seen that, without an interval adverbial, the present perfect places an event or state at some time in the past. The use of the perfect signals that the state of the reported event's having taken place (or the state of the reported state's having held) is a relevant part of the present circumstances – this is the result state reading. How the result state of the reported event or state is relevant to the present circumstances will determine how recent the past event or state is understood to be

Because the present perfect is in some sense about the present time, it can only combine with a time adverbial which denotes an interval including the present. When an interval adverbial modifies a state sentence, the sentence can have the continuing state reading, in which the reported state fills the interval up to the present.

Because the continuing state reading depends on the presence of an interval adverbial, it seems that the most basic reading of the present perfect is the result state reading: with some particular relevance to the present, an event or state of the kind described happened or held at some unspecified past time. The notion of an *unspecified* past time is emphasized in a traditional view of the present perfect, reviewed in the next section.

7.7.3 Definite and Indefinite Reference to Times

According to the traditional insight, in reporting past events, the choice between the simple past tense and the present perfect marks a distinction between definite and indefinite reference to times, as described in this comment from Webster (1789: 226–7):

'I have loved' or 'moved' expresses an action performed and completed, generally within a period of time not far distant, but leaves the particular

<u>point</u> of time wholly indefinite or undetermined. On the other hand, 'I loved' is necessarily employed, when a particular period or point of time is specified . . . 'I moved' is the definite time and 'I have moved' the indefinite.

We saw in Chapter 4 that indefinite or weak NPs are associated with novel reference, in contrast with the familiar reference of definite, or strong NPs. The definiteness contrast noted by Webster gives rise to clear familiarity effects along the same lines. The perfect denotes an unfamiliar time which cannot be identified with a previously mentioned time, as illustrated in (39).

(39)a Q: What did you do after dinner?
       A: # I have watched the news.

    b Q: What did you do after dinner?
       A: I watched the news.

    c I've never met a man that I didn't like.
    d I've never met a man that I haven't liked.

The response in (39a) is odd because the perfect *have watched* cannot be interpreted as referring to the same time as the previously mentioned and familiar *after dinner*: accordingly, the response doesn't seem to answer the question. Example (39c), attributed to Will Rogers, contrasts with (39d): the simple past tense *didn't* in (39c) can refer back to the time of meeting, which once mentioned, is familiar – the speaker liked every man at the time he met him. In contrast, the perfect *haven't liked* in (39d) cannot be identified with the familiar time of meeting, and the interpretation is that the speaker has liked every man he met at some stage, but not necessarily at the time of meeting.

Compare also the examples in (40):

(40)a Have you seen *Cats*?
    b Did you see *Cats*?
    c No, but I've seen it since.

The indefinite time reference with the perfect in (40a) has universal force in the question context, as in 'Have you ever seen *Cats*?'. The answer in (40c) is anomalous. In contrast, the simple past tense in (40b) makes reference to a definite time, here the season of a particular production of *Cats*, and the answer in (40c) is possible. These differences in reference compare directly with the NPs *a bike* and *the bike* in (41).

(41)a Have you ridden a bike?
    b Have you ridden the bike?
    c No, but I've ridden a different bike.

The indefinite reference in (41a) has universal force as in 'Have you ridden any bike?' (41c) is anomalous as an answer to (41a), but it is a possible answer in response to (41b), which asks a question about a definite identified bike.

The definiteness contrast may be the source of another effect noted with the present perfect, illustrated in (42a,b), repeated from (40).

(42)a Have you seen *Cats*?
    b Did you see *Cats*?

It has been suggested that the present perfect in (42a) shows present relevance, being an appropriate question if the show is still running and the hearer could still see it, while (42b) is appropriate where there is no present opportunity to see *Cats*, because the production has closed. But note that (42a) is also appropriate if the show is not currently running anywhere, and the question relates to any past or present production of the show. This reading does not require the understood background of a current season: it requires only that the questioner does NOT refer to a definite season which is completely in the past.

The definiteness contrast is particularly clear in examples like (43).

(43)a Tom hasn't read *Moby Dick*.
    b Tom didn't read *Moby Dick*.

The past tense in (43b) identifies a definite time identifiable from the context at which Tom didn't read *Moby Dick*, although he may have read it subsequently. This reading is represented in (44a). The present perfect in (43a) gives the same reading as an existential quantification under negation, as in (44b).

(44)a Tom didn't read *Moby Dick*.
       [The time t] $\sim$ READ(t, m) at t

    b Tom hasn't read *Moby Dick*.
       $\sim \exists (t < t^* \ \& \ $READ$(t, m)$ at t$)$
       'There is no past time at which Tom read *Moby Dick*.'

The analyses in (44) reveal a problem with the traditional logical analysis for simple tense, as pointed out by Barbara Partee with the famous example in (45).

(45)a I turned off the stove.
    b $\exists t (t < t^* \ \& \ $I turn off the stove at t$)$
    c I didn't turn off the stove.

d $\exists t \ (t < t^* \ \& \sim (I \ turn \ off \ the \ stove \ at \ t))$
    'For some time t such that t is earlier than now, I didn't turn off the
    stove at t.'

e $\sim \exists t \ (t < t^* \ \& \ I \ turn \ off \ the \ stove \ at \ t)$
    'There is no time t such that t is earlier than now and I turned off the
    stove at t.'

Recall that the traditional analysis for tense is just existential quantification
over times, so the past tense is analysed as 'for some time t such that t is
earlier than the time of utterance'. Accordingly, (45a) is represented as (45b).
Although the existential does not capture the definite time reference of a past
tense, if (45a) is true then (45b) is true. But the negative sentences cannot be
analysed with the existential, as shown in (45d, e). In principle, the quantifier
and negation may vary in scope, so both readings are considered. (45d) is
true iff there is any past time at all at which the speaker didn't turn off the
stove, including times before the speaker's birth, and (45e) is equivalent to 'I
have never turned off the stove'. Obviously neither of these readings is what
we understand a speaker to mean in saying (45c).

In short, the indefinite existential reading which was assigned to the
simple past tense is more suited to the present perfect. Moreover, the
analysis of the simple past tense should show that it makes reference to a
<u>definite</u> time.

An alternative approach to the semantics of tense is to treat time variables
as referring pronouns, rather than as variables bound existentially. Time
references are compared with pronouns along the lines of the examples
in (46).

(46)a   He'll never make it.
        (said while watching a man climb a ladder carrying two pots of paint,
        a scraper, a roller, a brush, a rag, putty, and sundry other items.)
    b   I left your mail on your desk.
    c   The plumber came and he'll send a quote.
    d   Everyone came to dinner last night and Jones got tipsy.

The pronoun *he* in (46a) refers to a definite person, identified from the
nonlinguistic context. In similar fashion the past tense of *left* in (46b)
refers to a definite time which is identified from the general context. The
pronoun *he* in (46c) is also definitely referring, but in this instance the
referent is identified through the linguistic antecedent *the plumber*. This
can be compared with the time reference of *got tipsy* in (46d), where
the time referred to is identified as the time of the dinner the previous
night.

We turn in the next section to the tense perfect, found only with the past
and future perfects.

7.8 THE TENSE PERFECT

The tense perfect is semantically a simple past tense. In the most basic case, a semantic past tense is expressed in a sentence by the syntactic past tense as in *John looked crazy*, but this option is not always available.

As we saw in Section 7.1, morphological tense appears only once in a verb group. If the verb group contains a modal, then the modal occupies the tense position and no further morphological tense marking can be placed on any other verb in the group. In this case a semantic past tense can be expressed by *have*, as in (47).

(47)   If he got in, *Jones must have broken the lock.*
       Jones must have broken the lock = □ Jones broke the lock
       'It must be the case that Jones broke the lock.'

The tense perfect is needed in (47) because it contains (semantically) both a modality and a past tense, and modal verbs always occupy the tense position, leaving the past tense to be expressed by *have*.

Tense *have* also appears in verb phrases which contain two semantic tenses, either a past-in-the-past or a past-in-the-future. These are illustrated in (48).

(48)a   Leda rang up at three. *She had arrived at noon and was still trying to* get a lift to the lodge.
   b   The car can't get to the station until three but *Leda will have arrived at noon*, so she'll have to wait.

In (48a) the narrative provides a past time, the time of Leda's phone call. From that time, which is already past from the time of speaking, Leda's arrival at noon is further in the past. These two past tenses are coded by the presence of tense perfect *have* and the syntactic past tense marked on the verb form *had*. The interpretation is diagrammed in (49).

(49)
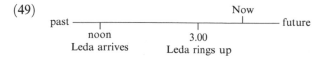

In (48b) the narrative provides the future time of three o'clock when the car arrives. At that time, Leda's arrival at noon is in the past. The sequence *will have* expresses the past tense inside the future tense, as diagrammed in (50).

(50)
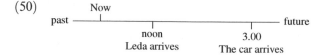

The adverbial *at noon* in (48) also shows that *have* in these examples is interpreted as a past tense. This can be checked by 'peeling off' the outer tense in *had arrived* and *will have arrived*, as in (51).

(51)a   Leda rang up at three. *She had arrived at noon* and was still trying to get a lift to the lodge.
        had arrived = past tense + *have* + *arrived*

   b   The car can't get to the station until three but *Leda will have arrived at noon*, so she'll have to wait.
        will have arrived = future tense + *have* + *arrived*

   The past tense in (51a) locates the past time identified as three o'clock, when Leda rang up. In (51b) the future tense of *will* locates the future time identified as three o'clock. The remainder of the sentence expresses what holds at three o'clock. The choices are in (52).

(52)a   Leda arrived at noon.   (said at three o'clock)
   b   # Leda has arrived at noon.   (said at three o'clock)

Example (52b) shows a clash between the aspectual perfect (remember that all present perfects are aspectual) and the adverbial *at noon*, which does not include the present time. The simple past in (52a), on the other hand, is compatible with *at noon*, so the simple past must be what is represented by *have* in (51). *Have* in (51) is a past tense under another tense. Accordingly, a temporal adverbial (*at noon*) with the tense perfect identifies the completely past time of the event.

7.9   REICHENBACH'S ANALYSIS

The most influential formal analysis of perfective *have* comes from Reichenbach's (1947) analysis of tense and aspect, based on the timeline image used above. Different verb forms denote arrangements of time points on the line, identified as the Speech time S, the Event time E, and the Reference Time R. Definitions for the simple past and future tenses are shown below.

(53)a   *simple past tense*
        John left.
        E,R_S or R,E_S

        event time _____ speech time
        reference time

b   *simple future tense*
   John will leave.
   S_R,E or S_E,R

   speech time _____ event time
                    reference time

Here the event time and reference time are the same time, placed at the same point on the timeline. Times separated by a comma are unordered and are located at the same time. Times separated by a dash are separated and ordered in time.

7.9.1   The Present Perfect

In Reichenbach's account the past event described by a present perfect verb form is *viewed from a present point of view or reference time*. Diagrammatically, the difference between a present perfect and a past tense is shown as in (54). In a present perfect the present time, or speech time, is the reference time or point-of-view time, while the reference time with the simple past tense is the time of the event.

(54)a   John has left.
         E_R,S

   b   John left.
         E,R_S

To account for the clash between present-excluding adverbials and the present perfect, as in *I have seen Jones last week*, Reichenbach proposed that a temporal adverbial modifying a perfect must always modify the reference time, rather than the event time. Assuming that all perfects have the same interpretation with adverbials, Reichenbach also applied this rule to the past perfect and future perfect. We return to this point below.

7.9.2   Past and Future Perfect

For the past-in-the-past and the past-in-the-future, the reference time marks the time of the outer tense. The past-in-the-past, or past perfect, is shown in (55).

(55)   Tom got there by noon, but *Molly had left at 10.30*.

   had left = past + have + *leave*
           = $past_1$ + $past_2$ + *leave*

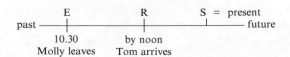

The first (outermost) past tense takes us back from the speech time to the reference time, the time of Tom's arrival, familiar and identifiable from being mentioned in the preceding clause *Tom got there by noon*. The second (embedded) past tense takes us back again from the reference time to the event time, the time of Molly's leaving. The event time is always the time of the main event reported in the sentence – Molly's leaving is the event reported in *Molly had left at 10.30*.

Note that Reichenbach's rule for temporal adverbials does not work in (55), as the adverbial *at 10.30* in the main clause *Molly had left at 10.30* modifies the event time of Molly's leaving, not the reference time as Reichenbach proposed. The reference time for *Molly had left at 10.30* is familiar and identifiable as the event time of Tom's arrival in the clause *Tom got there by noon*. Although the adverbial *by noon* does identify the time which is the reference time for *Molly had left at 10.30*, this is irrelevant for Reichenbach's rule, because *by noon* does not directly modify the event reported in *Molly had left*.

In fact, (55) with the diagrammed interpretation is an example of the tense perfect. The adverbial identifies the event time with the tense perfect, and identifies the reference time with the aspectual perfect. The aspectual perfect is illustrated in (56) below.

(56)   That evening the campers had already left.

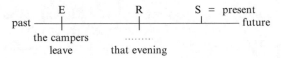

On the aspectual interpretation diagrammed here, the adverbial *that evening* identifies a past reference time which is not the time of the event of the campers leaving.

The future perfect also has both tense and aspectual readings. The tense future perfect is in (57) below, repeated from (48) above. As we have seen, the adverbial *at noon* identifies the event time, the time of Leda's arrival.

(57)   The car can't get to the station until three but *Leda will have arrived at noon*, so she'll have to wait.

```
                  S  =  present      E                R
      past ──────────┴──────────────┼────────────────┼──────── future
                                   noon           three o'clock
                              Leda arrives
```

The aspectual future perfect is illustrated in (58). Here the adverbial *at 10.30* identifies a future reference time which is not the time of the event of Leda's leaving.

(58) *Leda will have left at 10.30* – you will have to come before 9.00 if you want to see her.

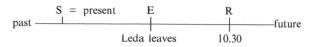

Following the diagrams, the representations for the past and future perfects are as in (59).

(59) past perfect   E_R_S
      future perfect   S_E_R

The timeline-based notation imposes an order on all three times, S, E and R. The future perfect is represented as S_E_R, but in fact the situations represented by E_S_R and E,S_R are also possible with the future perfect, as in (60).

(60) Loney says he's going out there, but *the tide will have washed any clues away*.

R = the time of Loney's arrival at the beach
S_E_R   The high tide is still to come, but will peak before Loney arrives.
E_S_R   The high tide peaked two hours ago.
E,S_R   The tide is full now.

In all of these scenarios Loney's arrival at the beach is in the future, and the high tide precedes Loney's arrival at the beach – this is all that is really required.

The future perfect is vague in a way which is compatible with all three orders for S, R and E in (60). Reasonably, the future perfect conveys only what is common to all of these situations, which is that S precedes R and E precedes R. The relationship between S and E is not determined. One way to deal with this problem is to represent the future perfect with a branching diagram, as in (61a), where the relative order of S and E is not fixed.

(61)a   future perfect   S__R
                          E⁄

    b   past perfect   E_R_S

 The central feature of Reichenbach's analysis is that perfect forms, unlike simple tense forms, denote a reference time which is separate from the event time. In addition, the aspectual reading for all perfects is characterized by a time adverbial identifying the reference time. This contrasts with the tense interpretation for past and future perfects, where a time adverbial identifies the event time.

EXERCISES

(A)   Tense Operators: Basic Review

Using the tense operators *Pres*, *Past* and *Fut*, write formulae for the following sentences. Omit the bracketed material.

(1)   Everyone likes icecream.
(2)   Jenny had met Claudia (already).
(3)   Some letters will have been destroyed.
(4)   Delia thinks Minnie is going to be sick.
(5)   (When we arrived at the flat), Jones had had breakfast.
(6)   Jones will have had breakfast.
(7)   (Harold began building his house that summer. On completing the house, ...)
       ...He would have spent $400,000.
(8)   (Clara began juggling when she was five. In a few years ...)
       ...she would be world class.

(B)   Reichenbach Diagrams: Basic Review

The Reichenbachian diagrams are:

present tense	E,R,S (or any order of E, R and S)
past tense	E,R_S or R,E_S
future tense	S_E,R or S_R,E
present perfect	E_R,S or E_S,R
past perfect	E_R_S
future perfect	S__R E

Give the Reichenbachian diagrams for the verb groups underlined below.

I have[1] to buy a present for Marcia. I suppose[2] I will get[3] something nice at the mall, but I can't afford to spend much because I haven't been paid[4] for that graphics job. They're really slack at that firm – if <u>I'd known</u>[5] about them before they <u>rang</u>[6] me I wouldn't have taken the job. By the time they pay me I <u>will have waited</u>[7] three months – it's a disgrace.

(C) Reichenbach Diagrams

Can you construct a Reichenbach diagram for the underlined verb group below? (Compare Exercise A, (7).)

(i)   John left for the front. By the time he would return, the fields <u>would have been burnt</u> to stubble.

(D) Reichenbach's Analysis: Discussion

Section 7.7.3 outlines the indefinite time reference property of the present perfect, contrasted with the definite time reference found with the simple past tense. In Reichenbach's analysis the simple past tense shows the time of the event as a reference time, while the event time with a present perfect is not a reference time. Can Reichenbach's reference time R be used generally to express the contrast between definite and indefinite reference to times?

(E) The Present Perfect: Discussion

Are the examples below fully consistent with the view that the present perfect, in contrast with the simple past tense, makes indefinite reference to times?

(1)   I haven't turned off the stove.
(2)   I haven't seen your dog.
(3)   I haven't seen the Grand Canyon.
(4)   I haven't had breakfast.
(5)   I haven't had chicken pox.

(F) The Present Perfect: Universal and Existential Readings

We saw in Section 7.7.2 that the continuing state and completely past readings of the present perfect can be analysed as universal and existential quantification over the times in an interval. Which of the examples below contain the proposed universal/existential ambiguity?

(1)   Gemma has been a juggler since she was five.
(2)   Jones has been a bank clerk since I saw him last.

(3)   Marcia was in Fiji last year.
(4)   Clive listened to the radio between 9.00 and 10.00.
(5)   Gemma will stay with Sally next week.
(6)   Since she was five Gemma has been a juggler.
(7)   Since I saw him last Jones has been a bank clerk.
(8)   Last year Marcia was in Fiji.
(9)   Between 9.00 and 10.00 Clive listened to the radio.
(10) Next week Gemma will stay with Sally.

(G)   The Present Perfect: Discussion

The present perfect is described here as placing an event or state at some past time in a way which is relevant to the present circumstances.

The present perfect might also be described as denoting an interval, beginning in the past and extending up to the present, which is filled with a state or situation. Either the described state or situation fills the interval, as in *Meiling has been here since Tuesday*, or the result state of a past event fills the interval – in *Jones has broken his ankle* the interval is filled with the state of Jones' having a broken ankle.

How well do these two analyses fit the examples below?

(1)   Kennedy has been dead.
(2)   Kennedy has been dead for many years.
(3)   Kennedy has been killed.
(4)   Kennedy has been killed for many years.

(H)   Quantification over Times

The logical definitions for the simple tenses introduce existential quantification over times, as in

John left
$\exists t(t < t^* \ \& \ \text{LEAVE}(j) \ \text{at} \ t)$

Presumably, other quantifiers may also bind t variables. Using quantification over times, give complete representations for the sentences below, including the underlined adverbs. Use the restricted quantifier notation introduced in Chapter 4. (Section 6.4.2 may also be useful here.)

(1)   When Mary phones Jimmy Bill <u>always</u> teases her.
(2)   Clive will <u>never</u> be a millionaire.
(3)   Marcia <u>usually</u> buys a hat when she shops.
(4)   When Clive tells a joke Marcia <u>seldom</u> laughs.
(5)   Mary <u>often</u> met Sam when she was jogging.

(I) Tense and Scope

A semantic tense may be represented as an operator at the beginning of a proposition. This suggests that the tenses are scopal expressions, like other expressions which also appear at the beginning of a proposition, such as modals, negation, and quantifiers.

Do the sentences below support the view that tenses are scopal expressions? (Write representations for the readings of the sentences.)

(1) All Torah's friends were rich then.
(2) The monarch will address Parliament in 2001.
(3) Only ten people on the course have previously been women.
     (Treat the sequence *only ten* as a complex quantifier determiner, and for simplicity, represent (3) with a simple past tense.)

(J) Tense and Scope

Analyse the scopal ambiguity in:

   The Pope will always be a Catholic

FURTHER READING

For general discussion of the meanings of all English tense and aspect forms, see Jespersen (1932), Leech (1971) and Palmer (1987).

For an accessible review of Reichenbachian theory, see Hornstein (1990), Chapter 1, and Mittwoch (1995).

The notion of an event's aftertime is based on Klein's (1992) post-time.

For the progressive, see Dowty (1977) and (1979), Chapter 3.

Emonds (1975) gives a syntactic analysis of the tense perfect, with many useful examples.

The referential analysis of tenses is developed particularly in Discourse Representation Theory, a theory which bridges semantics and pragmatics. A brief introduction to Discourse Representation Theory is Kamp (1995).

8 Events

This chapter reviews the notion, introduced by the philosopher Donald Davidson, that sentences with action verbs express reference to events. A wide range of linguistic phenomena can be analysed by appealing to reference to events, quantification over events, modification of events, the inner structure of events, different classes of events, and so on. Davidson's analysis of action sentences is generally considered to be the starting point for a number of event-based theories. Classes of events derived from a different tradition are discussed in the next chapter.

8.1 DAVIDSON'S ANALYSIS OF ACTION SENTENCES

Reference to events in the semantics of action sentences was introduced in Davidson's 1967 paper 'The Logical Form of Action Sentences'. His argument centres on the treatment of adverbials in examples like (1): the adverbials are *slowly*, *with a knife*, *in the bathroom*, and *at midnight*.

(1)   Jones buttered the toast slowly with a knife in the bathroom at midnight.

Recall that in Section 2.3.1 a distinction was drawn between the arguments of a predicate and adverbials appearing in the same sentence. The distinction was marked for the time being by omitting non-arguments altogether from the representation of atomic propositions, with the proviso that some analysis must be found for adverbials. But as Davidson points out, a standard logical analysis of the day would express the adverbials also as arguments to the predicate, so that, for example, *slowly*, *with a knife*, *in the bathroom*, and *at midnight* in (1) would be arguments of the predicate *buttered*, as in (2).

(2)   BUTTER(j, the toast, slowly, with a knife, in the bathroom, at midnight)

Now we also saw earlier that a predicate has a fixed number of argument places, and it must appear with the right number of arguments to form a well-formed proposition. If the representation in (2) is well formed, then the predicate BUTTER in (2) has six argument places. Presumably it cannot be the same predicate as the one in (3), which has only two argument places.

(3)   Jones buttered the toast.
      BUTTER (j, the toast)

Assume that the predicate in (3) is the most basic version of the meaning of the verb *butter*. Then when the verb *butter* appears with adverbials which are to be analysed as arguments, as in (2), we must suppose that the verb stands for a different predicate BUTTER with a different number of argument places. For each different set of arguments the verb *butter* can appear with, there must be a distinct predicate BUTTER as its meaning with the appropriate argument places to accommodate the arguments in the sentence. The different predicates BUTTER can be marked with primes, as in (4).

(4)a   Jones buttered the toast slowly.
       BUTTER′ (Jones, the toast, slowly)

   b   Jones buttered the toast slowly with a knife.
       BUTTER″ (Jones, the toast, slowly, with a knife)

   c   Jones buttered the toast slowly with a knife in the bathroom.
       BUTTER‴(Jones, the toast, slowly, with a knife, in the bathroom)

   d   Jones buttered the toast slowly with a knife in the bathroom at mid-
       night.
       BUTTER⁗(Jones, the toast, slowly, with a knife, in the bathroom, at
       midnight)

The argument structure in (4d) can be represented generally as in (5).

(5)   BUTTER⁗(butterer, butteree, manner, instrument, place, time)

There are several problems with this analysis.

First, a predicate closely selects its arguments – in a sense arguments fill spaces or gaps which are part of the meaning of the predicate. For example, in an act of buttering there must be someone or something which does the buttering and something which gets buttered. But the adverbial expressions are far more loosely connected to the predicate BUTTER. Although every action has to take place at some time and place, and no doubt in some manner, this is true of actions or events in general, and not specifically required of butterings.

Secondly, an action verb can be modified by a variety of adverbials in different combinations. To account for the possible combinations, this analysis must assume that each action verb is multiply ambiguous, with a distinct predicate for each of the modification contexts the verb can appear in. Presumably modification contexts differ in the kind of adverbials that appear as well as in number. For example, (6a) below has the arguments (butterer, butteree, manner) and (6b) has the arguments (butterer, butteree, instrument), so again, the two verbs *buttered* would express different predicates.

(6)a   Jones buttered the toast slowly
    b   Jones buttered the toast with a knife

Quite apart from the complexity of greatly increasing the number of predicates, it simply isn't convincing that all the appearances of the form *buttered* in (4) and (6) are different words. Our intuition is that the same predicate appears in all of them.

Davidson points out that sentences like those in (4) are related by entailments in a way which seems to require that the same predicate appears in all the sentences. A selection of these entailments is shown below.

(7)   Jones buttered the toast slowly with a knife in the bathroom at midnight.

The entailments of (7) include (8) and (9).

(8)   Jones buttered the toast slowly with a knife in the bathroom.
(9)   Jones buttered the toast slowly with a knife at midnight.

In turn, (8) entails (10) and (11).

(10)   Jones buttered the toast slowly with a knife.
(11)   Jones buttered the toast slowly in the bathroom.

And (10) entails (12), (13) and (14).

(12)   Jones buttered the toast slowly.
(13)   Jones buttered the toast with a knife.
(14)   Jones buttered the toast.

Davidson pointed out that every entailment of this kind resembles entailments which drop conjuncts, as in (15).

(15) $p \& q \rightarrow p$
       $p \& q \& r \rightarrow q \& r$

Explicitly, Davidson proposes that the entailment in (16a) is the same form of entailment as (16b).

(16)a 'Jones buttered the toast with a knife' entails 'Jones buttered the toast'.

   b 'Donna had icecream and Laura had a Coke' entails 'Laura had a Coke'.

There are two main points to this view. First, part of the entailing sentence is identical to the entailed sentence, as indicated in (17).

(17)a 'Donna had icecream and <u>Laura had a Coke</u>' entails '<u>Laura had a Coke</u>'.

   b '<u>Jones buttered the toast</u> with a knife' entails '<u>Jones buttered the toast</u>'.

Secondly, the parts of the entailing sentence which are dropped to produce the entailed sentence should be represented as logical conjuncts. This is straightforward for (17a), as shown in (18).

(18) 'Donna had icecream & Laura had a Coke' entails 'Laura had a Coke'.

   $p \& q \rightarrow q$

Neither of these points can be included in the analysis that treats adverbials as arguments of the verb. For one thing, the adverbial is not contained as a separate conjunct which can be dropped, because it appears as an argument to the verb. Secondly, according to the adverbials-as-arguments analysis, the verb *buttered* in (19a) below is not the same as the verb *buttered* in (19b), because they don't have the same argument structure, so the underlined sequences cannot actually be identical.

(19)a <u>Jones buttered the toast</u>.

   b <u>Jones buttered the toast</u> with a knife.

If the verbs *butter* in (19) are not the same verb, then the entailment from (19b) to (19a) must depend on a <u>lexical entailment</u> relationship between the two different verbs. In other words, under the adverbials-as-arguments analysis the entailment in (20a) below is a lexical entailment, like the entailment between *kill* and *die* in (20b), and not a formal entailment like (20c) as Davidson claims.

(20)a 'Jones buttered the toast with a knife' entails 'Jones buttered the toast'.

   b 'Jones killed Smith' entails 'Smith died'.

   c 'Tina screamed and strutted' entails 'Tina strutted'.

To replace the adverbials-as-arguments analysis, Davidson proposes that adverbials should be expressed as part of propositions conjoined to the central basic proposition, along the lines of (21).

(21)   Jones buttered the toast slowly with a knife
       BUTTER (Jones, the toast) & p & q
       p expresses 'slowly'
       q expresses 'with a knife'

The next step is to identify the propositions p and q which correspond to the adverbials. Davidson solves this problem by introducing reference to events into the representations for action sentences.

A very simple kind of reference to events is the pronoun reference illustrated in (22).

(22)a   Sally threatened Marcia.
        Oh that's nothing – she's always shooting her mouth off.
        No – <u>this was with a knife</u>.
    b   Jones buttered the toast – I think <u>it was in the bathroom</u>.

The underlined parts of these examples are sentences expressing simple propositions of the forms 'x was with a knife' and 'x was in the bathroom'. The subject pronoun *this* or *it* refers back to some entity which has already been mentioned. Davidson claims that this entity is an action or event, and the previous reference to the action or event is in the simple sentence reporting its occurrence, in this case *Sally threatened Marcia* and *Jones buttered the toast*. The expressions *with a knife* and *in the bathroom* are predicates on these events.

Davidson proposes that the event itself is one of the arguments of the action verb, in addition to the arguments we have identified so far, as illustrated in (23).

(23)a   Jones buttered the toast slowly with a knife in the bathroom at
        midnight.
    b $\exists e$ (BUTTER (Jones, the toast, e) & SLOWLY(e) & WITH(e, a
        knife) & IN(e, the bathroom) & AT(e, midnight))
    c   'There was an event, which was a buttering of the toast by Jones, and
        the event was slowly, and the event was with a knife, and the event
        was in the bathroom and the event was at midnight.'

The variable e is a restricted variable ranging over events, just as variables t range over times and variables w range over worlds. The event variable is existentially bound. The first conjunct is the atomic proposition containing the predicate from the main verb, the traditional arguments (that is, the butterer and the butteree) and the event as argument. The adverbials are expressed in separate conjuncts exactly parallel to the sentences in (22) above, *This was with a knife* and *It was in the bathroom*.

Now the entailments discussed above take the general form of p&q → q as shown below, where (24) entails both (25) and (26).

(24) Jones buttered the toast slowly with a knife.
      ∃e (BUTTER (Jones, the toast, e) & SLOWLY(e) & WITH (e, a knife))

(25) Jones buttered the toast slowly.
      ∃e (BUTTER (Jones, the toast, e) & SLOWLY (e))

(26) Jones buttered the toast with a knife.
      ∃e (BUTTER (Jones, the toast, e) & WITH (e, a knife))

In summary, Davidson argues that an action sentence contains reference to an event. The event itself is an argument of the verbal predicate in the underlying logical form of the sentence, along with the traditionally recognized arguments, which are still arguments of the verb. Adverbials such as time, manner and place are predicates on the event. Each adverbial predication is expressed in logical form as a separate conjunct. The presence or absence of adverbial expressions has no effect on the argument places of the verbal predicate. Consequently, there is no need to adopt the notion that action verbs are multiply ambiguous, each corresponding to many distinct semantic predicates, such as the verb *butter* corresponding to the predicates BUTTER, BUTTER′, BUTTER″, and so on.

8.2   NEODAVIDSONIAN DEVELOPMENTS

When Davidson's analysis was first presented it was quickly seen that his arguments concerning the nature of entailments applied more widely. Davidson argued that adverbials modifying events should be expressed in separate conjuncts in logical form. Similar examples suggested that the traditional arguments of the verb, particularly the subject and object of an action sentence, should also be expressed in separate conjuncts. This move to the so-called Neodavidsonian analysis makes quite radical changes to Davidson's original proposal.

8.2.1   Separation of Direct Arguments

One of the central motivations in Davidson's analysis is to establish the entailments noted above as instances of conjunct-dropping. Adverbials can almost always be dropped in this way. Apart from introducing the event variable, Davidson retained the traditional arguments of the verb, such as the subject and object, as arguments of the basic predicate, as in (27).

(27)   Jones buttered the toast.
       BUTTER (j, the toast, e)

Now the proposition 'Jones buttered the toast' also entails the two separate propositions 'Jones did some buttering' and 'the toast got buttered'. Both of these entailments seem to be of the conjunct-dropping kind, just like the entailments which support the separation of adverbials. In Davidson's representation these propositions cannot be isolated as separate conjuncts, and accordingly they cannot be represented structurally as separate entailments.

This point was made by Hector-Neri Castañeda (1967) with the examples in (28).

(28)a   I flew my spaceship to the Morning Star.
    b   I flew to the Morning Star.
    c   My spaceship was flown to the Morning Star.
    d   I flew.
    e   My spaceship was flown.

Castañeda noted that (28a) entails (28b–e). The entailments to (28b,d) involve dropping the object *my spaceship*, and the entailments to (28c, e) drop the subject *I*. These examples show that smaller entailments of the basic sentence can leave out the subject and the object, so it looks as if the subject and object should also be removed from the argument structure for FLY and expressed in separate conjuncts.

A Neodavidsonian representation for (28a) is shown in (29a), with a Davidsonian representation in (29b) for comparison.

(29)a $\exists e$ (FLY (e) & SUBJECT (I, e) & OBJECT (my spaceship, e) & TO (e, the Morning Star))
        'There was an event and the event was a flying and I was the subject of the event and my spaceship was the object of the event and the event was to the Morning Star.'

    b $\exists e$ (FLY(I, my spaceship, e) & TO (e, Morning Star))
        'There was an event of me flying my spaceship and the event was to the Morning Star.'

Given the Neodavidsonian representation in (29a), the entailments in (28) above are as in (30). (30a) entails (30b–e), (30b) entails (30d), and (30c) entails (30e).

(30)a I flew my spaceship to the Morning Star.
       $\exists e$ (FLY(e) & SUBJECT (I, e) & OBJECT (my spaceship, e) & TO (e, the Morning Star))

   b   I flew to the Morning Star.
       $\exists e$ (FLY(e) & SUBJECT(I, e) & TO (e, the Morning Star))

   c   My spaceship was flown to the Morning Star.
       $\exists e$ (FLY(e) & OBJECT(my spaceship, e) & TO (e, the Morning Star))

   d   I flew.
       $\exists e$ (FLY(e) & SUBJECT (I, e))

   e   My spaceship was flown.
       $\exists e$ (FLY(e) & OBJECT (my spaceship, e))

8.2.2 The Adicity of Verbal Predicates

The most important difference in the Neodavidsonian analysis is that the action verb is always a one-place predicate, with the event as its only argument. The traditional arguments identified in predicate logic, as outlined in Chapter 2, are no longer arguments of the verbal predicate. The established differences between one-place, two-place and three-place verbs are not represented in these logical forms.

The traditional logical view that, for example, GIVE is a three-place predicate, is matched in syntactic analysis by the established view that the verb *give* takes three NPs as syntactic arguments. The three-place nature of the verb *give* is expressed in Davidson's analysis by the three argument places (in addition to the event place) in the atomic proposition headed by GIVE, as in (31a) below. The same information in a Neodavidsonian analysis is spread across the representation, as in (31b).

(31)   x gives y to z
   a   GIVE (x, y, z, e)
   b   GIVE (e) & SUBJECT (x, e) & OBJECT (y, e) & TO (z, e)

The Neodavidsonian analysis is thus a kind of lexical decomposition, in that the verb itself is analysed into its semantic components, these being the arguments, taken separately, and the general nature of the event itself. The analysis is also called a **subatomic** analysis, in that the atomic proposition is more finely analysed. The traditional adicity of a verbal predicate attaches to the whole verb, not to the event predicate derived from the verb in a Neodavidsonian representation.

The difference between Davidsonian and Neodavidsonian forms in representing the obligatoriness of arguments is particularly important in analysing sentences with apparently missing arguments, such as the passive in (32b).

(32)a   John fed Fido.
   b   Fido was fed.

The Davidsonian form expresses the two-place verb *feed* as the three-place predicate FEED. All three argument places must be present with the predicate, and so the position of the feeder is filled by an existentially bound variable in the form for the passive sentence, as in (33b), meaning 'Fido was fed by someone or something.'

(33)a   John fed Fido.
       $\exists e\,(\text{FEED}\,(j, f, e))$

   b   Fido was fed.
       $\exists e\exists x\,(\text{FEED}\,(x, f, e))$

A Neodavidsonian form offers the choice of existentially quantifying the missing argument, as in (34b), or treating it as absent altogether, as in (34c).

(34)a   John fed Fido.
       $\exists e\,(\text{FEED}(e) \,\&\, \text{SUBJECT}\,(j, e) \,\&\, \text{OBJECT}\,(f, e))$

   b   Fido was fed.
       $\exists e\exists x\,(\text{FEED}\,(e) \,\&\, \text{SUBJECT}\,(x, e) \,\&\, \text{OBJECT}\,(f, e))$

   c   Fido was fed.
       $\exists e\,(\text{FEED}\,(e) \,\&\, \text{OBJECT}\,(f, e))$

If we choose the option in (34b), then the two analyses do not differ significantly in representing arguments as being obligatory. Once an argument place is established for a particular predicate, it is assumed to be always present in the logical representation even if it does not appear in the form of the sentence. Given that the Neodavidsonian form expresses arguments in separate conjuncts, the obligatory appearance of these conjuncts must be ensured in the symbolizations for verbs. For example, it must be stated that the translation of the verb *give* is (35a) and not (35b).

(35)a $\text{GIVE}\,(e) \,\&\, \text{SUBJECT}\,(x, e) \,\&\, \text{OBJECT}\,(y, e) \,\&\, \text{TO}\,(e, z)$
   b $\text{GIVE}\,(e)$

If definitions like (35) are included for all predicates to guarantee the appearance of the fixed number of arguments for any predicate, then the Davidsonian and Neodavidsonian forms mainly differ in the level of detail shown. So long as labels like SUBJECT and OBJECT are provided for the positions of variables in '(x, y, z, e)', we can translate back and forth between the two types of forms, using rules like (36). A prime is used to mark the difference between the two predicates GIVE.

(36) ∃e∃x∃y∃z (GIVE (x, y, z, e)) ↔ ∃e∃x∃y∃z (GIVE′(e) & SUBJECT(x, e)
      & OBJECT(y, e) & TO (e, z)))

The other option for the Neodavidsonian analysis, as in (34c), is to simply omit an argument which does not appear in a particular sentence. In effect, this is to claim that the apparent obligatoriness of certain arguments is purely syntactic, and not a semantic or logical matter. What you see is what you get, and the feeder is simply absent, both syntactically and semantically, in *The dog has been fed.*

The obligatoriness of arguments is assumed to reflect the intimate relationship between arguments and the predicate which takes them, as discussed in Chapter 2. Arguments 'fill gaps' in the meaning of a predicate, in contrast to adverbials which add extra, optional information, and can generally be omitted without the sentence being ill formed. Accordingly, a Neodavidsonian analysis which does not stipulate that argument conjuncts are obligatory treats both arguments and adverbials as being like adverbials, expressing optional information. If this is correct, then a sentence which is agreed to be odd because it lacks an argument, such as (37b), is ill-formed syntactically but not semantically.

(37)a Perry put more coal on the fire.
   b Perry put more coal.

This is one of the more controversial points in Neodavidsonian theory. Parsons (1990: 96–9) argues that the apparent obligatoriness of certain arguments does not hold up under scrutiny. For example, (38a) below entails (38b), with the Davidsonian forms in (38c, d). The entailment from (38c) to (38d) can be paraphrased as 'If Brutus stabbed Caesar then Brutus stabbed someone.'

(38)a Brutus stabbed Caesar.
   b Brutus stabbed.
   c ∃e (STAB (b, c, e))
   d ∃e∃x (STAB (b, x, e))

In the Davidsonian system the argument place for the stabbee is obligatory and must be included as an existentially bound variable in (38d). If it is not included, then the predicate STAB in (38c) is not the same as the predicate STAB in (38d) and the entailment from (38a) to (38b) is not represented. But according to Parsons, (38d) is the wrong form for *Brutus stabbed*, because (38d) is true only if Brutus stabbed someone or something, but Brutus could have stabbed and missed. In that case (38b) would be true but (38d) would be false. Explicitly, 'Brutus stabbed Caesar' entails not only 'Brutus stabbed someone', but also entails the distinct proposition 'Brutus stabbed'. (38d) represents 'Brutus stabbed someone', but cannot represent 'Brutus stabbed'. Here the Davidsonian system includes an argument which is not in fact fully obligatory.

The converse problem of a logically obligatory argument which is represented as optional is illustrated in (39).

(39)a   Brutus stabbed Caesar with a knife.
   b   Brutus stabbed Caesar.
   c $\exists e\,(STAB\,(b, c, e)\ \&\ WITH\,(e, a\ knife))$
   d $\exists e\,(STAB\,(b, c, e))$

In any version of Davidsonian theory it is agreed (as in linguistic theory generally) that *with a knife* is optional, and an adverbial. Accordingly, the entailment from (39a) to (39b) is of the conjunct-dropping kind. But given that a stabbing event always involves a weapon, the form in (39d) omits an argument which is logically necessary. Again, this mismatch suggests that the apparent obligatoriness of arguments is not really a semantic or logical matter.

Parsons also argues that language can express meanings which are not fully coherent, and in such cases entailments which may otherwise appear to be necessary can be suspended. He offers the example of reporting a dream, as in (40).

(40)   In a dream last night I was stabbed, although in fact nobody had stabbed me, and I wasn't stabbed with anything.

This is not intended as the report of a dream in which the stabbing happened prior to the dream's opening – it is an incoherent dream in which the situation of being stabbed is somehow separated from an assailant and a weapon, which are both absent. Parson's point is that although the dream is incoherent in the light of real experience, the language reporting it is not incoherent and can describe the impossible situation in the dream. A Davidsonian representation for the dream report would incorrectly include a variable 'someone' for the assailant, as in (41).

(41) $\exists e \exists x\,(STAB\,(x, p, e))$ (p = Parsons)

This creates a contradiction in the dream report '...I was stabbed by someone although in fact nobody had stabbed me', as in (42).

(42) $\exists e \exists x\,(STAB\,(x, p, e)\ \&\ \sim \exists y\,(STAB\,(y, p, e))...$

Parsons comments, 'My dream may have been incoherent, but I am not, and what I am saying should not contain a self-contradictory logical form.'

As we saw in Section 2.3.1, the obligatoriness or optionality of arguments is not as straightforward as it first appears. Arguments which are truly obligatory in all contexts where a particular predicate appears are hard to find. Other syntactic distinctions between arguments and adverbials are well established, and it may be that arguments and adverbials, although distinguished in other respects, do not contrast in semantic obligatoriness in the way that has been assumed. See also Exercise G at the end of this chapter for further discussion.

Whether or not arguments of a particular predicate are in fact obligatory, and if so, what such obligatoriness consists of, are questions for further research. For the present we will continue to assume that basic arguments are obligatory.

In the next section we reconsider the relations that hold between the arguments and the event, expressed so far as SUBJECT, OBJECT, TO and so on.

8.2.3 Relations to Events

In the notations used before this chapter, most of the symbols are directly borrowed from the English words they translate, including predicate symbols such as GIVE, CRAZY and SURGEON. As we have seen, the Neodavidsonian analysis decomposes the content of an action verb into parts which do not correspond with whole words in the sentence to be represented. In particular, we need symbols for all the predicates heading the added conjunct propositions.

The adverbials Davidson began with can be treated like noun or adjective predicates, so *slowly*, for example, can be represented as 'SLOW(e)' or 'SLOWLY(e)'.

Prepositional phrase adverbials can be analysed as in (43), using the preposition as the main predicate.

(43)a IN (e, the kitchen)
   b WITH (e, a knife)
   c AT (e, midnight)

This leaves the direct arguments of the verb to be dealt with, primarily the subject and object. For convenience, these were represented above as 'SUBJECT (x, e)' and 'OBJECT(y, e)', but there are problems with this.

Consider again the examples in (44) below.

(44)a I flew my spaceship to the Morning Star.
       ∃e (FLY(e) & SUBJECT (I, e) & OBJECT (my spaceship, e) & TO (e, the Morning Star))

b   My spaceship was flown to the Morning Star.
    $\exists$e (FLY (e) & OBJECT (my spaceship, e) & TO (e, the Morning Star))

In (44a) *my spaceship* is the object of the sentence, and the meaning expressed by this is represented as 'OBJECT (my spaceship, e)'. This content is part of (44b), which is entailed by (44a). To show the entailment as Davidson proposes, the sequence 'OBJECT (my spaceship, e)' must be uniformly represented in both (44a) and (44b). But in fact *my spaceship* is the subject of (44b), not the object, although it has the OBJECT reading because the sentence is passive.

We could handle the mismatch between the actual form of the sentence and the labels to be used in the logical representation by simply stipulating that 'OBJECT(y, e)' translates the object of an active verb and the subject of a passive verb. We should also add that 'SUBJECT (x, e)' translates the subject of an active verb and the *by NP* sequence in a passive sentence like *She was bitten by a spider*, where *a spider* corresponds to the subject of *A spider bit her*. This is confusing, because the terms *object* and *subject* are being used in different senses in syntax and semantics.

Strictly speaking, *subject* and *object* are syntactic terms which name the roles NPs play in sentences, as in 'The NP *my spaceship* is the subject of the sentence *My spaceship was flown.*' The labels we need for Neodavidsonian representations name the roles played in events by entities that NPs refer to, and SUBJECT and OBJECT are the wrong kind of label for this.

A possible (but somewhat controversial) alternative is to use the thematic relations labels from traditional linguistic theory.

8.3   THEMATIC ROLES

Thematic relations or **thematic roles** in linguistic theory are broad classes of participants in events. It is generally accepted that thematic role theory begins at least with the work of the Sanskrit grammarian Panini in 500–400 BC. Panini established classes of NPs according to the broad interpretation of their grammatical form, along the lines touched on in the previous section, where the subject of an action sentence is the doer of an action and the object is the undergoer of the action.

Although roles are primarily classified in interpretive or conceptual terms, evidence for the significance of thematic roles in language and for the identification of particular roles is mainly syntactic. Until recently, thematic roles have mainly been of interest to syntacticians and have scarcely appeared in semantic theory.

8.3.1 Traditional Thematic Roles

Thematic role theory in general is currently under revision. Some of the older traditional roles have more or less fallen out of use, while important roles are being divided into subtypes. The main point emerging in current research is that the terms we use for thematic roles are best seen as convenient abbreviations for components of the meanings of the verbs they appear with. For the present purpose the traditional roles listed in (45) will suffice, but thematic roles will be discussed in more detail in Chapter 10.

(45)   agent, patient, theme, source, recipient, goal, instrument, benefactive, experiencer, stimulus

The **agent** is the doer or actor in an event. In philosophy, notions of actors, agents and actions are strongly connected to notions of decision, intent and responsibility. The thematic role notion of agenthood is somewhat looser than this, and may overlap with other causing entities, such as the wind in *The wind stunted the saplings*.

The **patient** is the thing an action is done to. A typical patient is the thing touched in a contacting action. Agent and patient are illustrated in (46).

(46)a   <u>Jones</u> patted   <u>Fido</u>
   b   <u>Jones</u> stroked <u>Fido</u>
   c   <u>Jones</u> tapped   <u>the desk</u>
       (agent)   (patient)

There are two kinds of **theme**. A theme of motion is the thing which moves or is moved in an event, as in (47a, b). A change of state theme, as the name suggests, undergoes a change of state in the course of the event, as in (47c, d). The **goal** is the thing towards which movement is directed, as in (47a, b). The **recipient,** which is animate, receives something which is transferred or transmitted (that is, a theme of motion), as in (47e, f). The motion involved in the transfer of a theme to a recipient may be abstract or metaphorical, as in (47f). Recipients mainly occur with double object verbs, such as *give* and *teach*. The recipient is the first object in the double object sentence, as shown in (47f). The **source** is the thing away from which movement is directed, as in (47g).

(47)a   <u>Jones</u> rolled <u>the ball</u> <u>to the wall</u>
       agent   theme   goal

   b   <u>Clive</u> trickled <u>the honey</u> <u>onto the toast</u>
       agent   theme   goal

c John boiled the milk
   agent   theme

d John burned the paper
   agent   theme

e Sarah gave the parcel to Leo
   agent   theme   recipient

f Hilton taught the boys Japanese
   agent   recipient   theme

g Water poured out of the tap
   theme   source

In some cases an argument may fit the description for more than one role, particularly where one of the roles is agent. For example, *Sarah* in (47e) and *Hilton* in (47f) are sources as well as agents, and *Sally* in *Sally ran to the corner* is both an agent and a theme of motion. We return to this point in Chapter 10: for now, assume that the agent role outranks any other role an argument may bear, and such an argument is classed simply as an agent.

Thematic roles in Neodavidsonian representations are illustrated in (48) below.

(48)a   Clive sang a song to Marcia.
       $\exists e$(SING(e) & AGENT(c, e) & THEME(a song, e) & RECIPIENT (m, e))

       'There was an event and the event was a singing and Clive was the agent of the event and a song was the theme of the event and Marcia was the recipient of the event.'

   b   Sally ran to the shop.
       $\exists e$(RUN(e) & AGENT(s, e) & GOAL(the shop, e))
       'There was an event and the event was a running and Sally was the agent of the event and the shop was the goal of the event.'

The remaining roles are instrument, benefactive, experiencer and stimulus. The **instrument** is the thing used as a tool or means, marked in English by the preposition *with*, and the **benefactive** is the individual for whose direct benefit something is done. The **experiencer** is the entity, human or animal, which has an emotional or psychological state or experience, and the **stimulus** is the thing which triggers or is the target of an experiencer's psychological response. These roles are illustrated in (49).

(49)a   Jones buttered the toast with a knife
       agent   theme   instrument

b <u>Jones</u> buttered <u>another piece of toast</u> <u>for Hector</u>
   agent   theme   benefactive

c <u>Mary</u> was amazed at <u>the difference</u>
   experiencer   stimulus

d <u>Rats</u> frighten <u>Spot</u>
   stimulus   experiencer

e <u>Spot</u> is afraid of <u>rats</u>
   experiencer   stimulus

8.3.2 Thematic Roles, Arguments and Adverbials

Traditional thematic roles theory was concerned with the interpretation of NPs according to their grammatical characteristics, particularly the position in the sentence, the case marking, and the preposition, if any, preceding the NP. This approach applies to all the underlined NPs in (50) below.

(50) <u>Jones</u> buttered <u>the toast</u> with <u>a knife</u> in <u>the bathroom</u>.

Here, *Jones* is in subject position, indicating the agent of *buttered*, *the toast* is in object position, indicating the theme of *buttered*, *with* indicates that *a knife* is an instrument. *In* indicates that *the bathroom* is a location, and in some systems *the bathroom* would be assigned the locative role. These classifications make no distinction between arguments of the verb and adverbials, as traditional thematic roles apply to both.

More recently, linguists have assumed that thematic roles are closely related to the argument structure of particular predicates – the roles associated with a verb are determined by the verb's meaning, and thematic roles are assigned to arguments by verbs. This assumption focuses attention on agent, patient, theme, goal, experiencer and stimulus as the core roles for arguments of verbs. Roles such as instrument and benefactive are commonly assigned to adverbials and their status is unresolved.

8.3.3 The Generality of Thematic Roles

In addition to changing the representation of adicity, another major consequence of the move from Davidsonian to Neodavidsonian representations is the use of *general* labels for the relations between participants and events.

As we have seen, Neodavidsonian forms require some symbol or other to express the relation between a participant and the event, to fill the space marked '?' in (51b) below.

(51)a   Jones kicked Spot.
   b $\exists e (KICK(e)\ \&\ ?(j, e)\ \&\ ?(s, e))$

If we use the same sets of labels for different sentences, as in (52) below, this implicitly claims that the relation between, for example, the kicker and the kicking event is somehow the same as the relation between the patter and the patting event.

(52)a   Jones kicked Spot.
   b $\exists e (KICK(e)\ \&\ R1(j, e)\ \&\ R2(s, e))$
   c   Jones patted Spot.
   d $\exists e (PAT(e)\ \&\ R1(j, e)\ \&\ R2(s, e))$

No matter what labels are used, R1 and R2, SUBJECT and OBJECT or AGENT and PATIENT, if the same labels are used across sentences the generalization is expressed, that participants are involved in events in ways which count as the same across different types of events.

The use of general labels for event relations is criticized by some writers because it seems to be impossible to fix any constant content for such a label which holds across different types of events. For example, the NP *Jones* in all the sentences in (53) below is a candidate for the role of agent.

(53)a   Jones left early.
   b   Jones decided to leave early.
   c   Inadvertently, Jones left early and missed the speeches.
   d   Deliberately, Jones left early and missed the speeches.
   e   While under hypnosis, Jones left early and missed the speeches.
   f   Deliberately, Jones did nothing.

In (53a, c, d, e) Jones performed the action of leaving early, which is consistent with the basic characterization of an agent as the doer of an action. In (53b) Jones performed a mental action but no physical action is reported. In (53c, e) we see that conscious control or volition, traditional components of agency in the philosophical literature, are not required for thematic agency, although perhaps conscious control or volition must be possible in principle for actions of that kind. In (53f) we see that agency can apply where no action is reported at all – here, agency must stem from Jones' intention to do nothing. Clearly, it is very difficult to find a constant content for the role of agent which is logically entailed to be present in any report of an event with an agent. Quite generally, it seems impossible to construct workable *truth-conditional* definitions for general event roles, including established thematic roles.

Some writers propose that ways of being involved in events are in fact particular to the kinds of events. Then to be the agent of a kicking event is to bear the role agent-of-kicking, and to be the agent of a patting event is to bear the role agent-of-patting, and there isn't necessarily any common content between these roles. The differences can be marked by subscripting, as in the forms below.

(54)a Jones kicked Spot.
   b $\exists e\,(\text{KICK}\,(e)\,\&\,R1_{kick}(j,\,e)\,\&\,R2_{kick}(s,e))$
   c Jones patted Spot.
   d $\exists e\,(\text{PAT}(e)\,\&\,R1_{pat}(j,e)R2_{pat}(s,\,e))$

Current research suggests that the generalization expressed in any version of thematic roles theory is basically correct – arguments of verbs do fall into broad semantic classes, although the relevant classes are not always those identified by the traditional thematic relations introduced here. See Exercises C and D at the end of this chapter for more on the generality of roles. Thematic roles are discussed further in Chapter 10.

8.4 EVENTS AND PERCEPTION VERBS

Reference to events can account for the semantics of what are called naked infinitive complements to perception verbs (also called bare infinitives), as illustrated in (55) below. The naked infinitives are underlined.

(55)a Jones saw <u>Lina shake the bottle</u>.
   b Jones heard <u>the gun go off</u>.
   c Jones felt <u>the floor shake</u>.

The underlined sequence has the basic structure of a clause, with a subject (*Lina, the gun, the floor*) and a predicate. Without events, traditional logic would analyse such a sequence as a proposition, but this is inappropriate in these contexts. The whole underlined sequence describes what is seen, heard or felt, and a proposition cannot be physically perceived in these ways. Clearly, what is perceived is an event. Representations for (55) are shown in (56).

(56)a Jones saw Lina shake the bottle.
     $\exists e \exists e'(\text{SEE}(e)\,\&\,\text{EXPERIENCER}(j,\,e)\,\&\,\text{STIMULUS}(e',e)\,\&$
     $\text{SHAKE}(e')\,\&\,\text{AGENT}(l,\,e')\,\&\,\text{PATIENT}(\text{the bottle},\,e'))$

There was an event e and
there was an event e′ and
e is a seeing and
Jones was the experiencer of e and

e′ was the stimulus of e and
e′ was a shaking and
Lina was the agent of e′ and
the bottle was the patient of e′.

b Jones heard the gun go off.
∃e∃e′ (HEAR (e) & EXPERIENCER (j, e) & STIMULUS (e′, e) &
GO OFF (e′) & THEME (the gun, e′))

There was an event e and
there was an event e′ and
e was a hearing and
Jones was the experiencer of e
and e′ was the stimulus of e and
e′ was a going off and
the gun was the theme of e′

c Jones felt the floor shake.
∃e∃e′ (FEEL (e) & EXPERIENCER (j,e) & STIMULUS (e′, e) &
SHAKE (e′) & THEME (the floor, e′))

There was an event e and
there was an event e′ and
e was a feeling and
Jones was the experiencer of e and
e′ was the stimulus of e
and e′ was a shaking and
the floor was the theme of e′.

Note that these representations are accurate for genuine perceptions, not
for hallucinations, because they entail the existence (that is, the real occurrence) of the perceived event. For example, (56a) entails (57) below, and
similar entailments hold for (56b, c).

(57) Lina shook the bottle.
∃e′(SHAKE(e′) & AGENT (l, e′) & PATIENT (the bottle, e′))

To recap, the analysis here assumes that *Lina shake the bottle* in *Jones saw
Lina shake the bottle* is a kind of clause and denotes an event, which is the
second argument of the perception verb *saw*.

It has also been observed that the NP after a perception verb in sentences
like these reads like an argument to the verb, and the entailment in
(58a) should also hold. But the representation in (56a), repeated in (58b)
does not show this, as it does not show Lina as the stimulus of the seeing
event.

(58)a 'Jones saw Lina shake the bottle' entails 'Jones saw Lina'

  b Jones saw Lina shake the bottle.
$\exists e \exists e'$(SEE(e) & EXPERIENCER(j, e) & STIMULUS(e', e) & SHAKE(e') & AGENT(l, e') & PATIENT(the bottle, e'))

There was an event e and
there was an event e' and
e is a seeing and
Jones was the experiencer of e and
e' was the stimulus of e and
e' was a shaking and
Lina was the agent of e' and
the bottle was the patient of e'

However, a wider range of cases suggests that the apparent entailment in (58a) may be a commonsense inference in the particular case, rather than a general logical entailment of sentences of the same form. The candidate inferences in (59a–c) below for sentences of the same form are not obviously true on a normal reading, and (59d) is false.

(59)a 'Jones felt the floor shake' entails 'Jones felt the floor'
  b 'She heard the carpet rustle' entails 'She heard the carpet'.
  c 'She saw the wind blow the clouds away' entails 'She saw the wind'.
  d (The intruder was hiding behind the curtain)
     'I saw him twitch the curtain' entails 'I saw him'.

So it seems that the apparent entailment in (58a) is not a logical entailment, and it isn't a problem that such entailments are not shown in the representations in (56). Sequences such as *Lina shake the bottle* in *Jones saw Lina shake the bottle* denote events, as stated above. (See Exercise F for more on perception verbs.)

8.5 ADDING TENSE AND NP QUANTIFIERS

For the sake of simplicity, tense has been omitted from Neodavidsonian representations so far, and quantifier NPs have been left as unanalysed expressions in argument positions. When the detail from earlier analyses is included, the relative scope of various expressions needs to be decided.

First, suppose that the existence claim in '$\exists e$' is to be taken seriously, and that the way an event exists is that it occurs or takes place. The existence of an event is limited to the time at which it occurs, so that a past event, for example, goes out of existence when it is over, and a future event doesn't exist until it occurs. In that case, a tense operator always has scope over the existential quantifier binding the event variable, as the existence of the event is confined to the time expressed by the tense, for example:

(60)a   Jones left.

   b   Past $\exists$e (LEAVE(e) & AGENT (j, e))
'At a past time there was an event and the event was a leaving and Jones was its agent.'

   c   # $\exists$e Past (LEAVE (e) & AGENT (j, e))
'There is an event which at a past time was a leaving and Jones was its agent.'

Following findings in syntactic research which will not be reviewed here, we will assume that in fact the existential quantifier which binds the event variable always has narrow scope. We know that quantifier NPs and tense can interact in scope (see Exercises F and G, Chapter 7).

Putting these points together yields the following possible orderings.

(61)   NP quantifier – tense – $\exists$e
       tense – NP quantifier – $\exists$e

Neodavidsonian representations including tense are illustrated in (62).

(62)a   The president visited Harbin.

   b   [The x: PRESIDENT(x)] Past $\exists$e (VISIT (e) & AGENT (x, e) & PATIENT (h, e))
'For the x, such that x is the president, at a past time there was an event and the event was a visiting and x was the agent of the event and Harbin was the patient of the event.'

   c   Past [The x: PRESIDENT(x)] $\exists$e (VISIT(e) & AGENT (x, e) & PATIENT (h, e))
'At a past time, for the x such that x was the president, there was an event and the event was a visiting and x was the agent of the event and Harbin was the patient of the event.'

Tense can be more explicitly represented by quantification over times, with variables t standing for times. If a representation includes time variables, the relationship between an event and its time of occurrence can be represented by 'AT(e, t)', as in (63). (63b) corresponds to (62b).

(63)a   Jones will leave.
      $\exists$t$\exists$e (t*< t & (LEAVE(e) & AGENT (j, e) & AT (e, t))

b The president visited Harbin.
[The x: PRESIDENT(x)] ∃t∃e (t< t* & VISIT (e) & AGENT (x, e) & PATIENT (h,e) & AT (e, t))

EXERCISES

(A) Basic Review

Give the Neodavidsonian forms, including tense operators, for the following sentences.

(1) Marcia quickly shoved Clive into the cupboard.
(2) Marcia took the book from Clive.
(3) Clive broke some clods up roughly with a shovel.
(4) The tree will fall suddenly.
(5) Marcia saw Clive punch John.
(6) Kennedy's assassination shocked America.

(B) Adverbials: Discussion

Some adverbials do not seem to be predicates on events. For example, the Neodavidsonian formula for *John lied plausibly* would be

Past ∃e (LIE(e) & AGENT(j, e) & PLAUSIBLE (e))
'There was an event of John's lying and the event was plausible'.

but events are not the kind of thing we normally describe as plausible. Plausibility is usually a property of suggestions, assertions, theories and other things like propositions. If we paraphrase the sentence with *tell a lie* it becomes

John told a plausible lie.

This suggests that the lie, rather than the event of telling it, should be the thing modified by the adverbial.

In the sentences below, would you analyse the underlined expressions as predicates on the described event? If not, how would you analyse the adverbial?

(1) The Bedouin stole <u>silently away</u>.
(2) Jones woke up <u>in a foul mood</u>.
(3) Horace leaned <u>heavily on the counter</u>.
(4) They gathered <u>together in a huddle</u>.

(5)   Marcia <u>spontaneously</u> combusted.
(6)   John arrived <u>unexpectedly</u>.
(7)   Jones was <u>willingly</u> instructed by Clive.
(8)   Jones was instructed <u>willingly</u> by Clive.
(9)   Jones woke up <u>in a bar</u>.
(10)   Anita interviewed Barry <u>over coffee</u>.

(C)   Generalized Event Roles

Give the Neodavidsonian forms for the sentences below, ensuring that all the entailments listed here are accounted for in your representations.

(1)   entails (2)–(5), (3) entails (2) and (4).

(1)   Brutus stabbed Caesar in the marketplace.
(2)   Brutus did something.
(3)   Brutus did something to Caesar.
(4)   Something happened to Caesar.
(5)   There was a stabbing in the marketplace.

Which of the entailments among (1)–(5) above can be accounted for using Davidsonian representations?

(D)   Further Quantification over Events

Drawing on your solutions for (C), give the Neodavidsonian forms for the sentences below, including tense operators.

(1)   Everything John does is crazy.
(2)   Most of what happens to Marcia is funny.
(3)   Clive isn't going to do anything for Marcia.
(4)   Something awful is going to happen.

Does your representation for (3) entail all the following sentences and others like them?

(5)   Clive isn't going to buy flowers for Marcia.
(6)   Clive isn't going to sharpen a pencil for Marcia.
(7)   Clive isn't going to sing for Marcia.

(E)   A Different Kind of Scopal Ambiguity: Discussion

Modification by *almost* in the sentences below is ambiguous. Suppose that *almost* is an operator which takes scope over a proposition, and that its scope might be a complex proposition or any atomic proposition. Using

Neodavidsonian forms, how many readings can you represent for the sentences below?

(1)   Jones almost ran to the store.
(2)   Jones almost killed Bill.

(F)   Perception Sentences: Discussion

Using the Neodavidsonian analysis for perception sentences in Section 8.4, give representations for the sentences below.

(1)   Zapruder saw Oswald shoot Kennedy.
(2)   Zapruder saw Kennedy shot by Oswald.

Do the Neodavidsonian representations give the right results here?

(G)   Missing Arguments: Discussion

The underlined verbs in the sentences below have at least one argument (apparently) missing from the sentence. Identify the missing argument(s), and if you can, decide whether or not it is really semantically obligatory.

(1)   The cakes were eagerly <u>devoured</u>.
(2)   The boat was <u>sunk</u> to <u>collect</u> the insurance.
(3)   I <u>gave</u> at the office.
(4)   She <u>sliced</u> the cheese with a pocketknife.
(5)   She <u>sliced</u> the cheese.
(6)   I gave him a beer and he <u>drank</u>.
(7)   To <u>know</u> her is to <u>love</u> her.
(8)   Tom wrote Harry a note.
(9)   Tom <u>wrote</u> a note.
(10)   To <u>love</u> is to <u>exalt</u>.
(11)   To <u>love</u> is to <u>exult</u>.

FURTHER READING

Much of the discussion in this chapter draws on Parsons (1990), especially Chapters 1–6. This accessible work is the main source on the Neodavidsonian analysis. Chapter 7 of Kenny (1963) discusses the adicity of different kinds of predicate, and whether or not all arguments are really obligatory.

Problems about adicity in Neodavidsonian analyses and thematic relations in logical representations are discussed in Dowty (1989). Parsons (1995) responds to Dowty (1989).

Traditional thematic relations are reviewed in many introductory linguistics texts or syntax texts.

9 Aspectual Classes of Events

As we saw in Chapter 7, verbal aspect expresses characteristics of the internal structure of an event, independently of the event's placement in the past, present or future. English perfective *have* is called a perfect in grammatical tradition, though it isn't a clear case of semantic perfectivity in its aspectual readings, and it also has tense readings. Semantic perfectivity generally expresses the completeness of an event, or in other words, describes an event as having reached its natural conclusion or final boundary.

A weak perfectivity effect with *have* can be seen in the example below.

(1)a   I read the paper for a while.
       (I didn't finish reading it.)
   b   # I have read the paper for a while.
   c   I have read the paper.
       (I finished reading it.)

The adverbial *for a while* cannot modify events which have reached their natural conclusion, in this case the reading of the whole paper, and the perfectivity of *have read the paper* clashes with the adverbial in (1b), in contrast with the plain tense in (1a) which can have an unfinished event reading.

The English progressive was described in Chapter 7 as creating a temporal frame within which another time is placed, as illustrated in the examples repeated in (2).

(2)a   Alice reads the *Mail*.
   b   Alice is reading the *Mail*.
   c   When Alice arrives John will make coffee.
   d   When Alice arrives John will be making coffee.
   e   When Alice arrived John made coffee.
   f   When Alice arrived John was making coffee.

The progressives in (2d) and (2f) extend the making coffee event into a frame around the time of Alice's arrival, which happens during the coffee-making, in contrast with the simple tenses in (2c) and (2e), which report an arrival followed by a coffee-making. The present progressive in (2d) extends the paper-reading time around the time of utterance, giving the reading that the event is in progress at the time of speaking, in contrast with the habitual reading of the simple present tense in (2a). Other ways to describe this effect are to say that the progressive takes us into the internal process before the event's conclusion, or that the progressive emphasizes the duration of an event.

Setting aside the effects of perfective or progressive morphology, the aspectual characteristics of events (that is, their internal structures in time) are already coded to some extent in the basic verb phrases which are the predicates on events. Beginning with observations made by Aristotle, philosophers and linguists have developed a system of classifying events into aspectual event classes, also called **aktionsarten**, from the German *aktion* 'action' and *art* 'sort or type'. Four main classes have emerged in recent discussion, chiefly from the work of the philosophers Gilbert Ryle, Anthony Kenny and Zeno Vendler, particularly Vendler, who first proposed the four distinct categories of events most commonly in current use.

The four aspectual classes identified by Vendler include states, which are not really events. The term **eventualities**, coined by Emmon Bach, is used to cover events and states together, and strictly speaking the aspectual classes are classes of eventualities, though they are commonly referred to as event classes.

The classifications do not apply directly to eventualities themselves, but really apply to eventualities under a particular verb phrase description. An eventuality taken in itself may be described in different ways which place it in any of the four classes, depending on the verb phrase chosen to describe it or present it for attention. For simplicity I will refer to event classes and event characteristics, but strictly speaking these are classes and characteristics of eventualities under particular descriptions.

9.1 THE FOUR ASPECTUAL CLASSES

The chief characteristics which determine the classifications are bounding or boundedness, duration and change.

A **bounded** event has a shape which gives it a natural finishing point beyond which the same event cannot continue, because it is finished. An unbounded event has no inherent natural finishing point and can continue indefinitely. The distinction between bounded and unbounded is also called the **telic/atelic** distinction, from the Greek *telikos* 'final'.

A **durative** event occupies time, in contrast with a nondurative event which is idealized to a point in time.

The presence or absence of **change** marks the difference between heterogeneous and homogeneous events. A **heterogeneous event**, containing internal change, is not identical from moment to moment. A **homogeneous event** is unchanging from moment to moment, and all its parts are uniform.

These characteristics will become clearer as we proceed.

The four aspectual event classes are states, activities or processes, accomplishments and achievements.

States are illustrated in the sentences below.

(3)a   Brigitte is taller than Danny.
  b   The light is on.
  c   Clive knows my brother.
  d   Coal and coke are different.
  e   The cat is asleep.
  f   Your umbrella is in the hall.

States are unbounded or atelic – they have no natural boundaries or culminations which constitute finishing points. The situation of the light being on or the situation of Brigitte being taller than Danny can continue indefinitely.

States are durative – they occupy time, and can be said to last for minutes, weeks, years and centuries.

States are homogeneous – they have no internal variety or change. One moment of Clive knowing my brother is the same as another moment of Clive knowing my brother as far as the truth of 'Clive knows my brother' is concerned. This contrasts with a heterogeneous event such as the one described by 'Clive walked home'. The truth of 'Clive walked home' requires that he performed walking actions, so at one moment he had his weight on the left foot and his right foot swinging forward, while at another moment he had his weight on his right foot and swung his left foot forward. If different moments like this are not contained in an event then 'Clive walked home' can't be true of it.

Processes or activities are illustrated in (4).

(4)a   John walked in the garden.
  b   The leaves fluttered in the wind.
  c   Clive pushed a supermarket trolley.
  d   They chatted.
  e   The guests swam in the river.
  f   The visitors played cards.

Processes are unbounded and durative, like states, but unlike states they are heterogeneous. The heterogeneity of 'Clive walked home' applies to any walking event including the one reported in (4a). If 'The leaves fluttered' is true, then it must be the case that the leaves moved, so at one moment the leaves are in a certain position in space and at another moment they are in a different position.

Accomplishments are the eventualities with the clearest and most complex structure, consisting of a process or activity leading up to a culmination or finishing point. Accomplishments are illustrated in (5).

(5)a John built a house.
 b Marcia ate an apple.
 c Jones ran a mile.
 d We did the dishes.
 e The new incumbent made a speech.
 f Raffaele painted a triptych.

Accomplishments are the canonical bounded or telic events, in that the described process leads up to a culmination or outcome which finishes the event. For example, the event described in (5b) is finished when the whole apple is eaten, and the event described in (5f) finishes when the triptych is complete – even if Raffaele carries on painting on some other work, this later painting activity is not part of the event described in (5f).

Accomplishments occupy time, and are therefore durative, and given their internal structure, comprising a process followed by an outcome, they are clearly heterogeneous.

Achievements are illustrated in (6).

(6)a Clive realized that Deirdre was gone.
 b Then he recognized her.
 c They reached the summit.
 d Jones noticed a mark on the wallpaper.

Typically, an achievement is the transition from one state to another, such as the switch in (6a) from not knowing that Deirdre was gone to knowing that she was gone. Once Clive knows that Deirdre has gone the realization is complete and cannot continue, so the event is bounded. The same effect is found in the other examples, where the event is terminated as soon as the result state is established: in (6b) he remembers who she is, in (6c) they are at the summit, and in (6d) Jones is aware of a mark on the wallpaper. Accordingly, achievements are bounded. An achievement can also be described simply as the moment of the onset of a state. Once the state holds, the onset is over.

Achievements are idealized to occur at a nondivisible point in time, and lack duration. This is one of the points which focuses attention on the event-as-described rather than on the event itself in reality, as it is impossible for a real event to lack any duration. An achievement predicate represents an event as idealized to a point in much the same way that a city or town is idealized to a dot on a map. Although both the event and the town have inner structure in fact, the symbolization does not make it accessible.

In denoting a change or transition, an achievement is heterogeneous, although its heterogeneity cannot be described as a difference between one moment or another of the event's duration, given that an achievement has only one moment. The indivisible moment of change is the event.

The properties of the four classes are summarized in (7).

(7)	Change	Duration	Bound
State	−	+	−
Achievement	+	−	+
Activity/Process	+	+	−
Accomplishment	+	+	+

A fifth class of events is also proposed, falling between accomplishments and achievements, commonly called semelfactives. **Semelfactives** resemble both accomplishments and achievements in being bounded. They are like achievements in their brevity, but unlike canonical achievements they do not describe minimal moments of change between one state of affairs and another. Semelfactives are illustrated in (8).

(8)a   Jones rapped the table.
 b   Jones blinked.
 c   Jones coughed.
 d   The light flashed.

Semelfactives are also unlike accomplishments in not having a clearly identifiable process or activity stage leading up to the bounding culmination. The duration of an accomplishment is mainly occupied by its process stage. For example, in the accomplishment reported by *Mary ate an apple* the process of biting off, chewing and swallowing parts of the apple occupies most of the duration of the event, the final bound being the moment concluding the last swallow. A sentence like *Jones blinked* or *The light flashed* describes no comparable process. As we shall see in the next section, expressions which modify the duration of an event target the process stage of an accomplishment, but do not have this reading with semelfactives, indicating that semelfactives are distinct from accomplishments.

9.2   LINGUISTIC SIGNS OF ASPECTUAL CLASSES

The differences among aspectual classes are demonstrated by a number of syntactic tests, generally of two kinds: first, the effect of adverbials which target aspectual properties of events, such as their duration or temporal bounds, and second, the effect of tense and aspect verb forms on predicates of different classes.

9.2.1   Bounding and Duration

The chief adverbials which target bounding are of the form *in an hour/in ten minutes*. The duration of unbounded events is modified by adverbials with *for*, such as *for an hour/for ten minutes* – this is discussed further below.

With an accomplishment sentence an *in* adverbial modifies the duration of the event, as illustrated in (9a–c). With an achievement sentence an *in* adverbial is interpreted as stating the time which elapses before the event, which occurs at the end of the stated interval, as in (9d–f), although sentences like (9e,f) are more natural with *within five minutes* or *within three days*.

(9) accomplishments
    a He can eat a meat pie in 60 seconds.
    b They built the barn in two days.
    c Jones walked to town in 45 minutes.

    achievements
    d He recognized her in a minute or so.
    e Jones noticed the marks on the wallpaper in five minutes at most.
    f Jones lost his keys in three days.

These interpretations fall under the generalization that an *in* adverbial places a time point provided by the event within the stated interval, most commonly near or at the end of the interval. With both kinds of bounded event an *in* adverbial locates the bound of the event within or at the end of the stated interval. An achievement consists of its bound and no more, so the whole of an achievement modified by *in ten minutes* is understood to occur at the end of a ten-minute interval. An accomplishment modified by *in ten minutes* is described as ending at the end of a ten-minute interval, with the process stage of the event occupying the interval.

An unbounded event provides no inbuilt bound for an *in* adverbial to attach to, and sentences with this combination, as illustrated in (10), are commonly anomalous. As an alternative 'repair' reading, the onset of the event can be identified as the point of time anchoring the adverbial, so that, for example, (10a) reports that the couple began to be happy in two years. The '#' marks below indicate that the *in* adverbial cannot modify the event duration. For example, (10a) cannot mean that two years was the duration of the couple's happiness.

(10) states
    a # The couple were happy in two years.
    b # The room was sunny in an hour.
    c # Jones knew him well in five years.

    processes
    d # They walked in the park in half an hour.
    e # People waiting to buy tickets chatted in five hours.
    f # Jones pushed a supermarket trolley in 90 seconds.

The onset reading is far more natural with the future tense. Predicates of all event classes in the future tense can have an onset interpretation with *in* adverbials, as illustrated in (11).

(11) states
    a They will be happy in a year.
    b The room will be sunny in an hour.
    c Jones will know him in five years.

    processes
    d We will walk in the park in an hour.
    e They'll chat in a few minutes.
    f Jones will push the supermarket trolley in 90 seconds.

    accomplishments (ambiguous between onset delay and duration)
    g He'll eat a meat pie in an hour.
    h They'll build the barn in two weeks.
    i Jones will walk to town in 45 minutes.

    achievements
    j He will recognize her in a minute.
    k Jones will notice the marks on the wallpaper in a few minutes.
    l Jones will lose his keys in three days.

    semelfactives
    m Jones will rap the table in a minute.
    n Jones will blink in a minute.
    o Jones will cough in a minute.
    p The light will flash in ten minutes.

Given the freedom of onset readings for *in* adverbials with the future tense, *in* adverbials are generally used as a diagnostic with past tense sentences.

In addition to the onset reading, another repair reading for *in* adverbials with process sentences is to understand the event as bounded in some fashion. For example, if 'They walked in the park in half an hour' reports a routine walk which never varies, the walking event has a fixed form with an endpoint and the sentence can be given an accomplishment reading, with the *in* adverbial stating the duration of the event, giving a reading like 'They walked their usual route in half an hour'. The accomplishment readings of such sentences are not very natural. Generally, repair readings really demonstrate a hearer's strategy for trying to reconcile incompatible expressions. The chief point is that an *in* adverbial with an unbounded event cannot state the duration of the event unless the event is pragmatically understood as an accomplishment.

Semelfactives with *in* adverbials resemble achievements in that the adverbial cannot modify the duration of the event, but may express the interval which elapses before the event occurs. As with achievements, *within* adverbials are more natural with semelfactives on this reading, and past tense *in* adverbial sentences, as illustrated in (12), are somewhat anomalous.

(12) semelfactives
    a # Jones rapped the table in a minute.
    b # Jones blinked in a minute.
    c # Jones coughed in an hour.
    e # The light flashed in ten minutes.

For adverbials, on the other hand, measure the duration of basically unbounded events, and are anomalous with bounded events, as in (13).

(13) accomplishments
    a # He ate the meat pie for half an hour.
    b # They built the barn for two days.
    c # Jones walked to town for 45 minutes.

achievements
    d # He will recognize her for a minute.
    e # Jones noticed the marks on the wallpaper for five minutes.
    f # They reached the summit for half an hour.

There are two repair readings for bounded events with *for* adverbials, both of which adjust the reported event to an unbounded form. Achievements can be understood as denoting the onset of a state, and an achievement like *notice* in (13e) can be understood as denoting the result state of awareness. Accordingly, (13e) can be interpreted as 'Jones was aware of the marks on the wallpaper for five minutes'.

The commoner repair reading is to understand a bounded event as a series of repetitions. This is an alternative for *Jones noticed the marks on the wallpaper for a month*, reporting that Jones repeatedly noticed the marks for a month. An iterated reading for (13c), for example, is that Jones walked to town repeatedly for 45 minutes. Iterated readings are not very plausible for (13a–c) but are more natural for the accomplishment sentences in (14).

(14)a Sally painted the view from her window for five years.
    b The gang painted the bridge for ten years.

The central characteristic of semelfactives is that the iterated reading with *for* adverbials is the natural reading, as illustrated in (15).

(15) semelfactives
    a Jones rapped the table for a minute.

b Jones blinked for a minute.
c Jones coughed for an hour.
e The light flashed for ten minutes.

The only natural reading for (15a) is that Jones rapped the table repeatedly throughout a one-minute interval. (15b, c) have similar interpretations.

To sum up, *in* and *for* adverbials are diagnostic of boundedness. An *in* adverbial must be anchored by a time point which falls within the interval it identifies. With a bounded event predicate the endpoint of the event provides the anchor time. Generally the end of the event is understood to fall at the end of the interval, so that the interval is the whole duration of the event. With an achievement predicate the anchor time is the moment of the event's occurrence.

(16) Jones built a barn in an hour.
      Jones noticed the marks in an hour.

- *in an hour* identifies the interval t_1–t_3
- the anchor time t_2 must fall within the interval
- the event provides a bound as value for t_2
- *accomplishment*: $t_2 =$ endpoint, so the interval is the event duration
- *achievement*: $t_2 =$ occurrence time, so the interval is the event delay

Unbounded predicates (states and processes) are commonly anomalous with *in* adverbials because they do not provide any anchor time, having no endpoint. Occasionally a process predicate may be understood to describe an accomplishment event. Alternatively, the onset of the event or state may be understood as the anchor time.

(17) The room will be sunny in an hour.
      We will walk in the park in an hour.

repair reading for state/process: $t_2 =$ onset, so the interval is the event delay

The *take*+time construction illustrated in (18) below also selects bounded events, and is interpreted like *in* adverbials. With accomplishments the stated time is understood as the event duration, while achievements and semelfact-ives are understood to occur at the end of the stated interval.

(18) <u>accomplishments</u>
    a It took 60 seconds for him to eat the pie.
    b It took two days for them to build the barn.
    c It took 45 minutes for Jones to walk to town.

    <u>achievements</u>
    d It took a minute for him to recognize her.
    e It took five minutes for Jones to notice the marks on the wallpaper.
    f It took three days for Jones to lose his keys.

    <u>semelfactives</u>
    g It took a minute for Jones to rap the table.
    h It took a minute for Jones to blink.
    i It took an hour for Jones to cough.
    j It took ten minutes for the light to flash.

Although the temporal reading of (18d–j) is clear, the sentences are slightly odd in a way which suggests that the *take*+time construction primarily modifies only accomplishments. For example, (18g) suggests that throughout the minute before Jones rapped the table he was unsuccessfully striving to do so, and similarly with (18h, i). In (18d, e, f, j) there is a suggested background context in which an observer (possibly the narrator) is waiting throughout the interval for the described event to occur and assessing the interval as a delay. For example, (18e) does not have quite the same reading as (19a, b), which do not convey this hint of suspense.

(19)a After five minutes Jones noticed the marks on the wallpaper.
    b Five minutes later Jones noticed the marks on the wallpaper.

It may be that this effect arises because the *take*+time construction belongs with accomplishments, and the time before an achievement or semelfactive event occurs is interpreted as some sort of initial stage process of trying or being expected, converting the events into quasi-accomplishments.

    With unbounded events the *take*+time construction describes the interval to elapse before the onset of the state or process. This is a natural reading for (20c) below, paraphrasable as the accomplishment 'It took Jones five years to get to know him well'. The same sort of reading is found in (20a), 'It took two years for the couple to become happy'. As with achievements and semelfactives, the sentences suggest trying or expecting during the interval denoted by the time expression, and if this is unnatural, as in (20d–f), the sentences remain anomalous.

(20) <u>states</u>
    a   It took two years for the couple to be happy.

b   It took an hour for the room to be sunny.

c   It took five years for Jones to know him well.

<u>processes</u>

d   # It took half an hour for them to walk in the park.

e   # It took five hours for people waiting to buy tickets to chat.

f   # It took 90 seconds for Jones to push a supermarket trolley.

As above, (20d, f) can also have repair readings that convert the processes to accomplishments – 'walk the usual route' or 'push a trolley a certain known course'.

9.2.2   Tense and Verb Aspect

As we saw in Chapter 7, the interpretation of the simple present tense in English separates state predicates from all the others, as illustrated in (21).

(21)   <u>non-states</u>

     a   Heath bikes to work.

     b   Barry feeds the dogs.

     c   She writes with a fountain pen.

     d   She eats peas but she won't eat silver beet.

     e   He notices the little details.

     <u>states</u>

     f   He believes this rubbish.

     g   All those cupboards contain expensive equipment.

     h   Koalas live on eucalyptus shoots and leaves.

     i   The house stands on a bluff overlooking the upper harbour.

     j   I see the trucks coming.

Non-state sentences (accomplishments, achievements, processes and semel-factives) are generally interpreted as habitual in the simple present tense, apart from other special uses reviewed in Chapter 7 such as the historic present. States are interpreted as holding at the time of utterance, whether they are enduring states or temporary situations.

    The main verb aspect test for states is the progressive, which is tradition-ally held to be ill formed with state predicates. As we saw in Section 7.5, the progressive is well formed with a number of state predicates as in (22), and when contrasted with a simple tense form, indicates that the state is tempor-ary or brief.

(22)a   We live in London.

     b   We are living in London.

     c   The statue stands in the south quadrangle.

  d   The statue is standing in the south quadrangle.
  e   John's house sits at the top of a hill.
  f   John's house is sitting at the top of a hill.

However, canonical state predicates like those in (23) resist the progressive altogether.

(23)a   # Jones is knowing French.
   b   # This box is containing all my worldly goods.
   c   # Jones is being in Frankfurt.
   d   # They are having three children.
   e   # Brigitte is being taller than Danny.

The progressive also interacts with aspectual event classes in a number of other ways which will be discussed in Section 9.2.5 below.

Tests for state predicates are also found in the literature on stativity. **Stativity**, a property of linguistic expressions rather than of eventualities, is simply the property of denoting a state. All other expressions are non-stative. The distinction between statives and non-statives was first drawn by Lakoff (1965), quite independently of the traditional four aspectual classes under discussion here, although the class of states identified in both systems is the same. The chief difference is that Lakoff also included tests which primarily target agentivity, as discussed in the next section. States are generally not agentive, and for many years tests which showed a lack of agentivity were interpreted as tests for the presence of stativity. Strictly speaking, tests for stativity should include all the phenomena reviewed in this chapter which serve to identify state predicates.

9.2.3   Agentivity

Certain contexts semantically require a predicate which denotes an event with an agent. Although agentivity is thematic rather than aspectual, agentivity and aspectual class do not seem to be entirely independent. Agentivity is discussed in more detail in Chapter 10.

Agentive predicates are required in the complement to *persuade*, with adverbs like *carefully*, *deliberately*, *conscientiously*, in the imperative voice, and in the *what x did* construction. These tests are reviewed in more detail below.

Accomplishments and processes can appear with *persuade*, but achievements and states can not, as shown in (24).

(24)   <u>accomplishments</u>
   a   Jones persuaded him to eat the pie.
   b   They persuaded Jones to build a barn.
   c   Jones persuaded Mike to walk to town.

processes
d   Jones persuaded Tina to walk in the park.
e   Jones persuaded the group members to chat.
f   Dino persuaded Jones to push a supermarket trolley.

states
g   # Jones persuaded the couple to be happy.
h   # Lucas persuaded Jones to understand chaos theory.
i   # Jones was persuaded to hear the trucks coming.

achievements
j   # Jones was persuaded to notice the marks on the wallpaper.
k   # Jones was persuaded to recognize the woman in the doorway.
l   # Jones was persuaded to turn fifty.

Accomplishments and processes can be modified by adverbs like *carefully* or *deliberately*, but achievements and states can not, as in (25).

(25)   accomplishments
a   Jones deliberately ate the pie.
b   Jones built the barn carefully.
c   Mike deliberately walked to town.

processes
d   Tina deliberately walked in the park.
e   The group members chatted conscientiously.
f   Jones conscientiously pushed the supermarket trolley.

states
g.   # The couple were happy deliberately.
h   # Jones deliberately understood chaos theory.
i   # Jones carefully heard the trucks coming.

achievements
j   # Jones deliberately noticed the marks on the wallpaper.
k   # Jones carefully recognized the woman in the doorway.
l   # Jones conscientiously turned fifty.

Accomplishments and processes can appear in the imperative voice but achievements and states can not, as in (26).

(26)   accomplishments
a   Eat the pie!
b   Build a barn!
c   Walk to town!

processes
d   Walk in the park!

   e   Chat among yourselves!
   f   Push the trolley!

<u>states</u>
   g # Be happy!
   h # Understand chaos theory!
   i # Hear the trucks coming!

<u>achievements</u>
   j # Notice the marks on the wallpaper!
   k # Recognize the woman in the doorway!
   l # Turn fifty!

The imperative in (26g) is acceptable as a benediction rather than as a command, comparable to *May you be happy!* Imperatives of the form *be* + adjective are also often well-formed if they can be interpreted as containing so-called agentive *be*, as illustrated in (27).

(27)a   Be good!
    b   Be quiet!
    c   Don't be stupid!
    d   Be nice!

These are not commands to be in a certain state or have a certain property, but are really commands to behave in a certain fashion. Agentive *be* denotes behaviour and is really a process predicate.

Finally, only agentive predicates are appropriate in the *what x did* construction, as illustrated in (28).

(28)   <u>accomplishments</u>
      a   What Jones did was eat the pie.
      b   What Jones did was build a barn.
      c   What Mike did was walk to town.

<u>processes</u>
      d   What Tina did was walk in the park.
      e   What the group members did was chat among themselves.
      f   What Jones did was push a supermarket trolley.

<u>states</u>
      g # What the couple did was be happy/be rich.
      h # What Jones did was understand chaos theory.
      i # What Jones did was hear the trucks coming.

<u>achievements</u>
      j # What Jones did was notice the marks on the wallpaper.

k # What Jones did was recognize the woman in the doorway.
l # What Jones did was turn fifty.

To sum up, accomplishments and processes may be agentive, but states and achievements, even with a human subject, are generally not agentive (though this point will be discussed further in Section 10.3). In particular, achievements such as recognizing, noticing and realizing are mental events which happen to us without being under our control or attainable by effort or intention.

9.2.4 Internal Complexity

Accomplishments are the most complex events, having both duration and a final bound. Achievements are bounded but lack duration, while states and processes have duration but lack bounds. Accordingly, only accomplishments can finish or be finished, as finishing involves both duration and a natural termination, as illustrated below.

(29) a   Jones finished building his house.
   b # Jones finished noticing the marks on the wallpaper.
   c # Jones finished believing in colour therapy.
   d # Jones finished tapping the table.

Another consequence of the greater complexity of accomplishments is the range of ambiguities found with *almost*, as shown below (see also Chapter 8, Exercise E). One way to demonstrate the ambiguities here is to use Neodavidsonian representations. The variable s is used here for states. (Note that *almost* is not analysed as an operator in the (b) examples, but as part of the predicate.)

(30) <u>state</u>
    Jones was almost rich.
    a   Past Almost ∃s (RICH (s) & THEME (j, s))
        'There almost was a state and the state would have been a being rich and Jones would have been the theme of the state.'

    b   Past ∃s (ALMOST RICH (s) & THEME (j, s))
        'There was a state and the state was a being almost rich and Jones was the theme of the state.'

(31) <u>process</u>
    Jones almost swam.
    a   Past Almost ∃e (SWIM (e) & AGENT (j, e))
        'There almost was an event and the event would have been a swimming and Jones would have been the agent of the event.'

b   Past ∃e (ALMOST SWIM (e) & AGENT (j, e))
'There was an event and the event was an almost swimming and Jones was the agent of the event.'

(32)   <u>achievement</u>
Jones almost noticed the marks.

a   Past Almost ∃e (NOTICE (e) & EXPERIENCER (j, e) & STI-MULUS (the marks, e))
'There almost was an event and the event would have been a noticing and Jones would have been the experiencer of the event and the marks would have been the stimulus of the event.'

(33)   <u>accomplishment</u>
Jones almost ran to the corner.

a   Past Almost ∃e (RUN(e) & AGENT (j, e) & GOAL (the corner, e))
'There almost was an event and the event would have been a running and Jones would have been the agent of the event and the corner would have been the goal of the event.'

b   Past ∃e (ALMOST RUN(e) & AGENT (j, e) & GOAL (the corner, e))
'There was an event and the event was an almost running and Jones was the agent of the event and the corner was the goal of the event.'

c   Past ∃e (RUN(e) & AGENT (j, e) & ALMOST GOAL(the corner, e))
'There was an event and the event was a running and Jones was the agent of the event and the corner was almost the goal of the event.'

Both states and processes can show the ambiguity between the (a) reading, the state or event didn't actually happen or hold but almost did, and the (b) reading, what happened or held was almost swimming or almost richness. That is, in (30b) Jones is very well off but not quite rich, and in (31b) Jones paddled and did the breathing but didn't keep his feet off the bottom of the pool very long.

The representation in (32) reflects the intuition that noticing has an absolute quality that resists approximation – if you become aware of something to any degree you notice it. If this is correct, there is no kind of event which is an almost noticing, and *almost* can only modify the actual occurrence of the event, as in (32). An achievement such as *realize* may be gradable, in that if you come to strongly suspect that p is the case without being quite certain, then you almost realize that p.

Accomplishments, on the other hand, can show three readings for *almost*. As always, the modifier can target whether or not the event occurred at all, as in (33a), and can modify the predicate as in (33b) to describe the event as almost running – perhaps half walking and half running. In (33c) *almost* modifies the final bound expressed as the goal, so the distance Jones ran was almost to the corner. Another way to express the intended meaning in (33c) is to say that 'almost to the corner' denotes a place which was the goal of the event, in which case the final conjunct could be written 'GOAL (almost to the corner, e)'.

The additional ambiguity with accomplishments between (33b) and (33c) arises because an accomplishment has two identifiable parts, rather like a process grafted on to an achievement, so *almost* can target either the process or the outcome. The complexity of accomplishments is also demonstrated with some of the progressive effects discussed in the next section.

9.2.5   Interactions with the Progressive

One of the characteristics of the progressive is that it converts an accomplishment into an unbounded event, which is generally agreed to be the process part of the event. Progressives of accomplishment predicates are modified by *for* adverbials rather than by *in* adverbials, as in (34).

(34)a   Jones was building a house for six months.
   b   # Jones was building a house in six months.
   c   # Jones built a house for six months.
   d   Jones built a house in six months.

The *in* adverbial in (34b) is either anomalous, or given a repair reading in which Jones began to build a house at the end of six months, which would be more naturally expressed as 'Jones was building a house within six months'. This kind of reading is typical of process predicates.

The conversion of an accomplishment to its process stage removes the final bound, and so the completion of the event is no longer expressed. This is the source of the contrasting entailments in (35).

(35)a   'Jones was building a house' does not entail 'Jones built a house'.
   b   'Jones was walking in the park' entails 'Jones walked in the park'.

Because 'Jones built a house' is not progressive the sentence describes the whole accomplishment event including the completion of the house. 'Jones was building a house', on the other hand, describes only the process stage and does not entail that the event ever reached completion, so does not entail

'Jones built a house'. 'Jones walked in the park' and 'Jones was walking in the park' are both process reports, so each entails the other.

In addition to converting an accomplishment to a process, the progressive has its usual temporal frame reading as in (36).

(36)   Jones was eating a sandwich when I rang him.

The progressive predicate *eating a sandwich* describes the sandwich-eating process, without entailing that the sandwich was ever entirely eaten. In addition, the sandwich-eating process is stretched out to occupy a time interval containing the time of the phone call.

The class of achievements is the least widely accepted class, and some writers group achievements and accomplishments together. One of the main reasons to doubt that they are the same is the interaction of the progressive with achievement predicates. If the progressive converts a bounded event to its initial process stage, then it should be anomalous with achievement predicates because they have no process component. This prediction is borne out by canonical achievement predicates such as those in (37).

(37)a   # Jones was recognizing the woman when she sneezed.
   b   # Jones was noticing the mark on the wall when the doorbell rang.
   c   # Jones was noticing the mark on the wall for a few microseconds.
   d   # Jones was losing his key when I spotted him.
   f   # Jones was turning fifty when the clock struck.

However, a number of predicates which have been identified as achievement predicates easily take the progressive, as in (38).

(38)a   Jones was winning for the first three laps.
   b   Jones was dying for months.
   c   They are reaching the summit now.
   d   Flight 34 is now arriving at Gate 19.

The predicates *win (the race)*, *die*, *reach the summit* and *arrive* have been classed as achievements because they are considered to describe instantaneous transitions, but unlike achievements such as *notice*, *realize* and *recognize* they have clearly identified processes which normally lead up to them. To reach the summit one must approach it, to win the race one must lead the field at the final moment, to arrive one must approach the destination, and before dying one generally has a mortal illness or moribund episode. In other words, *win*, *die*, *reach the summit* and *arrive* describe the culminations of events which have the structure of accomplishments. The progressive of a bounded event predicate produces a predicate of the process stage, and in the cases in (38), unlike the examples in (37), there is a process to serve as the interpretation of the progressive form as a repair reading.

Progressives of achievements such as *arrive* and *reach the summit*, unlike progressives of accomplishments, can only denote an immediate prelude to the final event. That is, it isn't true to say that Flight 34 is arriving at Gate 19 if Flight 34 is still mid-journey. On the other hand, progressives of *win* can be interpreted to mean 'lead the field', and progressive *dying* can apply to a protracted final illness.

The temporal frame reading of the progressive emphasizes the duration of an event. As with *for* adverbials which modify duration, the progressive of a semelfactive is interpreted as repetition or iteration, as in (39).

(39)a Jones was tapping the table.
   b Jones was blinking.
   c Jones was coughing.
   d The light was flashing.

9.3 ASPECTUAL SIMILARITIES BETWEEN EVENT PREDICATES AND NPs

Aspectual event classes are commonly compared to different kinds of material entity denoted by different kinds of NP. Some of the structural parallels are reviewed in this section.

9.3.1 Countability and Boundedness

The distinction between bounded and unbounded event predicates has much in common with the distinction between count and mass NPs.

A count NP such as *a dog* or *a bicycle* denotes an individual with a definite form and spatial boundary. We can identify where a dog or a bicycle is bounded in space just as we can tell, given a group of dogs or bicycles, how many there are.

Bounded events are bounded in time by the characteristics specified in their predicates. We can tell when an event described by *eat an apple* begins and ends, and if Horace eats three apples one after the other, we can tell that there are three events of the *eat an apple* kind.

Unbounded events don't have inbuilt identifying boundaries which would allow us to count them. If Jones walks along the road for some indefinite time, there is no principle for identifying a *walk along the road* event that would allow us to mark where one such event ends during his walking and the next one immediately begins. Unbounded events are like the stuff or matter denoted by mass NPs such as *sugar*, *water*, *sand* or *porridge*. These events and substances have no inherent quantity or outer form.

As we saw in Chapter 6, mass substances, being homogeneous, are internally divisible into parts of the same kind. If you take a bucket of water and fill a glass from it, the word *water* applies equally to the contents of the glass, the original contents and the remaining contents of the bucket.

The same thing applies to unbounded events. If you take a stretch of time in which Jones is asleep and divide it into smaller intervals, 'Jones is asleep' describes what holds in the original interval and in any of the smaller intervals within it. Earlier, we distinguished processes from states by making processes heterogeneous and states homogeneous. But here we see that the unboundedness of processes makes them like homogeneous substances, so they should be homogeneous. The difference is a matter of scale – at a coarse level, processes are homogeneous, but at a finer level of detail they are heterogeneous. This point is discussed further in Section 9.4 below.

Individual objects and bounded events are not divisible into subparts of the same kind in this way. If you take a bicycle apart, none of the parts is itself a bicycle, and the NP *a bicycle* denotes only the original object before dismemberment. If you take a stretch of time which exactly contains the event described by 'Jones ate an apple', no smaller interval within that time is a time containing a 'Jones ate an apple' event, because in each of the smaller intervals only part of the apple is eaten. The smaller intervals contain the process which makes up all but the final point of the whole event – this process is described by the progressive, so 'Jones is eating an apple' describes the contents of the smaller subintervals.

Although substances have no inherent bounded form or quantity, these characteristics can be added by modification. Unbounded matter (cheese, cake, bread) can be expressed as having a bounded form as in (40a–c). Similarly, basically unbounded event predicates can be modified to describe an event with a bounded form, as in (40d–f).

(40) NP – bounded form
    a a block of cheese
    b a slice of cake
    c a loaf of bread

    event predicate – bounded form
    d walk + to the corner
    e beat the eggs + to a froth
    f pull the rope + off the hook

The modifiers in (40d–f) convert unbounded event predicates to bounded event predicates by fixing an outcome which ends the event. When aspectual event classes were first proposed they were considered to classify verbs rather than verb phrases. Contrasts like that between unbounded *walk* and bounded *walk to the corner* made it clear that at least the whole verb phrase must be considered. As we shall see in Section 9.3.2 below, the subject and object can also affect the aspectual character of a whole sentence.

The matter denoted by an NP with a mass noun can also be limited by a quantity expression, as in (41a–c). The parallel kind of quantity modification for events is in (41d–f).

(41) <u>NP – quantity</u>
    a a litre of milk
    b a pound of butter
    c a ton of coal

    <u>event predicate – quantity</u>
    d run + for twenty minutes
    e live in Singapore + until November
    f watch TV + until midnight

The quantity expressions in (41a–c) must be combined with mass nouns. Any singular count noun in such a context is interpreted as its mass counterpart or is anomalous, as shown in (42).

(42)a   a pound of apple/pumpkin/tomato
        (i.e. flesh or pulp, not a whole fruit)

    b   a ton of oak
        (i.e. timber, not a whole one-ton tree)

    c # a ton of truck

The parallel effect with event predicates and adverbials is seen with *for an hour* adverbials as reviewed in Section 9.2.1 above, and other time quantity adverbials such as *until November* and *all night*. If an event predicate cannot be given an unbounded reading the combination is anomalous.

(43)a   Jones walked for an hour.
    b # Jones ate the apple for an hour.
    c   Jones worked on his book until November.
    d # Jones finished his book until November.
    e   Jones watched TV all night.
    f # Jones signed the cheque all night.

As we saw in Section 9.2.1, a bounded event predicate combined with a time quantity adverbial may be interpreted as describing an event repeated indefinitely. Although slightly bizarre, a repetitive reading is possible for (43f) in which Jones signs the cheque again and again all night. Repetition readings are discussed in the next section.

9.3.2   Mass and Indefinite Plurality

A point that was raised briefly in Section 6.2.1 is that bare plurals are like mass NPs in denoting matter without inherent outer boundaries or quantity. Bare plurals can appear with mass quantifiers and in other contexts that exclude count NPs, as shown in (44).

(44)a   a lot of coal / a lot of people
    b   a roomful of coal / a roomful of chairs
    c   a pound of cheese / a pound of walnuts

    d # a lot of chair
    e # a roomful of first generation computer
    f # a pound of carriage clock

    g   There's sand all over the floor.
    h   There are dead cockroaches all over the floor.
    i # There's tree all over the road.

The similarity between mass substances and vague plural entities is not surprising, given that nonliquid substances are commonly made up of parts which can be isolated as individuals. Word pairs like mass *foliage* and plural *leaves* or mass *gravel* and plural *pebbles* denote the same matter. An unnumbered collection of individuals has the same structure as an aggregate substance, and both lack inherent form and quantity. Given this similarity, just as a vague plurality of objects is like a substance, a vague plurality of events is unbounded.

Where a time quantity adverbial requires an unbounded event to modify, an apparently bounded event predicate can be given a plural reading. There are several ways this can happen.

First, accomplishments and achievements can be interpreted as repetitions if repetition of the event is plausible, as in (45).

(45)a   Jones read *The House of Seven Gables* for years.
    b   The light came on all night.

The repetition interpretation is the standard interpretation for semelfactives modified by time quantity adverbials, as in (46).

(46)a   Jones coughed all night.
    b   Jones clicked his pen throughout the lecture.

A vague plural event reading can also be provided without repetition of the same event, as in (47a–c), contrasted with (47d–f). The adverbials *all night* and *all afternoon* measure durations of unbounded occurrences.

(47)a   People arrived at the club all night.
   b   Jones signed letters all night.
   c   Jones pointed out popular bookshops to Horace all afternoon.

   d # Harold arrived at the club all night.
   e # Jones signed the letter all night.
   f # Jones pointed out three popular bookshops to Horace all afternoon.

In (47a–c) the bare plurals *people*, *letters* and *popular bookshops* are the key to the plural readings. Each person that arrived at the club is the protagonist of a separate arrival, each letter that Jones signed is the patient of a separate letter-signing, and so on. Sentences like these describe a series of separate events of the same kind, and the vague plurality occupies the time interval like pebbles filling a bucket.

    Finally, mass NPs can be the key to unbounded readings, as in (48e, f) below, contrasted with (48a–d).

(48)a # A rock fell on the roof all morning.
   b # Several rocks fell on the roof all morning.
   c # Jones ate an apple all morning.
   d # Jones ate several apples all morning.

   e   Sand fell on the roof all morning.
   f   Jones ate porridge all morning.

9.4 HOMOGENEITY AND HETEROGENEITY

In Chapter 6 mass substances denoted by mass NPs such as *gold* and *water* were analysed as completely homogeneous, but as we shall see in this section, homogeneity is often not absolute. Strictly speaking, many mass substances are heterogeneous but count as homogeneous – the difference is a matter of degree of detail. The same consideration applies to events.

    States and processes are both durative and unbounded, but are separated aspectually by the distinction between homogeneity and heterogeneity. States are homogeneous, because one moment of a state is like any other moment, and they have uniform interiors. Processes are heterogeneous, because they have different kinds of internal parts, such as standing on the left foot, standing on the right foot, swinging the left foot, swinging the right foot, and so on, which make up the process of walking.

    The state/process distinction is paralleled by the distinction between homogeneous mass substances such as water, air and butter, and heterogeneous mass substances such as beef stew and fruit cake. Homogeneous substances are physically uniform to ordinary examination, while heterogeneous substances have recognizable nonuniform constituents, such as lumps of beef and carrot, or nuts and pieces of fruit.

As we have seen, activities still count as unbounded, and therefore parallel to mass NPs, even though they are heterogeneous, so absolute homogeneity is not required for events to be unbounded. The same consideration applies to heterogeneous substances such as fruit cake, which are homogeneous to some extent. If you break a piece of fruit cake into three pieces, each of them is fruit cake.

The difference between absolutely homogeneous events (states) and heterogeneous unbounded events (processes) can create difficulties for logical definitions of time quantity adverbials.

The time quantity adverbials which modify unbounded events have a universal quantificational character, as illustrated in (49), where *for three hours* is a time quantity adverbial, in contrast with *during the night*, which does not measure event time. (Time adverbials with universal quantificational readings are also discussed in Section 7.7.2.)

(49)a Jones snored during the night.
    b $\exists t$ (DURING (t, the night) & t<now & SNORE(j) at t)
      For some past time or times during the night, Jones snored at those times.
    c Jones snored for three hours.
    d $\exists t$ (t<now & THREE HOURS(t) & $\forall t'$(IN(t',t) → SNORE(j) at t'))
      There is a past time t which is three hours, such that for every time t' which is in t, Jones snored at t'

Universal quantification in (49d) is used to express the fact that the three-hour interval is understood to be the whole extent of the event, and Jones's continuous snoring filled up that time, or occurred at every moment in it. This contrasts with the existential reading of (49a), in which the night simply contains some times at which Jones snored.

As the definition is stated in (49d) there is no limit on how small a time can be sampled from the interval. Even the smallest moment within the interval must be a time of Jones snoring for 'Jones snored for three hours' to be true. But strictly speaking, this isn't possible, because snoring coincides with inhaling or exhaling, and we pause for some seconds between breaths. There are short periods in which no snoring is going on. It can be argued that the definition also doesn't work for 'Jones walked for hours', even if Jones is in continuous motion. If we cut up an event of walking quite finely we come up with subintervals that contain a single step or half step, which isn't enough to qualify as an instance of walking.

The proposal that mass substances are divisible into parts of the same kind runs into the same problem. A piece of fruit cake can be completely crumbled up to release nuts and pieces of dried fruit, which are not described by the predicate *cake*. You can cut a piece of fruit cake into smaller pieces of fruit cake, but this process of division cannot continue indefinitely.

The upshot is that mass substances have to be divided into smaller quantities on a scale which takes into account what kind of substance you are dealing with. At the coarse end of the scale, a warehouseful of furniture can be divided down to individual pieces of furniture, which are still quite large and still describable as furniture, but as soon as you start smashing up chairs and tables it is doubtful that the pieces of wood, metal, plastic and fabric that result from this can still count as furniture.

In the same way, processes have to be divided into subintervals on a scale that varies with the kind of process under consideration. The process of drinking a cup of coffee presumably needs to be divided into large enough chunks to contain some actual coffee-drinking, given the usual scenario of sitting over a cup of coffee while taking occasional sips. The definition in (49d) can stand so long as a pragmatic condition on the size of t' is included.

9.5   CLOSING COMMENT

Aspectual distinctions among event predicates first came to the attention of philosophers because of the different ways verbal aspect and tense are interpreted in combination with different event predicates. In particular, the goal of giving a simple uniform logical analysis for the present tense or for the progressive aspect or perfect aspect was made much more complicated by this apparent variety of interpretations. For these reasons the aspectual classification of events or event predicates has been of considerable interest in logic.

However, the aspectual classes themselves resist precise logical analysis. Parsons (see references below) represents boundedness in his Neodavidsonian theory, but there is no generally adopted way of representing all the characteristics of event classes in logic-based semantic representations.

It is likely that the four classes presented here are not essential to linguistic theory, and are just convenient shorthand for easily identifiable combinations of aspectual characteristics. The classifying features of boundedness, duration and change are the essential notions for analysing certain syntactic and semantic effects.

A similar reduction currently applies to the traditional thematic roles, as discussed in the next chapter: the roles themselves are probably not linguistically significant, except as abbreviations for clusters of more basic component properties. Nevertheless, with the proviso that they are subject to more detailed analysis, both aspectual event classes and thematic roles continue to be useful guides to thinking about linguistic phenomena.

EXERCISES

(A)   Review of Event Classes

Using the linguistic tests in Section 9.2, classify the sentences below as reporting accomplishments, achievements, states, processes or semelfactive events, and decide whether the events are singular or plural.

(1)   The door creaked open.
(2)   Sam got the joke about three minutes later.
(3)   Jerry is a great talker.
(4)   Elsa chewed her way through half a goat.
(5)   Liam picked at his food.
(6)   The cheese was rancid.
(7)   James read some of his strange poems.
(8)   A soft light shone on the hills.
(9)   Max pulled out a gun.
(10)   Donald heated the solution.
(11)   Donald heated the solution to 70 degrees.
(12)   Tim doodled on the tablecloth.
(13)   A strange mushroom appeared on the lawn.
(14)   Strange mushrooms appeared on the lawn.
(15)   A shabby warehouse complex came into view.
(16)   Anna was cracking nuts.
(17)   Anna cracked nuts with a hammer.
(18)   Macbeth became king.
(19)   Jones won the election.
(20)   People moved away.

(B)   *For* Adverbials

Some of the sentences below cannot be given a sensible reading. Which are the anomalous sentences, and what is the problem they have in common?

(1)   Jones found his keys for ten minutes.
(2)   Jones discovered new recipes for years.
(3)   Jones discovered the joy of cooking for years.
(4)   Jones thumped the TV for hours.
(5)   Jones walked to the corner for several hours.
(6)   Jones photographed the view for years.
(7)   Jones solved the mystery for weeks.
(8)   Jones turned the corner for 30 seconds.

(C)   Time Adverbials

As outlined in Sections 7.7.2 and 9.4, a time quantity adverbial can be analysed as a kind of universal quantifier. The force of the quantification is that an unbounded event occupies every part of the stated interval, as in *Jones walked for three hours*, which describes three hours of continuous walking. A bounded event predicate with a time quantity adverbial must be interpreted as a series of events filling the interval. If a plural event reading isn't possible a sentence with a bounded event predicate is anomalous, as in *Jones broke that pot for days*.

Other time adverbials have an existential reading – there is a time (or there are some times) in the stated interval at which the event occurs, but the event does not necessarily fill the interval.

Sort the adverbials listed in (1) into universal and existential interpretations. Use the test sentences in (2).

(1)   for a week, on Monday, since three o'clock, last week, until midnight, during the film, in May, all day, at night.

(2)   <u>unbounded</u>
    a   The light was/will be on.
    b   The radiator rumbled/will rumble.

    <u>bounded</u>
    c   The radiator broke down/will break down.
    d   That radiator exploded/will explode.

(D)   *For* Adverbials

Using the analysis in Section 9.4, write formulae for the sentences below.

(1)   Jones was rich for ten years.
(2)   Bill dithered for months.

Now consider the scopal ambiguity in (3) below.

(3)   For many years the emperor lived in luxury.

Construct formulae for both readings of (3).

(E)   Place Adverbials

Just as time quantity adverbials denote intervals which are filled by unbounded events, some place adverbials denote places filled by substances or by events which are spatially extended, for example:

(1) There's mud all over the floor.
(2) The combatants rolled all over the floor.
(3) There's heavy fog throughout the state.
(4) The war raged throughout the state.

Use variables l to represent locations or places and use $AT(e, l)$ to express 'e occupies location l'. Write formulae for (2) and (4).

The ambiguity of *For many years the emperor lived in luxury* in Exercise D is similar to a scopal ambiguity in (5) below. Write formulae for both readings of (5).

(5) Throughout the state the local newspaper is successful.

FURTHER READING

Early discussions of event classes are in Kenny (1963: Chapter 8) and Vendler (1967: Chapter 4). Dowty (1979: 51–71) reviews the event classes with many examples.

Parsons (1990: Chapter 9) gives an accessible discussion of the interpretation of the progressive with different event predicates. Dowty (1977) outlines a logical analysis of the progressive.

Van Voorst (1992) discusses the aspectual classification of psychological verbs according to the tests, with a wide range of data.

Jackendoff (1991) develops an analysis of the conceptual structure components which underlie boundedness and plurality in the concepts of both matter and events.

10 Thematic Roles Reviewed

Chapter 8 introduced a basic list of traditional thematic roles (agent, patient, theme, source, goal, recipient, instrument, benefactive, stimulus and experiencer) as simple labels for the ways entities are involved in or related to eventualities. This chapter outlines some of the key revisions in the theory of thematic roles that have emerged in more recent research.

10.1 THEMATIC ROLES, ARGUMENTS AND ADVERBIALS

As we saw in Section 8.3.2, thematic role theory originally applied to the interpretation of any NP in a sentence, according to its position in the sentence, its case form, or the preposition, if any, preceding the NP. The classification applied without distinction to arguments of the verb and to NPs in adverbial expressions. In addition to the adverbial-like role of instrument, thematic roles might in principle also be proposed for a wide range of adverbials, including those in (1) below from Blake (1930), cited by Dowty (1991: 548, fn. 3)).

(1)a additional role
       He gave him a sum of money <u>besides the cattle</u>.

   b substitutive role
       He gave me promises <u>instead of money</u>.

   c similative role
       He barked <u>like a dog</u>.

More recently, the narrower focus on verb arguments came from the use of thematic roles in syntactic theory to explain patterns in the syntax of verbs, which appear to be determined by verb meaning. Thematic roles came to be seen as part of, and determined by, the meaning of verbs, and assigned by verbs to their arguments.

If thematic roles are identified as roles assigned by verbs to their arguments, it seems to follow that thematic roles are assigned *only* to arguments, not to adverbials. One very strong expression of this view is the theory of theta roles and the theta criterion in Chomsky's (1981) influential Government and Binding (GB) theory of syntax.

The **theta roles** of GB theory combine two different properties of arguments, obligatoriness and thematic interpretation. For example, the verb *give* takes three arguments as indicated in (2a) below. Suppose that these arguments are assigned the thematic roles of agent, theme and goal, as listed in (2b). The extra move made in theta role theory was to combine these two characteristics in a verb's entry in the lexicon, as in (2c), so that the roles are fused with the argument places which mark the adicity of the verb.

(2)a GIVE (x, y, z)
  b agent, theme, goal
  c *give* < agent, theme, goal >

The identification of thematic role bearers with obligatory arguments is made explicit in the **theta criterion**, stated in a simplified form in (3).

(3)a Each theta role is assigned to exactly one NP.
  b Each NP receives exactly one theta role.

This principle states the familiar rule that a predicate must appear with exactly the right number of arguments to make a well-formed sentence or proposition – in other words, the adicity of a predicate must be satisfied. The extra move made here is to identify obligatory argument positions as thematic relations – the upshot is that bearers of thematic relations are obligatory.

It soon became clear that the early formulation of theta theory as outlined here was too condensed. In current theories of the lexicon, thematic or interpretive information about a verb is generally given separately from information about its syntactic adicity. For example, the entry for the verb *punch* would state that *punch* takes an agent and a patient, and also that *punch* takes a subject and direct object, which may be marked as obligatory. In addition, **linking** in the lexical entry establishes that the agent is realized as the subject, and the patient is realized as the object.

The focus remains on thematic roles as classes of arguments to verbs, rather than interpretation classes of sentence NPs in general. However, discussion of thematic roles often includes expressions which are not obligatory in the sentence, although they otherwise appear to be arguments of the verb. This commonly arises with **argument alternation**, also called **verbal diathesis**, as illustrated in (4).

(4)a Adam sprinkled glitter on the tree.
  b Adam sprinkled the tree with glitter.
  c Adam sprinkled the tree.

  d Jones cleared the table of papers.
  e Jones cleared papers from the table.
  f Jones cleared the table.

  g Louis served the quiche to the guests.
  h Louis served the guests with the quiche.

i   Louis served the quiche.
j   Louis served the guests.

The NP *glitter* is the direct object in (4a) and is assumed to be an argument. In (4b) *glitter* appears after the preposition *with*, and can be omitted as in (4c), so in (4b) *glitter* seems not to be an argument. But (4a) and (4b) have similar meanings and seem to contain the same verb *sprinkle,* with the same arguments, so the status of *glitter* in (4b) is marginal – it is argument-like but not obligatory. Similar patterns are found in the other examples in (4).

10.2   THEMATIC ROLES ARE NOT PRIMITIVES

The **primitive terms** of a theory are the theoretical terms which cannot be further analysed, or defined in terms of more simple notions – primitives have to be taken as unanalysed wholes.

Most of the thematic role labels have been used as if they were primitive terms, partly because they are very difficult to define, particularly in logical or truth conditional terms. The chief exceptions are the notions of agentivity and patienthood, which have long been analysed in considerable detail as clusters of properties. Agentivity and patienthood are important concepts in theories of the syntax of transitive and intransitive verbs, quite independently of a wider theory of thematic roles. Agentivity and patienthood will be discussed further in Sections 10.3 and 10.4.

For most thematic roles, the difficulty of defining role labels has been compounded by a lack of agreement on what labels there are, and given a particular sentence, what roles are borne by the NPs in it. Nevertheless, it has long been clear that thematic roles are not primitives, and that the information they contribute to the meaning of a sentence can be represented in more detail. This requires a subatomic analysis, resembling in some ways the Neodavidsonian representations introduced in Chapter 8, but breaking down the meaning of the verb itself to a greater extent.

10.2.1   An Alternative Subatomic Analysis

Recall that a Neodavidsonian representation decomposes the verb into a simple predicate on the event and the separate thematic relations to the event, as in (5) below.

(5)a   Jones killed Stimson.
   b $\exists e\,(KILL\,(e)\ \&\ AGENT\,(j,\ e)\ \&\ THEME\,(s,\ e))$

An alternative representation for *Jones killed Stimson* breaks the verb *kill* down into smaller components more closely corresponding to subevents –

parts of the whole event – in such a way that the relations of the arguments to the killing event are expanded, as in (6).

(6)a [DO(j)] CAUSE [BECOME [NOT ALIVE(s)]]]
  b A DOing by Jones causes it to BECOME the case that Stimson is NOT ALIVE.

The verb *kill* is broken down into the components DO, CAUSE, BECOME, NOT and ALIVE, arranged in a framework with positions for two entities, here Jones and Stimson.

The component predicates such as DO and CAUSE are elements of sublexical analysis, and are not the same as the meanings of the corresponding English words, *do*, *cause*, and so on. Perhaps the most important difference here is the mismatch between CAUSE and *cause*. The verb *cause* can be used for any type of causation, including **direct or manipulative causation** and **indirect or influential causation**. If Jones breaks a pot by striking it with a hammer, then he directly causes the pot to break, and we can say 'Jones broke the pot'. *Break* in this sentence is a causative verb, containing the direct causation predicate CAUSE. But if Jones bumps into Stimson who is carrying the pot, making Stimson drop the pot on the floor and break it, then Jones indirectly causes the pot to break. In this case we can say 'Jones caused the pot to get broken' or 'Jones caused Stimson to break the pot', but we can't say 'Jones broke the pot'. In short, the predicate CAUSE expresses direct causation, and the event [DO(x)] which is the first argument of CAUSE in (6) is a directly causative action.

10.2.2 Defining Thematic Roles

The information that Jones is the agent and that Stimson is the theme is represented in (6a) by characteristic parts of the formula, called **schemata**. The **schema** in (7a) shows that the agent is the first argument of DO. A change of state theme is the argument which comes to be in a state, as in the schema in (7b).

(7)a agent = x: DO [x, ..]
  b change of state theme = y: BECOME [STATE (y)]

A sentence expressing movement to a location can be analysed as in (8), with the GO predicate.

(8)a Jones pushed the wheelbarrow to the wall.
  b [DO PUSH (j, the wheelbarrow)] CAUSE [GO (the wheelbarrow, [AT (the wheelbarrow, the wall)])]

According to (8b) Jones does something, further specified as pushing the wheelbarrow, which directly causes the wheelbarrow to go to be at the wall. The theme of movement is generally defined by the schema in (9a) and the goal is defined in (9b).

(9)a   theme of movement = y: GO (y, [AT (y,z)])
   b   goal = z: GO (y, [AT (y,z)])

The patient role can be defined for now as the second argument of the DO predicate, as in (10).

(10)a   Jones patted Fido.
    b   DO PAT (j, f)
    c   patient = y: DO (x, y)

Taken together, (8b), (9a) and (10c) show that the wheelbarrow in 'Jones pushed the wheelbarrow to the wall' has both patient and theme of movement properties, because Jones pushes it and also moves it to another location. In 'Jones pushed the wheelbarrow (but it didn't budge)' the wheelbarrow has only the patient role. This overlap between theme and patient has been a target of criticism in the literature on thematic roles, because it isn't clear how the two roles are to be distinguished. As we shall see presently, these roles overlap because they operate in different systems.

10.2.3   Defining Verb Classes

The version of thematic roles theory used here assumes that roles are generalized. In other words, a role such as theme can be identified in a wide range of sentences with different verbs, in contrast with particularized roles which are defined for particular verbs. In a particularized role system the role of the lake in 'The lake froze' is theme$_{freeze}$, the role of the butter in 'The butter melted' is theme$_{melt}$, and they are not the same role. A theory of generalized roles entails that there are general verb classes, such as the class of all verbs that take an agent and a theme, or the class of all verbs that take an experiencer and a stimulus, and so on. These verb classes can also be defined by the generalized definition schemata which represent the content of roles. Some of these classes are illustrated below.

(11)   Inchoative (verbs of becoming)
        BECOME [STATE (y)]

    a   The lake froze.
        BECOME [FROZEN (the lake)]

    b   The butter melted.
        BECOME [MELTED (the butter)]

   c The pot broke.
      BECOME [BROKEN (the pot)]

(12) Agentive verbs (verbs of doing)
     DO (x)

   a Jones laughed.
      DO LAUGH (j)

   b Jones chewed the string.
      DO CHEW (j, the string)

   c Jones walked.
      DO WALK (j)

   d Jones broke the pot.
      [DO (j, the pot)] CAUSE [BECOME [BROKEN (the pot)]]

(13) Agentive causative
     [DO (x)] CAUSE [. . .]

   a Jones broke the pot.
      [DO (j, the pot] CAUSE [BECOME [BROKEN(the pot)]])

   b Jones dragged Fido outside.
      [DO DRAG (j, f)] CAUSE [GO (f, [AT (f, outside)])]

   c André levelled the parterre.
      [DO (a, the parterre)] CAUSE [BECOME [LEVEL (the parterre)]]

(14) Non-agentive causative
     CAUSE (x, [BECOME [STATE(y)]]

   a The sun melted the icecream.
      CAUSE (the sun, [BECOME [MELTED (the icecream)]])
   b The storm broke the window.
      CAUSE (the storm, [BECOME [BROKEN (the window)]])

(15) Stative verbs
     STATE (x)

   a Lisa is tall.
      TALL (l)
   b The pie is cold.
      COLD (the pie)

Note that the verbs in (12) and (13) show that agentive verbs can differ in whether or not they actually describe the action of the agent. In (12a–c) and

(13b) the DO predicate is modified to specify the nature of the agent's action, but in (12d), (13a) and (13c) the verb only describes the endstate of the theme, and DO stands for some unspecified action of the agent.

The representations in (14) are intended to show that sun melts icecream and storms break windows through their inherent properties, and not by performing causative actions. These kinds of causers, distinct from agents, are often called natural forces. Differences between (13) and (14) will be raised again in Sections 10.3 and 10.4 below.

10.2.4 Signs of Aspectual Event Classes

Analyses of the kind shown here also reveal aspectual properties of predicates. The unbounded eventualities, states and activities, have the simplest representations, as in (16).

(16)a   Jones laughed.   activity (agentive)
        DO LAUGH (j)

   b   The wind blew.   activity (non-agentive)
        BLOW (the wind)

   c   Maria is tall.   state
        TALL (m)

   d   Fido is outside.   state
        AT (f, outside)

The change of state found in achievements and many accomplishments is represented by the BECOME predicate. Accomplishments are distinguished from achievements by the presence of a process stage, shown in (17b) as 'DO BUILD (j)]' and (17c) as 'BURN (the wood)]'.

(17)a   Jones noticed the mark.
        BECOME [AWARE (j, the mark)]

   b   Jones built a house.
        [DO BUILD (j)] CAUSE [BECOME [BE (a house)]]

   c   The wood burned to ash.
        [BURN (the wood)] CAUSE [BECOME [ASH (the wood)]]

The clause which is the argument of BECOME marks the endstate of an achievement. The clause which is the argument of BECOME or the second argument of GO marks the endstate or location which bounds an accomplishment. The endstates in (17) are 'AWARE (j, the mark)', 'BE (a house)' and 'ASH (the wood)'. The endstate with a motion accomplishment is the final location of the theme, shown in (18) as 'AT (f, outside)'.

(18)a   Jones pushed Fido outside.
   b   [DO PUSH (j,f)] CAUSE [GO (f, [AT(f, outside)])]

Some inchoative verbs can be interpreted as predicates of accomplishments, with both a durative process and an endstate, or they can be interpreted as predicates on events idealized to a simple transition, in which case they are achievements. For example, *The lake froze* is represented as an accomplishment in (19a), with a separate clause for the freezing process, and as an achievement in (19b), repeated from (11a) above.

(19)a   The lake froze.   (accomplishment)
      [FREEZE (the lake)] CAUSE [BECOME [FROZEN (the lake)]]

   b   The lake froze.   (achievement)
      BECOME [FROZEN (the lake)]

10.2.5   Aspect and Types of Thematic Role

The subatomic analyses presented here, using schemata of the same kind to characterize both thematic roles and aspectual classes, invite comparisons between the two ways of classifying events, by their typical thematic roles and their aspectual structure. Such comparison reveals that not all basic roles are of equal significance in aspectual terms – in fact the key aspectual role is theme, and goal is aspectual if it is present.

The schemata repeated in (20a,b) below show that the predicate BECOME identifies both the change-of-state theme role and the inchoative verbs which take change-of-state themes. The endstate clause with an inchoative, '[STATE (y)]' identifies the final state of the theme, which is the bound of the event.

(20)a   inchoative   BECOME [STATE (y)]
   b   theme of change = y: BECOME [STATE (y)]

The GO schema in (21) below identifies the theme of movement and the goal. The endstate of the theme being at the goal, expressed in the endstate clause '[AT (y, z)]', is the final bound of the event. In (21c) *to the wall* is a goal phrase in traditional thematic role theory, and *outside* in (21d) might also be classified as a goal.

(21)a   theme of movement = y: GO (y, [AT(y, z)])

   b   goal = z: GO (y, [AT(y, z)])

   c   Jones pushed the wheelbarrow to the wall.
      [DO PUSH (j, the wheelbarrow)] CAUSE [GO (the wheelbarrow, [AT (the wheelbarrow, the wall)])]

    d   Jones pushed Fido outside.
       [DO PUSH (j, f)] CAUSE [GO (f,[AT(f, outside)])]

In contrast to theme and goal, the agent role is not associated with either boundedness or unboundedness, as shown by the range of contexts for agentive DO in the examples repeated below.

(22)   <u>bounded event</u>:
     a   André levelled the parterre.
       [DO (a, the parterre)] CAUSE [BECOME [LEVEL (the parterre)]]

     <u>unbounded event</u>:
     b   Jones laughed.
       DO LAUGH (j)

     c   Jones chewed the string.
       DO CHEW (j, the string)

The only aspectual significance claimed for the agent role, as reviewed in Chapter 9, is the common observation that states and perhaps achievements are non-agentive. Although this is a common tendency, we will see in Section 10.3.1 below that states may be agentive. In fact, the agent role has no clear aspectual correlation, unlike the theme and goal roles. There are two kinds of thematic role, only one kind being positively associated with aspect.

On different grounds, Jackendoff (1987) also separates the traditional thematic roles into two groups. Apart from agent, patient, stimulus and experiencer, the roles in the traditional inventory are largely based on a *spatial* mapping of the event, centred on the image of a theme of movement moving from a source to a goal. The source, theme and goal type of role inventory characterize what is sometimes called a **localist theory of thematic roles**, where the roles are based on positions and movements in physical or metaphorical space. In Jackendoff's revision roles of this sort form the **thematic tier**, also called the **event tier**. Aspectually significant roles fall in the event tier. The actor role, incorporating the traditional agent, and the patient role constitute the **action tier**. Roles from the two tiers can coincide in the same argument, as illustrated in (23).

(23)a <u>Laura</u> gave <u>the photograph</u> to <u>Donna</u>.
      actor   patient
      source   theme   goal

    b <u>Donna</u> took <u>a book</u> from <u>the shelf</u>.
      actor   patient
      goal   theme   source

The actor/agent and patient roles are explored further in Sections 10.3 and 10.4. The action tier expresses the origin or centre of dynamism in the event, proceeding from the actor and directed towards the patient, if there is one.

The thematic or event tier, previously conceptualized in terms of physical space, is reanalysed by some writers as primarily aspectual, based on the unfolding and culmination of an event in time. So, for example, the key property of a goal phrase is not so much that an entity moves to the goal in space, but that the state of a moved entity being at the goal bounds the event in time. The aspectual nature of themes is further illustrated in section 10.5.

10.3   AGENTIVITY

The traditional tests for agentivity target different properties of supposed agents which do not always coincide. Real agents in the philosophical sense are identified by volition and control, the target properties for the tests to be reviewed in Section 10.3.1 below. Other candidates for linguistic agentivity are identified by the broader tests reviewed in Sections 10.3.2 and 10.3.3.

10.3.1   Volition and Control

Most of the tests that were used to demonstrate agentivity in Section 9.2.3 pick out conscious and deliberate action, most obviously the adverb *deliberately* and other adverbs such as *carefully* and *conscientiously*. Similar tests are the *persuade* context and the imperative voice. Examples of these tests from section 9.2.3 are repeated below.

(24) *persuade* contexts
    a   Jones persuaded him to eat the pie.
    b   They persuaded Jones to build a barn.
    c   Jones persuaded Mike to walk to town.
    d   Jones persuaded Tina to walk in the park.
    e   Jones persuaded the group members to chat.
    f   Dino persuaded Jones to push a supermarket trolley.
    g # Jones persuaded the couple to be happy.
    h # Lucas persuaded Jones to understand chaos theory.
    i # Jones was persuaded to hear the trucks coming.
    j # Jones was persuaded to notice the marks on the wallpaper.
    k # Jones was persuaded to recognize the woman in the doorway.
    l # Jones was persuaded to turn fifty.

(25) agentive adverbs
    a   Jones deliberately ate the pie.
    b   Jones built the barn carefully.

c   Mike deliberately walked to town.
d   Tina deliberately walked in the park.
e   The group members chatted conscientiously.
f   Jones conscientiously pushed the supermarket trolley.
g   # The couple were happy deliberately.
h   # Jones deliberately understood chaos theory.
i   # Jones carefully heard the trucks coming.
j   # Jones deliberately noticed the marks on the wallpaper.
k   # Jones carefully recognized the woman in the doorway.
l   # Jones conscientiously turned fifty.

(26)   imperative voice
a   Eat the pie!
b   Build a barn!
c   Walk to town!
d   Walk in the park!
e   Chat among yourselves!
f   Push the trolley!
g   # Be happy!
h   # Understand chaos theory!
i   # Hear the trucks coming!
j   # Notice the marks on the wallpaper!
k   # Recognize the woman in the doorway!
l   # Turn fifty!

The fourth test used in Chapter 9, the *what x did* test, through the general verb *do* picks up doings or performances in general, but doesn't specifically target the contribution of consciousness or will, as we shall see in Sections 10.3.2 and 10.3.3.

(27)   *what x did* context
a   What Jones did was eat the pie.
b   What Jones did was build a barn.
c   What Mike did was walk to town.
d   What Tina did was walk in the park.
e   What the group members did was chat among themselves.
f   What Jones did was push a supermarket trolley.
g   # What the couple did was be happy/be rich.
h   # What Jones did was understand chaos theory.
i   # What Jones did was hear the trucks coming.
j   # What Jones did was notice the marks on the wallpaper.
k   # What Jones did was recognize the woman in the doorway.
l   # What Jones did was turn fifty.

The examples in (24)–(27) were selected to illustrate the correlation between agentivity and aspectual event class. Although the reason is unclear, generally achievements and states are non-agentive, though accomplishments and processes frequently are agentive. In fact, things are a little more complicated than this.

States can be agentive if they contain the key agent properties of volition, or willingness, and control of one's participation in a state, even where no action at all is reported. This is illustrated in (28).

(28)a What you must do is be absent that day.
   b He persuaded me to be absent that day.
   c I was deliberately absent that day.
   d # He's being absent today.
   e What you must do is be ready.
   f Jones persuaded us to be ready.
   g We were ready deliberately.
   h # They are being ready right now.

Examples (28d,h) are included to show that *be absent* and *be ready* are not interpreted here as agentive *be* processes of behaviour such as *be nice*, *be noisy* and *be quiet*, which take the progressive form.

The presence of a human subject can lend an agentive interpretation to a wide range of predicates, and many predicates cannot be classed in isolation as either agentive or non-agentive. For example, the temporary state predicate *lie* in (29) below is interpreted as agentive or non-agentive according to the subject, though otherwise the meaning is the same.

(29)a What Jones is doing is lying on the floor.
   b # What the newspaper is doing is lying on the floor.

Prototypical agents combine volition and conscious control of the action with physical action or force, often action or force directed at or affecting another entity. Action or force in the absence of consciousness or volition characterizes lower ranking agents which are commonly inanimate.

Both canonical volition and control agents and lower ranking agents can be identified by tests which exploit the vague thematic content of the general verbs *do* and *happen*, as in the contexts illustrated in (30)–(36). Briefly, the subject of *do* is an agent and the object of *happen to* or *do to* is a patient.

(30) Brutus killed Caesar.

(31)a What Brutus did was kill Caesar.
   b # What Caesar did was Brutus killed him.

(32)a   Brutus killed Caesar, therefore Brutus did something.
    b # Brutus killed Caesar, therefore Caesar did something.

(33)a   What happened to Caesar was that Brutus killed him.
    b # What happened to Brutus was that he killed Caesar.

(34)a   Brutus killed Caesar, therefore something happened to Caesar.
    b # Brutus killed Caesar, therefore something happened to Brutus.

(35)a   Brutus did something to Caesar.
    b   What Brutus did to Caesar was that he killed him.

(36)a   What did Brutus do? He killed Caesar.
    b # What did Caesar do? Brutus killed him.
    c # What happened to Brutus? He killed Caesar.
    d   What happened to Caesar? Brutus killed him.

These tests are used to illustrate the discussion in the next section. Note that the DO predicate in the representations in Section 10.2 expresses the volitional agentivity demonstrated here. The quasi-agents discussed in the next two sections are represented in Section 10.2 with the CAUSE predicate rather than DO.

10.3.2   Inanimate Forces

Much of the discussion in this section and the next section is based on Cruse (1973), although I have reinterpreted some of his examples. The first kind of inanimate force is a natural force such as a storm or wind, illustrated in (37).

(37)a   The wind opened the door.
    b   What the wind did was open the door.
    c   The wind did something to the door.
    d # What happened to the wind was that it opened the door.
    e   What happened to the door was the wind opened it.
    f ? The wind opened the door therefore the wind did something.

Inanimate forces are also found in machines which work under their own power, unlike tools which are directly manipulated.

(38)a   This machine stamps holes in the uppers.
    b   What this machine does is stamp holes in the uppers.
    c   This machine does something to the uppers.
    d # What happens to this machine is it stamps holes in the uppers.
    e   What happens to the uppers here is this machine stamps holes in them.

A second kind of inanimate force with agent-like properties is a projectile, as in (39).

(39)a   The stone broke the window.
   b   What the stone did was break the window.
   c   The bullet smashed John's collar-bone.
   d   What the bullet did was smash John's collar-bone.

Projectile force distinguishes a flying stone or a thrown hammer from an instrument being directly manipulated by an agent. The difference is illustrated in the following examples, where a projectile has agent properties but an instrument does not.

(40)a   John broke the window with the hammer...
      # The hammer did something to the window.
      # What the hammer did was break the window.

   b   As a result of the explosion, a stone flew across the road and broke the window.
      The stone did something to the window.
      What the stone did was break the window.

On the other hand, a projectile does not have the autonomy of a natural force. This contrast shows up in the examples below, where *itself* can only appear with autonomous forces. Assume that the stone in (41e) and the hammer in (41f) are thrown projectiles.

(41)a   The fire spread itself rapidly through the building.
   b   The sea, by eating away the shore, inches itself closer to the village.
   c   The waves dashed themselves against the rocks.
   d   The wind flung itself down the valley.
   e   # The stone smashed itself through the window.
      (The stone smashed through the window.)
   f   # The hammer crashed itself against the wall.
      (The hammer crashed against the wall.)

10.3.3 Inherent Causal Properties

The *do* test is also sensitive to the interplay of forces in a state such as that in (42) below. (42a,b) are taken from Cruse.

(42)a   What these columns do is support the weight of the pediment.
   b   # What happens to these columns is that they support the weight of the pediment.
   c   Those columns don't do anything, they're just ornamental.

In (42a) the columns resist the gravitational pull on the pediment by their strength, derived from their design and construction. This may be the same kind of agentivity as the quasi-agentivity based on the inherent design or construction of instruments, found in examples such as those in (43).

(43)a   The key opened the door.
   b   What does this key do? It opens the cellar door.
   c   What this key does is open the cellar door.
   d   What does this doohickey do? It gets the cores out of apples / You core apples with it.
   e   I tried that thing out and it cored the apples quite well.
   f   What does this thing do? It crushes garlic / You crush garlic with it.
   g   I used that gizmo and it crushed the garlic OK.
   h   What does this pen do? It writes on glass.

The examples in (43) attribute some kind of agentivity to an instrument which fulfils the function it was specifically designed for, or enables the user to carry out that purpose. This kind of agentivity may depend to some extent on the degree of specialization in the design of the instrument. If an instrument is not designed for a specific purpose it cannot be the subject of a predicate describing that purpose. A well-known example of this is that it seems to be impossible to express implements like spoons and forks as instrument-agents, as shown in (44).

(44)a   Gina ladled the gnocchi out with a spoon.
   b # The spoon ladled the gnocchi out.
   c # What that spoon does is ladle pasta.
   d   Gina stirred the soup with a spoon.
   e # The spoon stirred the soup.
   f # What that spoon does is stir soup.

Note that where the agent-instrument is expressed as the subject of a sentence the predicate must describe the design-related purpose of the instrument, not the action performed by the user, as shown in (45).

(45)a   Tom channelled the wine into the bottle with a funnel.
   b   The funnel channelled the wine into the bottle.
   c   Tom poured the wine into the bottle with a funnel.
   d # The funnel poured the wine into the bottle.
   e   Tom pricked the onions with a fork.
   f   The fork pricked the onions.
   g   Tom ate the onions with a fork.
   h # The fork ate the onions.

The best prototype of instrument-agent seems to be a key, as in *The key opened the door*. More than most instruments or tools, a key is designed for a specific purpose (that is, to open a particular lock) in such a way that it is very difficult to open a lock without the right key. The key significantly enables the door-opening event to proceed, and the predicate *open the door* applies naturally to a key which fits the lock in the door.

Objects may also have unintended inherent properties in their design or construction, which support the use of *do* in examples like those below. (These examples are also from Cruse.)

(46)a   Why does the door do that?
        What?
        Fly open every time the wind blows.

   b   Why does the vase do that?
        What?
        Keep falling off the shelf.

The questions here with *do* suggest that the door flies open repeatedly because of some property of the door, such as a faulty latch, and the vase falls off the shelf because it is inherently unstable in some way. The quasi-agentive interpretation is not sufficiently agentive to support the *do something* replacement, as in (47a, d) below. Example (47c) shows that *the door* in *The door kept flying open every time the wind blew* can also have a patient reading, and similarly for *the vase* in (47f).

(47)a ? The door kept flying open every time the wind blew, therefore the door did something / kept doing something.
   b   What the door did was keep flying open every time the wind blew.
   c   What happened to the door was it kept flying open every time the wind blew.
   d ? The vase kept falling off the shelf, therefore the vase did something/kept doing something.
   e   What the vase did was keep falling off the shelf.
   f   What happened to the vase was that it kept falling off the shelf.

In summary, variants of the *do* test are sensitive to a range of types of linguistic agentivity, characterized by different criterial properties. The highest ranking agents are conscious, deliberate, controlling performers of their deeds. These agents must be animate. Volition alone may be sufficient to make an event with a human protagonist agentive, as in 'What John is doing is lying on the floor'. Natural forces are seen to act through their own autonomous force but have no control or volition. Projectiles have force which powers the events in which they are the actors, but projectile force isn't autonomous. Instruments and artefacts can have quasi-agentivity attributed to them in the states of affairs or events they are designed to bring about or be used in, so long as their design is sufficiently specific to the task.

A final property which is considered to be weakly agent-like is movement relative to another entity, as illustrated in (48). In these data, the possibility of an argument appearing in the subject position, alone or in a coordinated NP with *and*, is taken to be a sign of some degree of agentivity.

(48)a   The truck collided with the lamppost.
   b # The lamppost collided with the truck.
   c # The truck and the lamppost collided.
   d   The truck collided with the bus.
   e   The bus collided with the truck.
   f   The truck and the bus collided.
   g   The ship collided with the iceberg.
   h   The iceberg collided with the ship.
   i   The ship and the iceberg collided.

Only *the truck* can be the subject or included in the subject of *collide* in (48a–c) because the truck moves while the lamppost is stationary. (48d–i) show that where a collision involves two moving objects, both NPs can be the subject or included in the subject of *collide*, even though only the ship has powered movement in (48g–i).

10.4   THE ACTOR/PATIENT DIVISION

Agentivity is not a simple unified property, but a cluster of properties which characterize different kinds of agentivity. Some of the factors which have been identified as contributing to agentivity are listed in approximate rank in (49), beginning with the strongest indicators of agentivity.

(49)   <u>animate only</u>
- volition – voluntary involvement in an event or state
- control over involvement in an event or state
- wilful initiator or instigator of an event
- consciousness, sentience, perception (cf. experiencer)

<u>animate or inanimate</u>
- initiator, instigator or causer of an event or state
- source of force directed at or against another entity
- entity which moves, coming into contact with another entity which is stationary

- entity which moves in a stationary background, or relative to another entity which is stationary

For many writers the term *agent* can apply only if properties in the animate set are present. The whole set of properties in (49) more accurately identifies what is called the super-role or **macrorole of Actor**, including true agents.

A **Patient macrorole** is also identified by a range of properties. Component factors in the Patient macrorole have not been so extensively discussed, apart from various kinds of theme which are included in it. A provisional list of suggested Patient properties is given in (50), with themes at the highest rank.

(50)   theme
- change of state to an endpoint in the event; total change of state
- movement to a stated endpoint location
- change of state in the event, not necessarily to an endpoint
- 'affectedness': affected or altered in some way by an event or state

non-theme patient
- stationary target of contacting movement or action of another entity
- target of force directed from another entity
- lack of control or causal influence in the event or state

The central significance of the Actor and Patient macroroles in language is the way the roles correlate with assigning one argument to the subject and the other argument to the object in a **transitive sentence** – that is, a sentence with a verb that takes a syntactic subject and a syntactic direct object, as illustrated in (51).

(51)   SUBJECT: OBJECT:
           ACTOR   PATIENT
    a   The killer   shot   the victim.
    b   The machine   punched   the leather.
    c   The wind   opened   the door.
    d   The knife   cut   the plastic.
    e   The pen   marked   the glass.
    f   The columns   supported   the roof.

The fixing of Actor and Patient macroroles works in two main ways. First, high-ranking Actor factors such as volition and control identify classical true agents, just as high-ranking Patient factors, chiefly complete change of state, identify true themes. These higher ranking factors are independent of each other – for instance, there is no obvious relation between a total change of state and the presence of volitional involvement. The lower ranking Actor and Patient factors are not independent of each other in the same way, and both measure comparative degrees of agentivity. In other words, lower ranking factors rank two arguments in a transitive sentence as more or less dynamic, or agent-like. Lower ranking patients, then, are negatively specified as less dynamic than the other argument, giving many non-theme patients the vague 'elsewhere or other' character loosely described as 'the thing verbed'. That is, the agent is the more dynamic argument of a transitive sentence, and the patient is the most involved non-agent, or runner-up.

10.5 ASPECT AND THEMES

The move to understand thematic roles in aspectual terms is centred on various kinds of theme, as it can be shown that the two most important aspectual properties, bounding and duration, are closely associated with the theme. The relationship between themes and event duration is revealed with accomplishment predicates that take change-of-state themes. These accomplishment predicates include verbs of change of state (*melt, freeze*), verbs of consumption or destruction (*eat, drink, destroy, demolish, burn*) and verbs of creation (*build, compose, write*).

The process part of the accomplishment operates on the theme by degrees, in such a way that the event must finish when the theme is totally affected or 'used up' by the process. (With verbs of creation, the theme is totally affected by the process when it is fully created.) In this image, the unfolding of the event by stages in time, up to its culmination, correlates with the theme's changing state in stages throughout the event, up to the end.

Themes which correlate in this way with the duration or gradual unfolding of a bounded event are called **incremental themes**, described in Tenny (1994) as 'measuring out' the event. For example, consider the event described in 'Jones ate the pie'. The stages of the event's being a quarter, a half and three-quarters elapsed in time correlate broadly with a quarter, a half, and three-quarters of the pie being eaten.

The correlation is also shown in certain examples with *half* or *halfway*.

(52)a   Jones ate the apple halfway.
   b   Jones built a shed halfway.
   c   The butter half melted.
   d   The wood half burned before the rain put the fire out.
   e   Otto played the sonata halfway.

In these examples the halfway point of the potential complete event correlates with a halfway division in the theme itself. If Jones ate the apple halfway then he ate half the apple, and what Jones built in (52b) was half a shed. A half-shed need not be a complete shed split down the middle, but can be the basic supporting structure constituting half the whole structure. 'The butter half melted' can be interpreted to mean that the whole block of butter was uniformly softened to a thick sauce-like consistency, but it can also mean 'Half of the butter melted'. Similarly, (52d) can be interpreted as 'Half the wood burned', and (52e) reports that Otto played the first half of the sonata.

The alternative interpretation of 'The butter half melted' as 'the butter was (uniformly) softened to a thick sauce-like consistency' shows that change-of-state themes can also undergo change uniformly, rather than changing part by part. On the most likely interpretations for the examples in (53) below, the themes undergo uniform change. Themes which change in this way are sometimes called **holistic themes**, in contrast with incremental themes.

(53)a The water heated to boiling point.
   b The cut grass withered in the sun.
   c The wine had matured halfway.

In (53a), for example, the halfway point in the event would not be a point at which half the water is at boiling point and the other half is still cool, but a point at which the water is uniformly at a temperature halfway to boiling point. In (53c) the halfway point is a time at which all the wine is uniformly half-matured, not a point at which half the wine is matured and the other half is still too young.

Both incremental and holistic themes show how the unfolding of the event in stages through time is determined by the gradual progress of what happens to the theme. In addition, for both kinds of theme, the endpoint is reached when the whole theme is in the final state, and the event cannot progress any further.

The theme determines the final bound by reaching its final state. In the incremental theme examples above, the theme measures out the event and determines the endpoint by being used up in some fashion by the event process. For the theme to measure the event in this way, the theme itself must supply a measure by being a specific or bounded quantity. For example, in an *eat an apple* event, we know that the event ends when the apple is consumed, and we know such a point must come because an apple is a definite bounded amount of apple substance. But if the theme of an accomplishment is not itself a bounded quantity, it cannot supply a bound for the event, and the event is unbounded. This is illustrated in (54)–(56).

(54) bounded: theme of specific quantity
   a   Jones wrote a letter in five minutes.
   b # Jones wrote a letter for five minutes.
   c   Jones wrote three letters in five minutes.

    d # Jones wrote three letters for five minutes.
    e   Jones ate two icecreams in two minutes.
    f # Jones ate two icecreams for two minutes.
    g   Jones demolished the shed in an hour.
    h # Jones demolished the shed for two hours.

(55)   unbounded: mass theme
    a   Jones wrote drivel for hours.
    b # Jones wrote drivel in an hour.
    c   Jones ate icecream for hours.
    d # Jones ate icecream in a minute.
    e   Jones demolished brickwork for days.
    f # Jones demolished brickwork in an afternoon.

(56)   unbounded: bare plural theme
    a   Jones wrote letters for hours.
    b # Jones wrote letters in an hour.
    c   Jones ate peanuts for hours.
    d # Jones ate peanuts in a minute.
    e   Jones demolished sheds for days.
    f # Jones demolished sheds in an afternoon.

EXERCISES

(A) Basic Review: Subatomic Representations

Using the kind of representations introduced in Sections 10.2.1–4, analyse the sentences below.

(1)   Peter ran inside.
(2)   Simon was hungry.
(3)   Charlie flew the kite into the tree.
(4)   Mary made Lucy laugh.
(5)   Padmini ground the spices to powder.
(6)   The wood half burned.
(7)   Jones left Paris.
(8)   The car left the road.

(B) Intransitive Verbs and Adjectives: Discussion

The past participles of intransitive verbs can sometimes be converted into adjectives, and sometimes cannot. From the data below, can you identify a thematic criterion for converting a past participle into an adjective?

his tent had collapsed	a collapsed tent
the milk has curdled	curdled milk
the leaves have fallen	fallen leaves
his ankles have swelled	swollen ankles
the flowers have wilted	wilted flowers
the plan had failed	a failed plan
the windowframe had twisted	a twisted windowframe
the shirt had wrinkled	a wrinkled shirt
the carpet had rotted	a rotted carpet
the door had stuck	a stuck door
the puddles had frozen	frozen puddles

people have talked	# recently talked people
the patient had coughed	# a coughed patient
the light has flashed	# a flashed light
several competitors have run	# several run competitors
a few dogs had barked	# a few barked dogs
children had played	# played children
a patient had sneezed	# a sneezed patient
the audience had clapped	# a clapped audience
a bystander had shouted	# a shouted bystander
the bull had charged	# a charged bull

(C)   Verbs of Eating: Discussion

The sentences below show a general difference between *nibble* and *swallow*.

(1)a   Bugs nibbled the lettuce leaf.
  b   # Bugs nibbled the lettuce leaf down.
  c   Bugs nibbled at the lettuce leaf.

(2)a   Benjamin swallowed the pill.
  b   Benjamin swallowed the pill down.
  c   # Benjamin swallowed at the pill.

Using these examples as a guide, sort the verbs below into groups according to whether they appear with *at* and /or *down*. What is the general meaning type for each class of verbs?

   chew, bolt, gulp, gnaw, swig, munch, sip, slurp, snarf, suck, guzzle, gobble, pick, hoover, lick, wolf.

In each example below, which, if any, of the Patient macrorole factors are present in the underlined NP?

(3)a	Bugs nibbled *the leaf*.
 b	Bugs nibbled at *the leaf*.
 c	Benjamin swallowed *the pill*.
 d	Benjamin swallowed *the pill* down.

(D) Verbs of Change: Discussion

Examples (1)–(4) below show that *grow*, *develop*, *evolve* and *hatch* can take either a source or a goal as the single complement, while *alter*, *change*, *convert* and *transform* can take only a goal, as shown in (5)–(8).

(1)a	The acorn grew <u>into an oak tree</u>.
	goal
 b	An oak tree grew <u>from the acorn</u>.
	source

(2)a	The bud developed into a leaf.
 b	A leaf developed from the bud.

(3)a	Some reptiles evolved into birds.
 b	Birds evolved from reptiles.

(4)a	The eggs hatched into larvae.
 b	Larvae hatched from the eggs.

(5)a	The lake altered into a marsh.
 b	# A marsh altered from the lake.

(6)a	The tadpole changed into a frog.
 b	# A frog changed from the tadpole.

(7)a	The ironing board converted into a card table.
 b	# A card table converted from the ironing board.

(8)a	The ironing board transformed into a card table.
 b	# A card table transformed from the ironing board.

Grow verbs and *alter* verbs also differ in the contexts illustrated below. In each set, either the *alter* verbs in (e–h) are somewhat anomalous in the context, or the examples do not have the same kind of meaning as a *grow* verb in the same context.

(9)a	The acorn grew.
 b	The bud developed.
 c	The reptile evolved.
 d	The eggs hatched.

e   The lake altered.
f   The tadpole changed.
g   ? The ironing board converted.
h   ? The ironing board transformed.

(10)a   The tree is fully grown.
 b   The leaf is fully developed.
 c   The bird is fully evolved.
 d   The larvae are fully hatched.

 e   The marsh is fully altered.
 f   The frog is fully changed.
 g   ? The card table is fully converted.
 h   ? The card table is fully transformed.

(11)a   The tree has finished growing.
 b   The leaf has finished developing.
 c   The bird has finished evolving.
 d   The larvae have finished hatching.

 e   ? The marsh has finished altering.
 f   ? The frog has finished changing.
 g   ? The card table has finished converting.
 h   ? The card table has finished transforming.

What general difference in meaning between these groups of verbs might be responsible for this difference?

(E)   *See, Look* and *Watch*: Discussion

The examples below show some of the different contexts in which *see, look* and *watch* appear.

(1)a   Jake saw Loretta.
 b   # Jake saw at Loretta.
 c   # Jake rudely/carefully saw Loretta.
 d   # It was rude/careful of Jake to see Loretta.
 e   # Jake saw towards Loretta.
 f   Jake saw Loretta through the window.
 g   Jake saw through the window/around the corner/over the wall.

(2)a   # Jake looked Loretta.
 b   Jake looked at Loretta.
 c   Jake rudely/carefully looked at Loretta.
 d   It was rude/careful of Jake to look at Loretta.
 e   Jake looked towards Loretta.

f   Jake looked at Loretta through the window.
g   Jake looked through the window/around the corner/over the wall.

(3)a   Jake watched Loretta.
  b   # Jake watched at Loretta.
  c   Jake rudely/carefully watched Loretta.
  d   It was rude/careful of Jake to watch Loretta.
  e   # Jake watched towards Loretta.
  f   Jake watched Loretta through the window.
  g   Jake watched through the window.
        Jake watched around the corner.
        Jake watched over the wall.

Using these examples as a guide, sort the verbs below into classes, according to the contexts they appear in.

> *peer, gawk, spot, scan, sight, study, glare, eye, glance, observe, peep, stare, examine, glimpse, peek, perceive, goggle, witness, spy, gaze, leer, notice, scrutinize, squint, inspect, survey*

What is the general kind of meaning for each class?
What is the thematic role (if any) of the underlined expression in the examples below?

> If any of the underlined expressions is a Patient, what are the relevant Patient factors?

(4)a   Jake saw <u>Loretta</u>.
  b   Jake looked <u>at Loretta</u>.
  c   Jake watched <u>Loretta</u>.
  d   Jake leered <u>at Loretta</u>.
  e   Jake looked <u>over the wall</u>.
  f   Jake watched <u>through the window</u>.

(F)   Verbs of Attaching: Discussion

The examples (1a–c) below with *join* can have roughly the same meaning, but (2b, c) with *glue* cannot have roughly the same meaning as (2a).

(1)a   join A to B
  b   join A with B
  c   join A and B

(2)a   glue A to B
  b   glue A with B
  c   glue A and B

Using these examples as a guide, sort the verbs below into groups according to the *join* type and the *glue* type.

anchor, connect, hitch, nail, fuse, pin, lash, clasp, link

What is the general type of meaning for each group of verbs? How does the general meaning fix the contexts the verbs can appear in?

FURTHER READING

Event participants and thematic roles are discussed in Chapter 6 of Saeed (1997).

Dowty (1979: 38–51) reviews the classic generative semantics analysis of *kill* as 'cause to become not alive', from McCawley (1968). Dowty's Chapters 2 and 3 give a technical analysis of the aspectual predicate classes using the predicates DO, BECOME and CAUSE.

The first section of van Valin (1990) presents an analysis of aspectual classes defined in subatomic analyses, based on Dowty (1979).

An influential recent source on the agent and patient macroroles is Dowty (1991). This paper is fairly accessible, and reviews thematic theory and its problems in some detail. Cruse (1973) on agentivity is a very readable short paper.

Jackendoff (1991) updates his theory of Conceptual Structure, introduced in Jackendoff (1983). Much of the discussion concerns the realization of arguments and thematic roles, with detailed discussion of the semantics of particular verbs. Chapter 7 deals with the action tier. This is a little more advanced than Jackendoff (1983).

The language of young children, revealing the processes of acquisition of argument structure and thematic patterns, is discussed in great detail in Pinker (1989). This work covers general issues in linguistic theory, and is accessible.

Levin and Rappaport Hovav (1992) discuss the agent-like and theme-like properties of subjects of verbs of motion, and Levin and Rappaport Hovav (1991) discuss the *clear* and *wipe* verbs. The first of these assumes a considerable background in syntax.

Tenny's theory is summarized in Tenny (1992).

11 Implicature and Explicature

As previewed in Chapter 1, this chapter takes up some of the main issues in the relationship between semantics and pragmatics, or between the literal meaning of the expressions the speaker utters and the extra information, taken from the context, which is needed to understand exactly what was said or what was meant.

The modern field of pragmatics is very strongly influenced by the work of the philosopher Paul Grice, who outlined a theory of inferences that hearers draw to arrive at a full understanding of what a speaker meant by an utterance, especially in those cases where what is meant goes well beyond the literal meaning of what is uttered. This kind of communication is dramatically illustrated in Grice's famous example of a letter of reference.

> A is writing a testimonial about a pupil who is a candidate for a philosophy job, and his letter reads as follows: 'Dear Sir, Mr X's command of English is excellent, and his attendance at tutorials has been regular. Yours, etc.'

The utterly condemnatory nature of this testimonial is so clear that it is worth pointing out how positive the literal content is. Having an excellent command of English and attending tutorials regularly are both positive qualities for a potential teacher. The two compelling points about this example are, first, that the negative overall impact of the letter seems to be quite separate from the actual mildly positive content, and second, that given the context, any English speaker who knows what a testimonial letter is would understand this letter in the same way – the negative interpretation is in some fashion systematic, not arbitrary.

In Grice's theory the extra information conveyed here, roughly that Mr X is no good at philosophy, is **implicated** by A or by A's letter, or is an **implicature** of A's letter. As this example shows clearly, implicature is quite different from entailment, as the content of the letter in no way entails that Mr X is no good at philosophy.

Gricean implicature is a systematic part of communication which involves the interplay between what a speaker actually said and certain broad rules, shared by speakers and hearers, which govern communication. The details of Grice's proposal are reviewed in the next section.

11.1   GRICE'S CONVERSATIONAL IMPLICATURE

Grice's theory of implicature includes two main kinds of implicature which he called conversational implicature and conventional implicature. This discussion concerns only conversational implicature, which is by far the more important.

Grice proposed that communicative utterances and exchanges, typically in conversation but not confined to conversation, are in accordance with a general principle of cooperation.

The Cooperative Principle
Make your conversational contribution such as is required, at the stage at which it occurs, by the accepted purpose or direction of the talk exchange in which you are engaged.
or
Be helpful.

The Cooperative Principle is observed in the application of four more specific maxims which fall under it, commonly called Grice's Maxims.

Maxim of Quality (also called the **Maxim of Truthfulness**)
Try to make your contribution one that is true.
1   Do not say what you believe to be false.
2   Do not say that for which you lack evidence.

Maxim of Quantity (also called the **Maxim of Informativeness**)
1   Make your contribution as informative as is required (for the current purposes of the exchange).
2   Do not make your contribution more informative than is required.

Maxim of Relation (also called the **Maxim of Relevance**)
Be relevant.

Maxim of Manner (also called the **Maxim of Clarity**)
Be perspicuous.
1   Avoid obscurity of expression.
2   Avoid ambiguity.
3   Be brief. (Avoid unnecessary prolixity.)
4   Be orderly.

(In the discussion below I shall use the Maxim names given in brackets.)

In a communicative act, (typically talking but also writing) the assumption that the speaker obeys the Cooperative Principle and the Maxims adds further information about the utterance itself. The utterance can be taken to be currently relevant, true and informative, and the hearer can draw inferences based on these assumptions. Knowing that these ways of drawing inferences are available, the speaker can speak in such a way as to encourage inference drawing, and thus deliberately convey the content of inferences. When the speaker deliberately phrases an utterance to lead the hearer to draw a certain inference, the content of that inference is implicated by the speaker – implicature is a deliberate communication tactic.

Alternatively, the speaker may say something that clearly does not obey all the Maxims, in such a way that both the speaker and the hearer are mutually aware of this. Even so, the assumption that the Maxims should be obeyed is still in force, and the obvious breaking or violating of a Maxim is itself a salient feature of the utterance from which inferences may be drawn, in accordance with the speaker's intentions. Whether a Maxim is observed (obeyed) or violated, if it plays a clear role in the way a speaker sets up an implicature, the Maxim is said to be **exploited** by the speaker. These points should become clearer with the discussion of examples below.

First, consider again A's letter of reference for the unfortunate Mr X. In the context of writing a reference for Mr X's application for a philosophy job, A should have written about Mr X's abilities in philosophy, and his failure to do so flagrantly violates the Maxim of Informativeness. He simply does not give the information required. In addition to the Maxims, there is a general agreement that references should be positive – if you cannot write a positive reference you should encourage the applicant to find another referee if possible. So A is constrained not to be too openly critical of Mr X in his letter. All these background assumptions are just as familiar to A's academic colleagues to whom Mr X has applied for a job. A's failure to comment on Mr X's philosophical abilities, which is a violation of the Maxim of Informativeness, clearly signals, as A intends, that something is wrong. A has had to choose between writing negatively or violating the Maxim of Truthfulness by writing positively about Mr X's philosophy, and caught on the horns of this dilemma, he has chosen to violate the Maxim of Informativeness. His readers can with little difficulty recover the message that A considers Mr X to be a poor philosopher.

Further examples of implicatures based on Grice's Maxims are illustrated in the next few sections.

11.1.1   Clarity

Suppose that Marcia and Clive are at a party, and have the following exchange.

(1)   C: Who are those two standing by the door?
        M: That's my mother and her husband.

If the couple referred to were Marcia's parents in a stereotypical nuclear family, the phrase *my mother and her husband* used by Marcia would refer to them, but this would be an odd way for her to describe them, and would violate the Maxim of Clarity. Assuming that she is in fact obeying Clarity and also Truthfulness, her reason for speaking this way is that she doesn't judge it true to say 'Those are my parents', and in particular, the man is not a parent to her. The obvious inference to be drawn is that the man is not her father.

Compare this example with (2) below.

(2) Alan is the male offspring of my parents.

Here the circumlocution *male offspring of my parents* just expresses the same content as the phrase *my brother*, but in a more obscure way. It cannot be understood as an exact way of expressing a slightly different meaning, unlike *my mother and her husband*. Here Clarity is violated, probably signalling the avoidance of the phrase *my brother* with its connotations of sibling closeness and affection, and the speaker implicates that she doesn't like her brother.

A standard illustration of Clarity violation is (3).

(3) They don't allow dogs at that B-E-A-C-H.

The speaker in (3) signals that utterance of the word *beach* is to be avoided, presumably because the dog (assume there is a dog) recognizes the word and will infer that a trip to the beach is in the offing. The central point of Clarity devices like (3) is that the way of speaking is clear to the intended audience, but unclear to a potential audience, and what the speaker implicates is that what is said should be kept from the potential audience.

11.1.2 Truthfulness

The Maxim of Truthfulness is taken by Grice to be of higher priority than the other Maxims, providing the background against which they come into play, and generally taking precedence over the others if there is a clash. Observing Truthfulness is not usually cited as giving rise to particular implicatures on its own, although one instance would be the rhetorical device mentioned in Chapter 2 and repeated below.

(4) If that's a genuine Picasso then the moon is made of longlife food product.

The implicature here, that that is not a genuine Picasso, requires the initial assumption that the whole conditional is true, which we can attribute to the assumption that Truthfulness is observed. The consequent is mutually accepted by speaker and hearer as false, giving a true conditional with a false consequent. Accordingly, the antecedent must also be false, hence the implicature 'That's not a genuine Picasso'.

The observance of Truthfulness at the cost of another Maxim is illustrated in examples like (5).

(5)   A: Where's the city branch of Woolworths?
      B: Oh, somewhere near the Peacock Mall.

Assume that A and B both know that A wants to go to Woolworths, so she wants to know exactly where Woolworths is. B gives less information than is required and so violates Informativeness, but preserves Truthfulness by saying as much as he knows, rather than giving explicit but false instructions for getting to Woolworths. In contrast to 'I don't know' or silence, B's response shows a helpful attitude, gives correct but limited information, and implicates that he doesn't know more precisely where Woolworths is, or he would have said.

11.1.3   Informativeness

The Maxim of Informativeness has two clauses, 'Make your contribution as informative as is required' and 'Do not make your contribution more informative than is required'. The first clause, requiring the speaker to give enough information, is identified as the basis of a wide range of implicatures known as scalar implicatures. **Scalar implicatures** typically arise with terms denoting quantities or degrees of attributes which can be graded on some scale of informative weakness and strength. The term *scalar implicature* was coined by Laurence Horn, whose theory of implicature is reviewed further in Section 11.3 below.

A classic scale giving rise to scalar implicature is the one shown in (6).

(6)   (weak) $<$ *some, most, all* $>$ (strong)

The scale indicates that *some* is typically used to make a weaker, less informative statement than *most*, and *most* is typically used to make a weaker, less informative statement than *all*.

With a scalar implicature it is assumed that the speaker obeys Informativeness and makes the strongest statement consistent with what he or she knows or believes to be the case. The speaker's use of an expression on an information strength scale implicates the negation of any higher term on the same scale. For example, assume that the students in a particular course have just had a test. Their teacher is asked 'So how did the students do on the test?' The possible answers in (7) have different scalar implicatures.

(7)a   Most of them passed.
       implicature: Not all of them passed.

   b   Some of them passed.
       implicature: Not all of them passed.
       implicature: It isn't the case that most of them passed.

   c   Two or three did very well.
       implicature: Not more than two or three did very well.

On the scale illustrated here, the relative informational strength of the expressions can also be defined in terms of entailment. 'All the students passed' entails 'Most of the students passed' and 'Some of the students passed' but not vice versa, so *all* is informationally stronger on the scale than *most* and *some*. Similarly, 'Most of the students passed' entails 'Some of the students passed' but not vice versa, so *most* is informationally stronger than *some*.

Further examples of scalar implicature 'no more than stated' are given in (8)–(14). The appropriate scales of informational strength are informally indicated.

(8)   Sam got a passing grade on the test.
       implicature: He didn't do any better than a passing grade.
       <pass, very good, excellent>

(9)   It's quite warm out.
       implicature: It isn't hot.
       <warm, hot, sweltering>

(10)   I tried to contact Don several times.
       implicature: I didn't manage to contact Don.
       <try, manage>

(11)   I've read halfway through the book.
       implicature: I haven't read any further than halfway.
       <barely started, halfway, three-quarters through, finished>

(12)   Diane can carry 30 pounds in her pack.
       implicature: She can't carry any more weight than 30 pounds.
       <20 pounds, 30 pounds, 40 pounds, ...>

(13)   (Receptionist to patient seeking an urgent appointment)
       Dr Evans could fit you in tomorrow afternoon at 2.00.
       implicature: He can't see you any sooner.

(14)   Milk and sugar?
       One sugar, thanks.
       implicature: I don't want any milk (not both milk and sugar).
       <sugar, milk and sugar>

Example (13) shows that the appropriate scale for a scalar implicature may depend on the context. Here the patient wants to see the doctor as soon as possible, so the most informative response the receptionist can make is to identify the earliest available time. In a different context, as in (15) below, the relative informational strength of different time expressions is reversed, and the most informative utterance identifies the latest possible time.

(15)   The machine is playing up a bit – when do you want those negatives?
       I suppose first thing tomorrow would be OK.
       implicature: We need the negatives no later than first thing tomorrow.
       < this afternoon, first thing tomorrow, tomorrow afternoon, ...>

Scalar implicature is unlike other kinds of conversational implicature in being commonly associated with particular groups of words or expressions, such as *some* and *all*. Nevertheless, even these implicatures depend on the context, as illustrated in (16) and (17).

(16)a   Some cast members want to see you after the show.
    b   The photographer wants some cast members for the photo.

(17)a   Some of you are working well.
    b   If some of you work solidly the mess could be cleared by tomorrow.

Here the (a) member of each pair has the expected implicature 'not all', but the (b) member has no such implicature. It is likely that the photographer would like the whole cast or most of the cast in the photo if possible, and if some of you can clear the mess by tomorrow, certainly most of you or all of you could clear the mess in the same time or sooner.
    Scalar implicature is discussed further in section 11.3.1.

We turn next to Relevance.

11.1.4   Relevance

Relevance is most commonly seen to be at play in implicature where a speaker makes a remark which appears at first sight to be irrelevant, but is fully understood only on the assumption that it is relevant, as in (18).

(18)   A: Where's Bill, do you know?
       B: His coat's gone.

Given that A inquired after Bill and not his coat, B's response does not seem to answer the question. But assuming that both A and B know that Bill doesn't leave the building except to go home, and further assuming that Bill does not wear his coat inside the building, B's response is relevant to the question of Bill's whereabouts – B implicates that Bill has left for the day.

A different kind of Relevance implicature is shown in (19).

(19)   A: Why don't you see if Bob might join you in your new venture?
       B: I try to stay clear of shady operators.

Here B's remark about shady operators is relevant to A's suggestion concerning Bob only if Bob is a shady operator, and accordingly, B's utterance implicates that Bob is a shady operator.

Relevance is in fact an all-pervading consideration, not only in making and understanding implicatures, but also in understanding the basic content of what a speaker actually said. This is illustrated in (20).

(20)   A: I'm sick to death of going to the laundromat.
       B: The man should be coming tomorrow.

The general background context is that the washing machine in A and B's flat has broken down, and A's remark introduces the laundry problem as a topic. B's apparently irrelevant remark can then be understood to mean that the washing machine repairman should come to the flat the following day to repair the washing machine. Unlike an implicature, this content is a more explicit version of what B actually said. A possible implicature here, relevant to A's remark, is that A won't need to go to the laundromat again, provided that the repairman does come and mend the machine. The role of Relevance in understanding what was actually said will be discussed in section 11.4.

11.2   LATER DEVELOPMENTS

Grice's theory remains the main starting point for discussions of pragmatically conveyed meaning, although the original theory and Maxims as stated above have been extensively re-evaluated and revised.

Grice's four Maxims do not have equal importance in generating implicatures. As we have seen, the main kind of implicature attributed to Clarity is the 'warning of potential listeners' device, which isn't a major part of day-to-day communication. Truthfulness, although said to underpin the functioning of all the other Maxims, does not often play the main part in giving rise to implicatures, apart from its possible contribution to ironical utterances. Most of the work is done by Informativeness and Relevance.

Informativeness and Relevance are not clearly separate and independent principles. If you are to obey Informativeness, you must know exactly how much information is required, so as not to give too much or too little information. But surely information which is not required (that is, on the topic but too much) is irrelevant to the current purpose, and information which is required is relevant to the current purpose. If you give too little information it is because you omit information which is relevant to the purpose, and therefore required. So Informativeness and Relevance are interdependent.

Sections 11.3 and 11.4 outline two main approaches to implicature since Grice, both emphasizing in different ways the importance of Informativeness and Relevance, and the interdependence between them. The first approach takes Informativeness as the basis for a new theory of implicature, incorporating Relevance into a more general principle. The second approach develops a technical notion of Relevance as the central key to understanding and interpretation in general, including, but not confined to, the understanding of implicature.

11.3   HORN'S Q PRINCIPLE AND R PRINCIPLE

Horn observes that human language design can be partly characterized as the product of a tension between cost and benefit, or the need to achieve a balance between economy and effectiveness. This dual constraint is expressed quite clearly in the two clauses of Grice's Informativeness Maxim, which enjoin the speaker to say not too little (clause 1) and not too much (clause 2). In other words, clause 1 imposes a lower limit on the amount of information expressed by the speaker and clause 2 imposes an upper limit.

Horn retains Grice's Maxim of Quality (that is, Truthfulness) as a background rule, and proposes two general Principles, based on the two-way contrast in Informativeness, to replace Grice's other three. Horn's Principles do not express exactly the same constraints as Grice's, but they are loosely related as indicated below.

The Q principle
Make your contribution SUFFICIENT:
Say as much as you can (given both Quality and **R**)

The Q Principle collects Grice's Maxims:
        Quantity 1:   'Make your contribution as informative as is required (for the current purposes of the exchange)'
        Manner 1:   'Avoid obscurity of expression'
        Manner 2:   'Avoid ambiguity'

The R Principle
Make your contribution NECESSARY:
Say no more than you must (given **Q**)

The R Principle collects Grice's Maxims:

Relation:	'Be relevant'
Quantity 2:	'Do not make your contribution more informative than is required'
Manner 3:	'Be brief (avoid unnecessary prolixity)'
Manner 4:	'Be orderly'

The theory sorts implicatures into two main classes corresponding to the principle which drives the implicature.

11.3.1 Q-Implicatures

Assuming that the Q Principle is obeyed, the hearer accepts that the speaker made the most informative statement that could be made in the circumstances. Accordingly, the hearer infers that a stronger statement would not be warranted, and an implicature on the lines of 'but no more' is added to the speaker's statement. Given that the Q Principle is most closely based on Grice's Informativeness, scalar implicatures, introduced in section 11.1.3, are the main kind of Q-implicature. Further illustrations are given in (21) below.

(21)a It's possible he'll be elected
    Q-implicature: It's not likely / not certain he'll be elected.

  b Harold is as tall as Tom.
    Q-implicature: Harold is not taller than Tom.

  c We recorded most of the tunes.
    Q-implicature: We didn't record all of the tunes.

  d That performance was very good.
    Q-implicature: That performance was not outstanding.

  e I believe he'll be here on Wednesday.
    Q-implicature: I don't know for a fact that he'll be here on Wednesday.

Q-implicature in Horn's theory also gives the exclusive interpretation of *or*. Recall that the truth table for logical disjunction defines inclusive *or*, often glossed as 'and/or', which does not fit with exclusive uses of *or*, as in (22a).

(22)a That tree is native to either China or India (I can't remember which).
  b No, I think you'll find it's native to both countries.

On the exclusive interpretation, (22a) is false if the tree is native to both China and India, and (22b) contradicts (22a), but *pvq* is true if both *p* and *q* are true.

The key to the exclusive *or* implicature is that *and* and *or* form a strength scale: *p&q* entails *pvq*, but not vice versa.

(23)

p	q	p ∨ q	p & q
T	T	T	T
T	F	T	F
F	T	T	F
F	F	F	F

The truth of *p&q* guarantees the truth of *pvq* (top line). But *pvq* is also true on lines 2 and 3 where *p&q* is false, so *pvq* does not entail *p&q*. Accordingly, *and* and *or* form the scale in (24).

(24)   (weak) < *or, and* > (strong)

Now suppose I say 'Jones bought a Coke or an icecream.' On the inclusive logical disjunction reading, I allow for all of the following:

(25)a   He bought a Coke only.
   b   He bought an icecream only.
   c   He bought a Coke and an icecream.

If I know what Jones bought, and in fact he bought a Coke and an icecream, according to the Q Principle I should have said 'He bought a Coke and an icecream', because that is the strongest statement of the facts I could make, even though in that case 'Jones bought a Coke or an icecream' on the inclusive reading would still be true. So the choice of *or* instead of *and* signals that the stronger statement with *and* would not be true. The hearer infers the Q-implicature 'Jones did not buy a Coke and an icecream'. The logical representation for exclusive *or* shows the two parts clearly.

(26)a   (p ∨ q) & ∼(p & q)   exclusive interpretation
   b   p ∨ q   what was said
   c   ∼ (p & q)   'not both' implicature

11.3.2   R-Implicatures

The R Principle, on the other hand, enjoins the speaker to say no more than is necessary. If the hearer assumes that the R Principle has been obeyed, this can serve as the basis of implicature which goes beyond what the speaker actually said to a much stronger statement along the same lines. As one might expect, R-implicatures include devices of suggestive understatement, such as those illustrated in (27).

(27)a This essay is not entirely satisfactory.
   R implicature: This essay is entirely unsatisfactory.

   b He isn't very bright.
   R implicature: He's thick.

   c He needs to go somewhere.
   R implicature: He needs to use the lavatory.

   d not at all bad (in fact, very good)
   not bad   (in fact, pretty good)
   not too bad   (OK)
   not too good (in fact, pretty bad)
   not good   (in fact, bad)

A major kind of R-implicature Horn proposes is a pragmatic account of what syntacticians have called **Neg-Raising**. The Neg-Raising phenomenon is illustrated in (28)–(30) below.

(28)a I don't think John has left town.
   b I think John hasn't left town.

(29)a I don't imagine the price will stay down.
   b I imagine the price will not stay down.

(30)a I don't expect to see you tomorrow.
   b I expect I won't see you tomorrow.

The (a) sentences are Neg-Raising sentences. Strictly speaking, the negations in these sentences should apply to the main verb, as in *don't think*, *don't imagine* and *don't expect*, simply to deny that the speaker has a thought content of the sort specified. So for example, (29a) would be expected to mean that the speaker lacks the thought 'The price will stay down', which would be compatible with the speaker having no opinion about the price at all. But in fact these sentences are generally interpreted as if the negation were in the lower clause, so that (a) and (b) in each pair are interpreted as having the same meaning.

The term *Neg-Raising* for the (a) sentences is based on a syntactic analysis in which the negation originates in the lower clause and is subsequently raised to the main clause. For example, 'I do not think John has left town' is derived from 'I think John has not left town' by moving *not*. According to the Neg-Raising analysis, the negation really belongs in the lower clause, and so a 'Neg-Raised reading' interprets the negation in the <u>lower</u> clause, before it is moved.

Whether or not the Neg-Raised interpretation is available depends on the predicate in the main clause. In the sentences in (31)–(33) below the main verb does not allow Neg-Raising, as is shown by the fact that the (a) and (b) sentences in each pair do not have the same interpretation.

(31)a   He doesn't claim to have all the answers.
   b   He claims not to have all the answers.

(32)a   It wasn't possible to sit near him.
   b   It was possible to not sit near him.

(33)a   Jones didn't manage to stop the car.
   b   Jones managed to not stop the car.

The Neg-Raised interpretation is informationally stronger than the non-Neg-Raised interpretation. As we saw with scalar implicatures in Section 11.1.3, a difference in informational strength can be demonstrated by the presence of one-way entailments – an informationally stronger statement entails a weaker statement, but not vice versa. This is illustrated in (34)–(36) below.

(34)   I don't think John has left town.
    <u>Neg-Raised interpretation</u>
    a   'I have the thought "John has not left town"'

    <u>non-Neg-Raised interpretation</u>
    b   'I lack the thought "John has left town"'

(35)   I don't imagine the price will stay down.
    <u>Neg-Raised interpretation</u>
    a   'I have the thought "the price will not stay down"'

    <u>non-Neg-Raised interpretation</u>
    b   I do not have the thought "The price will stay down"'

(36)   I don't expect to see you tomorrow.
    <u>Neg-Raised interpretation</u>
    a   'I have the thought "I won't see you tomorrow"'

    <u>non-Neg-Raised interpretation</u>
    b   'I do not have the thought "I'll see you tomorrow"'

In each example, assuming that the speaker is cognitively coherent, (a) entails (b), but (b) does not entail (a). For example, if I lack the thought that John has left town, this does not entail that I have the thought that he has not left town – I may have no view on the matter at all. In Horn's analysis, the literal meaning of these sentences is the non-Neg-Raised interpretation, consistent with the actual order of the words in the sentence. The informationally stronger Neg-Raised interpretation is an R-implicature, strengthening what was actually said.

To sum up, Horn's system centres on two principles, similar to the two clauses of Grice's Informativeness Maxim, which tend to produce opposite effects. Observing the Q-Principle ensures that the speaker will give enough information. The hearer who assumes that the Q Principle has been obeyed is led to infer limiting 'no more than I said' implicatures. Observing the R-Principle ensures that the speaker does not go into unnecessary detail or voice what is obvious and easily recovered. The hearer who assumes that the R-Principle has been obeyed is led to infer elaborating, 'at least as much as I said and more' implicatures – the utterance is recognized as an understatement.

The next section introduces the notion of Relevance in Relevance Theory, which is a major current alternative to Gricean and revised Gricean theories.

11.4 RELEVANCE THEORY

Relevance Theory, developed originally by Deirdre Wilson and Dan Sperber, accounts for the hearer's understanding of an utterance, including implicatures, in terms of cognitive information processing. The emphasis is not so much on the external context in which an utterance is made as on the internal context, this being the hearer's current knowledge, beliefs, assumptions, hypotheses, and cultural and social conventions, in the form of mental representations of propositions. For simplicity, I shall refer to all these contents as the hearer's current assumptions. Recall also that the hearer stands for both hearers and readers. The concept of Relevance used in Relevance Theory is illustrated in the next section.

11.4.1 Cognitive Effect and Processing Effort

An incoming message interacts with the hearer's current assumptions to a greater or lesser degree. For example, I could break off at this point to comment that I'm not using footnotes in this book.

(37) I'm not using footnotes in this book.

You may have already noticed this, but you probably don't care about it one way or the other. It has no apparent bearing on the current issue, which is how Relevance Theory works, nor on any other issue at hand. So this information will not cause you to change your mind about anything, or draw any new inferences, or add a new proposition to your existing stock. In different circumstances you might wonder why the writer had pointed out such a trivial thing, but in this case it is obviously presented as an example sentence, so that speculation doesn't arise. In short, the content of 'I'm not using footnotes in this book' probably has minimal **cognitive effects** for you – that is, it doesn't interact with your current assumptions to produce any effects. In this, it has little significance to you at this point.

Now take a different case. Suppose that friends of Tom have invited him to come with them to an afternoon showing of a new film. One of the group, Jenny, says

(38)   The movie ends at 3.50.

Tom's current assumptions include the information that he has a lecture at four o'clock, and it takes ten minutes to walk from the cinema to the lecture room. Tom now infers that if he goes to the film and leaves immediately at the end he should be on time for the lecture. So he decides to go to the film.

In this case the utterance in (38) interacts significantly with Tom's current assumptions. In particular, the new information combines with existing current assumptions to lead to new inferences, and ultimately to the decision to see the film.

Take a third and very different case. Alan and Bridget, a married couple, have an old friend Chester who they haven't seen for a while. Alan has recently begun to suspect that Bridget is having an affair, though he has no idea who with. One of Bridget's annoying habits is to read aloud bits of what she is reading in bed – Alan usually doesn't listen. One night she reads this passage:

> The magnolia likes to spread itself over two and even three stories. It is the kind of shrub for whose sake any outmoded old parsonage, however riddled with dry rot and beetle, should be acquired with enthusiastic pride. If the owner starts inquiring 'How should I prune my magnolia?' a preservation order, to include every twig, must be served on him forthwith. He should be grateful for being allowed to live in permanently darkened rooms, when the darkness springs from so august an umbrage.
> (Christopher Lloyd (1985), *The Well-Tempered Garden*
> (revised edn), Penguin, pp. 235–6)

Some days later, Alan runs into Chester by chance. After initial greetings, the conversation proceeds:

(39) A: We haven't seen you since, it must be just before you moved. We haven't even seen the inside of the house. Have you had to do much work on it?

    C: Ah, yes! The rat-ridden rectory! Fortunately the august umbrage is over the garage so it can stay. Of course I had to paint the whole interior, but the house is terrific.

Chester's remarks about the rat-ridden rectory and the august umbrage are unclear to Alan, but they sound familiar. The thought nags him that he has heard something similar recently, perhaps a quote . . . something about a magnolia tree, some gardening book . . . 'so august an umbrage', that was it, odd that Chester should quote the same thing a few days later, he never reads gardening books, that's for sure . . . Suddenly Alan is convinced that Bridget has recently quoted the same passage to Chester about his new house – they have seen each other without her mentioning it – Chester is her lover!

Here Chester's rather obscure remark triggers a chain of speculation for Alan. In casual chat we quite often let an unclear remark go by, but Alan latches onto this allusion and worries at it, makes the connection with a recent utterance of Bridget's to which he wasn't even listening properly, and comes to a startling conclusion which may have far-reaching consequences. In short, the utterance interacts very significantly with Alan's current assumptions.

These three examples, 'I'm not using footnotes', 'The movie ends at 3.50', and 'the august umbrage can stay', can be ranked in two ways. First, they differ in the cognitive effects for the hearer, according to the extent to which the new information interacts with the hearer's current assumptions to produce changes in the hearer's stock of assumptions, including further assumptions derived by inference, and possibly decisions to act. Secondly, they can be ranked according to how much processing effort they provoke in the hearer.

'I'm not using footnotes in this book' presumably produces almost no cognitive processing, providing trivial information which may not be new and stimulating no inferences.

'The movie ends at 3.50' produces a moderately complex reasoning process but presumably does not involve much mental effort for Tom. For one thing, the existing assumptions which were also used were easily accessible to Tom's calculations; either they were connected to the familiar scenario of going to the local cinema or to Tom's plans for the afternoon, both counting as part of the topic of the conversation of the moment.

The last example produced quite an extensive processing effort for Alan, including the identification of a misquoted passage as one he had recently heard but not attended to, the creative leap to the assumption that Chester also heard the quote from Bridget, and the inference that Bridget has seen Chester without mentioning it, and that this demonstrates their guilt.

So the utterances can be compared on two scales, as in (40).

(40)

	cognitive effect (benefit)	processing effort (cost)
footnotes	minimal	minimal
movie	moderate/high	low/moderate
umbrage	high	very high

The probability that a hearer will actually follow a potential processing path presented by an utterance to draw further inferences from it (in association with existing assumptions) depends on the balance between cost and benefit. Generally, a hearer will process an utterance, achieving cognitive effects from it, only if the processing cost is not too high for the benefit gained.

The technical notion of **Relevance** on which Relevance Theory is based is defined in terms of the balance between cost and benefit. A highly relevant utterance (that is, relevant for the hearer) has high cognitive effects for low processing cost, and an utterance of low relevance has a processing cost which outweighs its potential cognitive effects. Relevance, then, is a property of utterances from the hearer's point of view, reflecting whether or not it is worth the hearer's trouble to work for understanding and for further inferences.

The discussion so far has not included the role of the speaker as a deliberate communicator, in particular as a deliberate implicator. Essentially, implicature arises where the speaker is confident that a potential utterance would be highly relevant for the hearer, and takes advantage of this. In normal successful communication all utterances are relevant, as both the speaker and hearer mutually recognize. If an utterance is relevant for the hearer, then the hearer will perform the required processing to achieve the anticipated cognitive effects, including the drawing of inferences. So the speaker has only to make the utterance to cause the hearer to arrive at the anticipated and intended inference(s).

Of the examples above, only 'The movie ends at 3.50' is a reasonable candidate for implicature.

'I'm not using footnotes in this book' produced little or no cognitive effects anyway.

In example (39), 'the august umbrage can stay', it is clear that Chester certainly did not intend to communicate to Alan that he had been seeing Alan's wife. So this is not an instance of implicature, which is a deliberate communicative tactic on the speaker's part. Even if Chester had intended to betray the secret, (39) was arguably so costly in terms of processing effort that Chester would not be justified in expecting Alan to follow the chain of reasoning through, even though the cognitive effects were substantial. For one thing, he couldn't count on Alan remembering the quote, assuming he knew Alan had heard it.

But 'The movie ends at 3.50' is just right. The moderately low processing effort is justified by the cognitive effect. Jenny (the speaker) could confidently anticipate that Tom would perform the required processing and could judge that the utterance would be highly relevant for Tom, so long as she was familiar with Tom's background assumptions – chiefly, the distance from the cinema to the lecture hall and Tom's four o'clock lecture. So when Jenny said 'The movie ends at 3.50' she implicated 'You can see the film and be back in time for your lecture'.

11.5 LEVELS OF INFERENCE: IMPLICATURE AND EXPLICATURE

In discussing implicature so far, we have more or less taken for granted the meaning of what a speaker said, and worked forward from there to analyse the implicature. This gives two main propositions forming the communication. The **explicature** is what the speaker expressed explicitly, or what was said. Whether the speaker spoke truly or not rests on the truth or falsity of the explicature. The implicature is what the speaker conveyed implicitly, or in common parlance, what was implied.

Attention in pragmatics has generally focused on the role of contextual information in implicature, as defined in this two-way contrast, which suggests that pragmatics has little part to play, if any, in determining the explicature. One might assume, as Grice appeared to assume, that the explicature is just the literal meaning of the words the speaker uttered, given by core semantics.

But in fact there is almost always a gap between the literal meaning of an utterance and the explicature. Traditional semantics has long acknowledged three main areas in which contextual information is needed to establish a proposition for which truth conditions can be given: the disambiguation of ambiguous expressions, the assignment of reference to variables, and the interpretation of indexical expressions.

11.5.1 Disambiguation, Reference Assignment and Indexicality

Disambiguating ambiguous expressions is straightforward. Both lexical and structural ambiguity can be resolved by pragmatic considerations to identify which of two meanings a speaker actually expresses, as in (41).

(41)a They've got that creamy duck on special at Forresters.
   b Everyone should bring a pencil.

The phrase *that creamy duck* in (41a) is lexically ambiguous. For example, if Forresters is a restaurant, *that creamy duck* refers to their special dish, roast duck in a spiced cream sauce. If Forresters is a fabric store, *that creamy duck* refers to a cream-coloured strong cotton twill. The structural ambiguity in

(41b) is a quantifier scope ambiguity, which common sense resolves here in favour of the surface order of the quantifiers, so we understand that each person should bring a separate pencil. Disambiguation in context also applies to most personal names such as *Bruce* and *Violet* – context allows the hearer to discern whether the speaker is talking about, for example, Violet Trefusis or the hearer's Aunty Vi.

The assignment of reference to variables includes personal pronouns and may also include simple tense time references, as illustrated in Section 7.7 with the examples repeated below.

(42)a He'll never make it.
       (said while watching a man climb a ladder carrying two pots of paint, a scraper, a roller, a brush, a rag, putty, and sundry other items.)
   b   I left your mail on your desk.
   c   The plumber came and he'll send a quote.
   d   Everyone came to dinner last night and Jones got tipsy.

The general context supplies the person referred to by *he* in (42a) and the time referred to by the past tense of *left* in (42b). The pronoun *he* in (42c) and the past tense of *got drunk* in (42d) both pick up the reference of some expression earlier in the sentence. In (42c) *he* takes the same referent as its antecedent, *the plumber*, and in (42d) the time at which Jones got drunk is the time of the party mentioned in the first conjunct. Here, the referent for the variable is identified through a linguistic context, but the connection between the variable (pronoun or time variable) and the expression it depends on is still established pragmatically, not by any automatic syntactic or semantic rule. In some cases the reference of a pronoun is established by syntactic rules, but not in the examples given here.

Indexical expressions, also called **deictic expressions**, are expressions which depend on the context of utterance in some systematic way for their interpretation. The classic examples of indexicality or deixis are words and expressions like those in (43).

(43) yesterday   today   tomorrow
      last week   this week   next week
      last year   this year   next year

      I, we   you, youse, y'all

      here
      now

      this, these   that, those

The central anchoring points of an utterance are the identity of the speaker, the identity of the hearer(s), the time and place of the utterance, and the position of the speaker. The expressions in (43) are interpreted in relation to these key points. For example, *yesterday* refers to the day before the day of utterance, *this morning* refers to the morning of the day of utterance, *you* refers to the hearer(s), and so on. *This, these, that* and *those* are deictic where the contrast between them is interpreted in terms of nearness to or distance from the speaker, as in *this one (here)* and *that one (over there)*. Demonstrative uses of *this, these, that* and *those*, canonically associated with a pointing gesture, are also deictic in that their reference depends on the gesture, which is a feature of the immediate context of utterance.

Tense is also indexical, as past, present and future are calculated as earlier than, overlapping with, or later than the time of utterance. As we have seen, in addition to placing the time spoken of in the past or future, simple tenses also commonly trigger the hearer to use wider contextual information to identify the specific time a speaker is talking about.

The term *indexicality* is also often used in formal semantic theory to cover a much wider range of contextual dependence, including the assignment of reference to variables and names, and the identification of the domain for a restricted quantifier. In addition to the expressions given in (43), many writers class definite descriptions as indexical, because definite descriptions can be used in context to refer in a name-like way.

The contribution of these kinds of contextual information to the explicature is illustrated in (44).

(44)   I saw Jean's new plane yesterday.
       (uttered 6 p.m., 25 October 1937)

The literal meaning for (44) is approximately as given below.

(45)   'At a time before the time of utterance and overlapping the day before the day of utterance, x_{1s} saw Jean's aeroplane or woodscraping tool which was just born, recently manufactured or recently acquired.'

The notation 'x_{1s}' represents 'first person singular', and the ambiguous words *plane* and *new* are shown as disjunctions.

Pragmatic information can now be added to make this more precise, as follows:

(46)   (The speaker is Irma Smith. The hearer knows that Irma visited Jean Nagy, a friend of Irma's from woodwork classes, in the morning of 24 October 1937. The time of utterance = 6 p.m., 25 October 1937.)

       I refers to Irma Smith
       Jean refers to Jean Nagy

the past tense of *saw* identifies an event time before 6 pm, 25 October 1937

yesterday refers to the day before the day of utterance = 24 October 1937

the time of the event is during the day of 24 October 1937

add background context:
the time of the event is during Irma's visit to Jean Nagy on the morning of 24 October 1937

disambiguation:
her new plane refers to a woodscraping tool which Jean has recently bought

Now we can compare Irma's utterance (47a), the literal meaning of Irma's utterance (47b), and the explicature for Irma's utterance, as represented in (47c). The truth condition for what Irma said is (47c).

(47)a 'I saw her new plane yesterday'.
    b 'At a time before the time of utterance and overlapping the day before the day of utterance, x_{1s} saw Jean's new aeroplane or wood-scraping tool which was just born, recently manufactured or recently acquired.'
    c 'During the morning of 24 October 1937 while visiting Jean Nagy, Irma Smith saw a woodworking tool which Jean Nagy had purchased shortly before 24 October 1937.'

We have identified five components of interpretation as summarized in (48).

(48)1 The literal meaning of the words uttered.

    2 First pragmatic level:
reference assignment to variables, including tense; disambiguation of ambiguous expressions, including names; interpretation of indexical expressions, giving the explicature as output.

    3 The explicature, the main truth condition for what was said.

    4 Second pragmatic level:
further inferences taking the explicature as input, giving implicatures as output.

    5 The implicature(s).

So far, the operations in the first pragmatic level, which provide input to the explicature, are not the same as the operations of the second pragmatic level, which construct implicatures. Given that the explicature is the main truth condition for an utterance, it is obviously desirable if possible to have a clear picture of the explicature – what is actually said – distinguished from the implicature – what is additionally implicated/inferred. This distinction depends to a considerable extent on the distinction between the first and second pragmatic levels. Accordingly, the question arises whether or not any further processes, usually associated with conversational implicature, also operate at the first level. This question is discussed in the next section.

11.5.2   Further Pragmatic Contributions to Explicature

The discussion in this section is based on work by Robyn Carston, particularly her paper 'Implicature, explicature and truth-theoretic semantics' (1988).

Carston draws attention to a range of examples which demonstrate the need for further pragmatic input to explicatures, in addition to the pragmatic contributions to explicature outlined in the previous section. To begin with, there are vague statements like (49).

(49)   The park is some distance from my house.

To calculate the explicature, we apply the familiar processes of reference assignment, disambiguation and interpretation of indexicals. In this example the quantifier NP *the park* will also be interpreted in context as referring to a particular park. This gives (50) as the purported explicature, assuming the park to be Hyde Park and the speaker to be Soames Forsyte.

(50)   A distance exists which is the distance between Hyde Park and 62 Montpelier Square.

Now recall that whether or not Soames speaks truly depends on the truth of the explicature, so Soames speaks truly if and only if (50) is true. But given that the house is not actually in Hyde Park, obviously there is *some* distance between the house and the park, even if the park is right across the street from the house. So if (50) really is the explicature, Soames speaks truly even if he lives across the street from the park, which runs counter to our strongest intuitions: surely in uttering 'The park is some distance from my house', Soames actually said that his house and the park are quite a large distance apart. (What distance counts as large will also depend on the context.) If in fact he lives across the street from the park, he spoke falsely. Suppose that an acquaintance has asked if Soames walks in the park frequently. In this case the explicature for (49) might be something like (51).

(51)   The distance between Hyde Park and 62 Montpelier Square is so great
       that it would not be convenient to walk from 62 Montpelier Square to
       Hyde Park (and back again) in order to walk in Hyde Park.

The extra information in (51) is not drawn from assigning reference to
variables, interpreting indexical expressions or resolving ambiguity. Similar
examples are in (52).

(52)a   It will take us some time to do this.
        (a long time)

   b   They have money.
        (a lot of money)

   c   Hold the noise down for a minute, I think I heard something.
        (something other than the noise you are making, and unexpected or
        requiring investigation).

The need to enrich the explicature is also demonstrated by examples like
(53).

(53)a   We don't have enough rice.
   b   The park is too far from the house.

Here the words *enough* and *too* signal that the amount of rice and the
distance to the park are estimated in relation to some purpose or projected
action which is not mentioned. This content is provided explicitly in (54),
where the underlined parts are complements to *enough* and *too*.

(54)a   We don't have enough rice to make curry and rice for three people.
   b   The park is too far away from the house to walk the distance in half
        an hour.

Again, whether or not the speaker speaks truly depends on the extra content.
    The third kind of example Carston raises concerns the interpretation of
and. One of Grice's main purposes in identifying implicature was to consign
the variability of interpretation of *and*, *or* and *if* to pragmatics. If this can be
done, then the logical analyses (that is, the meanings given by the truth
tables) can be retained as the actual semantic content of these words.
    Different interpretations for *and* are illustrated in (55)–(58). In each pair,
the underlined part of the (b) example shows the extra information added to
logical conjunction.

(55)a   Alice opened the wine and poured a glass.
   b   Alice opened the wine and after that poured a glass.

(56)a   Jackie has won the Golden Kiwi and she's going to pay off the mortgage.

   b   Jackie has won the Golden Kiwi and <u>as a consequence</u> she's going to pay off the mortgage.

(57)a   Stephen was tuning his bike and he was listening to the cricket.

   b   Stephen was tuning his bike and <u>simultaneously</u> he was listening to the cricket.

(58)a   We looked into your Mr Sutton and he has been fiddling his taxes for years.

   b   We looked into your Mr Sutton and <u>consequently we discovered that</u> he has been fiddling his taxes for years.

It has been suggested that *and* should be treated as an ambiguous word, with many readings including those shown in (55)–(58). In fact, the readings associated with *and* in these sentences do not depend on the presence of *and*, but are chiefly conveyed by the order in which the clauses appear, as shown in (59).

(59)a   Alice opened the wine. She poured out a glass.

   b   Stephen was tuning his bike. He was listening to the cricket.

   c   We looked into your Mr Sutton. He has been fiddling his taxes for years.

This shows that the variable readings are pragmatically associated with the combination of sentences in a certain order (along with *and* where it appears), rather than semantically coded in *and*. Carston's main point is that this pragmatic content is not implicature, but must be included in the explicature. The evidence for this is reviewed below.

The distinction between explicature and implicature is clearly shown with *yes/no* questions and responses in rebuttal or agreement. Implicature in these frames is illustrated in (57).

(60)   (Jones is generally scruffy, but tidies himself up from time to time when he has a girlfriend. His friends are familiar with this pattern.)

   a   A: Jones has transformed himself again recently.

        (implicature: Jones has a new girl.)

      B: No he hasn't.

   b   A: Has Jones tidied himself up lately?

      B: Yes, he has.

The point here is that B's response in rebuttal in (60a) can only target the explicature, and so contradict the assertion that Jones has tidied himself up.

It cannot be understood to contradict the implicature, meaning 'No, he hasn't got a new girl'. In the context, A's question in (60b) can implicate the query 'Has Jones got a new girl?', and again, B's response can only address the explicated question about Jones' appearance, not the implicated question about Jones's love life.

The extra content with *and* does not behave like implicature in similar examples, as shown in (61). Here the 'subsequently' content, giving the order of events, is used.

(61)   A: (*to director*) I light her cigarette and she smiles, right?
      B: No, she smiles and you light her cigarette.

Here it is clear that the order of events is the target of B's response, which indicates that the 'subsequently' content is included in the explicature.

Carston cites more complex examples which show that the extra content associated with *and* can be crucial in determining the logical properties of utterances. Her examples include (62) below.

(62)a   If the old king died of a heart attack and a republic was declared Sam will be happy, but if a republic was declared and the old king died of a heart attack Sam will be unhappy.

    b   p = the old king died of a heart attack
       q = a republic was declared
       r = Sam will be happy

    c $((p\&q) \rightarrow r) \& ((q\&p) \rightarrow \sim r)$

Recall that if the extra 'subsequently' content of *and* is implicature, then the content of *and* at the level of explicature is simply logical conjunction, where *p&q* is equivalent to *q&p*. Then, with the values for *p* and *q* as given in (62b), the sentence in (62a) has the form in (62c), which is a contradiction. But it is clear that (62a) spoken or even written on any occasion is not understood as contradictory, and can be true. So the explicature expressed by any use of this sentence must include the 'subsequently' content pragmatically associated with *and*. Similar examples from Carston's paper are given below.

(63)a   He didn't steal some money and go to the bank; he went to the bank and stole some money.

    b   p = he stole some money
       q = he went to the bank

    c $\sim (p\&q) \& (q\&p)$

(64)a   It's better to meet the love of your life and get married than to get married and meet the love of your life.

   b   p = x to meet the love of x's life
       q = x to get married

       (p&q) is better than (q&p)

   c   'x is better than y' entails '$\sim x = y$'

(65)a   Either she became an alcoholic and her husband left her or her husband left her and she became an alcoholic, I'm not sure which.

   b   p = she became an alcoholic
       q = her husband left her

   c   ((p&q) v (q&p)) & $\sim$((p&q) & (q&p))

In summary, both the explicature and the implicature(s) (if any) may include pragmatic content, and so the domain of pragmatics is not confined to what Grice identified as implicature. Moreover, pragmatic content in the explicature may go beyond the assignment of reference to variables, disambiguation and the interpretation of indexical expressions.

11.5.3   Differentiating Explicature and Implicature

We now return to a point that was raised earlier. If we are to confidently identify the explicature (what was said) and distinguish it from any implicatures (what was implied), we want to separate the two kinds of pragmatic processes that contribute to the two levels.

Now a key property of implicature as first discussed by Grice is that implicatures are fully distinct from and logically independent of what the speaker actually says. For example, the explicature of the utterance 'The movie ends at 3.50' is a completely independent proposition from the implicature 'You (Tom) can see the film and still attend your 4.00 lecture' – neither of these propositions entails the other. The lack of a logical relationship between explicature and implicature was the chief point that required explanation, given that we seem to derive one from the other.

As Carston points out, the explicature and the literal meaning of an utterance are not independent and distinct in this way, as the explicature is an elaborated form of the literal meaning. Example (46), repeated below in (66), shows that the explicature entails the literal meaning, but not vice versa. The literal meaning would entail the explicature only if the two were identical.)

(66)a   'I saw her new plane yesterday.'

   b   **literal meaning:** (day of utterance = 25 October 1937)

'At a time before the time of utterance and overlapping the day before the day of utterance, x_{1s} saw Jean's new aeroplane or wood-scraping tool which was just born, recently manufactured or recently acquired'.

c **explicature:**
'During the morning of 24 October 1937 while visiting Jean Nagy, Irma Smith saw a woodworking tool which Jean Nagy had purchased shortly before 24 October 1937.'

In short, an explicature entails the literal content of the expression uttered, but an implicature does not. Accordingly, Carston proposes that explicature is characterized by its lack of functional independence from the literal sense.

The pragmatic processes which contribute to the explicature are all ways of filling in a framework provided by the literal sense. The literal sense is still contained in the explicature and entailed by it. The linguistic form of the utterance provides clues guiding the construction of the explicature, and accordingly Carston characterizes the pragmatic processes at this level as 'linguistically directed enrichment'.

The main pragmatic processes in constructing the explicature are summarized below.

i. Assigning reference to variables
   linguistic trigger: pronouns, tense, etc.

ii Disambiguation:
   linguistic trigger: ambiguous words, including names or ambiguous structures

iii Interpreting indexical expressions
   linguistic trigger: indexical expressions such as *you*, *tomorrow*, tense, etc.

iv Filling in ellipsis
   linguistic trigger: syntactic ellipsis, such as *There isn't enough (for what?)*, *It's too hot (for what?)*, etc.

11.6 CLOSING COMMENT

The main theme of this chapter is to show that pragmatically derived meaning, variable from one context to another and from one set of participants to another, is not separate from what we take to be the basic meaning of what a speaker says. Generally, language is not a complete coding device into which we translate completely specified propositions for transmission, and the literal meaning of a sentence as analysed by basic semantic theory falls far short of what a speaker would communicate by uttering that sentence on a particular occasion. Even setting aside what we implicate, insinuate, suggest, or hint, much of the time what we plainly say is dramatically underdetermined by the literal meaning of the words we utter.

This is not to claim that human language <u>cannot</u> encode more precise explicatures as the literal meaning of sentences. While talking to her friend, instead of 'I saw Jean's new plane yesterday', Irma Smith could have said 'The present speaker, Irma Smith, during the morning of the twenty-fourth day of the month of October in the year numbered 1937 in the Julian calendar incorporating the Gregorian correction (being the day prior to the day on which the speaker, Irma Smith, is speaking), while visiting Jean Nagy did see a woodworking tool used for shaving timber which Jean Nagy purchased between three and five days prior to the twenty-fourth day of the month of October in the year numbered 1937 in the Julian calendar incorporating the Gregorian correction (being the day prior to the day on which the present speaker, Irma Smith, is speaking)'.

Irma Smith could have expressed herself more explicitly, but fortunately she didn't have to.

The expressive power of natural language rests largely on its interaction with context, and on what does not need to be explicitly stated. If language was not designed to be interpreted in a context (that is, if it was not indexical in the broader sense), every name would have to have a unique bearer, every use of a definite description would have to completely identify the referent, every use of a quantifier would have to state the background set, all ambiguous words such as *bank*, *settle*, *drive*, *duck*, which normally give us no problems, would have to be replaced with nonambiguous sets of words, each with one meaning only, and so on. To express the range of meanings we can now express, a language would have to have a vocabulary so vast that it might well defeat human powers of memory. We would be constantly groping for the right word.

Without indexicality, we couldn't use demonstratives to refer. Faced with some unidentified object, we couldn't ask 'What is that?', because we couldn't use *that* to refer. Speaking of past and future events without indexicality would be extraordinarily difficult, perhaps impossible, as the very concepts of past and future are indexical. In any case, the fully explicit expression of what we want to say would require an unmanageable degree of prolixity.

As things are, the literal meaning of a sentence lays down a framework which determines the set of propositions, perhaps infinitely many, that a speaker can express by uttering the sentence. But the context allows the hearer to identify which of these propositions the speaker actually expressed.

EXERCISES

(A)   Basic Review of Grice's Maxims

In the dialogue below, identify the implicatures (if any) of each utterance, and state how Grice's Maxims are involved in calculating them. The different utterances are numbered for convenience.

1   Adam: I need a hand to get this piano upstairs.
2   Barry: Oh ... my practice starts in ten minutes.
3   Adam: Mmm ... I wonder if Jim next door is home.
4   Barry: The Volkswagen is in the drive.
5   Adam: Do you think it's a bad time to ask?
6   Barry: Well, he really hates missing the six o'clock news.
7   Adam: I'll wait till you get back.

(B)   Q- and R-Implicatures: Discussion

As we saw in Chapter 2, *if* can be interpreted as 'if and only if', written as *iff*. This is a likely interpretation for *if* in

   If the fingerprints match then Jones is guilty.

Assume that the basic meaning of *if* is logical implication, and the biconditional interpretation arises through implicature. In Horn's system, is this R-implicature or Q-implicature, and why?

(C)   More Q- and R-Implicatures: Discussion

The frames illustrated below are considered to be diagnostic of informational strength scales such as < *some all* >, on which scalar implicature is based.

(1)   Some of them, if not all of them, have left.
(2)   Some of them, indeed all of them, have left.
(3)   Some of them, even all of them, have left.
(4)   # All of them, if not some of them, have left.
(5)   # All of them, indeed some of them, have left.
(6)   # All of them, even some of them, have left.

Can the examples below be reconciled to the notion of strength scales, and if so, how?

(7)   Three workers, if not two/indeed two/even two, will finish this in a day.
(8)   This soap dissolves in hot, indeed warm water.

(9)   If everyone or even anyone objects then we'll reconsider the plan.
(10)   If every tree, indeed any tree, is felled we are likely to lay charges.

(D)   Basic Review of Explicature and Implicature

Analyse the literal sense, the explicature and the implicatures (if any) of the italicized utterance in each example below. Use informal paraphrases like the ones used in Section 11.5. Identify the information added at each level and state how it is provided.

(1)   A group of friends are about to go out for dinner to a busy restaurant where they don't have a table booked. Alan has wandered off and started reading the paper. Lucy comes to find him.
      Lucy: *Everyone's waiting.*

(2)   Amy and Brian are making a list of people to invite to a picnic on Sunday.
      Brian: ...and I'll ring Gareth and Carrie and Leo.
      Amy: *Oh but she'll bring Donald.*

(3)   Amy and Brian are making a list of people to invite to a picnic on Sunday.
      Brian: ...and I'll ring Gareth and Carrie and Leo.
      Amy: *...and she'll bring Donald.*

(4)   Morse: We know the documents were locked in that cabinet at four and found to be missing at six thirty when Donald Barrett needed them for the meeting. The secretary had the afternoon off and left at twelve, which leaves Barrett, Jeremy Lamb and Maria McLeay in the office at some time in the afternoon.
      Lewis: *Lamb doesn't have a key.*

(E)   Relevance in Narrative Interpretation: Discussion

The mechanisms for recovering pragmatic meaning in conversation seem also to operate in other linguistic texts, such as narrative. In the passages below, identify all the gaps in the literal meaning which you can fill from context. Do you think the information you add belongs in the explicature or the implicature?

(1)   I am glad Rex never saw a trained police dog jump. He was just an amateur jumper himself, but the most daring and tenacious I have ever seen. He would take on any fence we pointed out to him. Six feet was easy for him, and he could do eight by making a tremendous leap and hauling himself over finally by his paws, grunting and straining; but he

lived and died without knowing that twelve-and sixteen-foot walls were too much for him. Frequently, after letting him try to go over one for a while, we would have to carry him home. He would never have given up trying.

> (James Thurber (1945), 'Snapshot of a Dog' in *The Thurber Carnival*, London, Penguin)

(2)   We went out at the French doors and along a smooth red-flagged path that skirted the far side of the lawn from the garage. The boyish-looking chauffeur had a big black and chromium sedan out now and was dusting that. The path took us along to the side of the greenhouse and the butler opened a door for me and stood aside. It opened into a sort of vestibule that was about as warm as a slow oven. He came in after me, shut the outer door, opened an inner door and we went through that. Then it was really hot.

> (Raymond Chandler (1939), *The Big Sleep*, London: Hamish Hamilton)

(F)   Implicature and Explicature: Discussion

Section 11.5.3 outlines ways of differentiating the explicature and implicature(s) of an utterance. Is the distinction made here compatible with Horn's theory of Q and R implicatures, outlined in section 11.3?

(G)   Context Dependence: Discussion

The example below, repeated from section 11.5, was an illustration of an explicit utterance, in an attempt to make the literal meaning express the explicature. Is the passage below in fact quite independent from pragmatic input?

> The present speaker, Irma Smith, during the morning of the twenty-fourth day of the month of October in the year numbered 1937 in the Julian calendar incorporating the Gregorian correction (being the day prior to the day on which the speaker, Irma Smith, is speaking), while visiting Jean Nagy did see a woodworking tool used for shaving timber which Jean Nagy purchased between three and five days prior to the twenty-fourth day of the month of October in the year numbered 1937 in the Julian calendar incorporating the Gregorian correction (being the day prior to the day on which the present speaker, Irma Smith, is speaking).

FURTHER READING

For pragmatics and implicature, see Levinson (1983), Blakemore (1992), and other introductions to pragmatics. A general discussion of the Maxims is in Green (1990). The most commonly cited of Grice's papers is 'Logic and Conversation' (1975). Neale (1992) provides an accessible review of Grice's philosophy of language.

Horn's theory of Informativeness-based Implicature is outlined in Horn (1984) and in sections of Horn (1989). A similar view is outlined in Chapter 3 of Gazdar (1979).

The main work on Relevance Theory is Sperber and Wilson (1986), revised edition (1995). Blakemore (1992) is a students' introduction to Relevance Theory, and Blakemore (1995) provides a summary of the theory. A précis of the theory is also given in Sperber and Wilson (1996).

Pragmatic inputs to implicature and explicature are discussed in Carston (1988). A detailed discussion of pragmatic inference is in Wilson and Sperber (1986). Lakoff (1971) provides an extensive discussion of the interpretation of conjunction with *and*.

Bibliography

Abbott, B. (1997) 'Definiteness and Existentials', *Language*, **73**, 103–8.

Adams, E. W. (1970) 'Subjunctive and Indicative Conditionals', *Foundations of Language*, **6**, 89–94.

Allan, K. (1980) 'Nouns and Countability', *Language*, **56**, 541–67.

Allan, K. (1986) *Linguistic Meaning*, vols 1 and 2 (London and New York: Routledge & Kegan Paul).

Allwood, J., Andersson, L.-G. and Dahl, O. (1977) *Logic in Linguistics* (Cambridge: Cambridge University Press).

Anderson, A. R. (1951) 'A Note on Subjunctive and Counterfactual Conditionals', *Analysis*, **12**, 35–8.

Anderson, J. R. (1995) *Cognitive Psychology and its Implications*, 4th edn (New York: W. H. Freeman).

Asher, R. E. (ed.) (1994) *The Encyclopaedia of Language and Linguistics* (Oxford and New York: Pergamon Press).

Audi, R. (ed.) (1995) *The Cambridge Dictionary of Philosophy* (Cambridge: Cambridge University Press).

Bach, E. (1989) *Informal Lectures in Formal Semantics* (Albany: SUNY Press).

Bach, E., Jelinek, E., Kratzer, A., and Partee, B. H. (eds) (1995) *Quantification in Natural Languages*, vols 1 and 2 (*Studies in Linguistics and Philosophy* 54) (Dordrecht, Boston and London: Kluwer).

Barwise, J. and Cooper, R. (1981) 'Generalized Quantifiers and Natural Language', *Linguistics and Philosophy*, **4**, 159–219.

Bennett, M. and Partee, B. H. (1978) 'Towards the Logic of Tense and Aspect in English' (Indiana: Indiana University Linguistics Club).

Berg, J. (1988) 'The Pragmatics of Substitutivity', *Linguistics and Philosophy*, **11**, 355–70.

Bertinetto, P. M., Bianchi, V., Dahl, O., and Squartini, M. (eds) (1995) *Temporal Reference: Aspect and Actionality*, vols 1 and 2 (Turin: Rosenberg & Sellier).

Blackburn, S. (1994) *The Oxford Dictionary of Philosophy* (Oxford: Oxford University Press).

Blakemore, D. (1992) *Understanding Utterances: An Introduction to Pragmatics* (Oxford: Blackwell).

Blakemore, D. (1995) 'Relevance Theory', in Verschueren, J. et al. (eds) (1995), 443–52.

Bunt, H. C. (1985) *Mass Terms and Model-Theoretic Semantics* (Cambridge: Cambridge University Press).

Carlson, G. (1984) 'On the Role of Thematic Roles in Linguistic Theory', *Linguistics*, **22**, 259–79.

Carlson, G. and Pelletier, F. J. (eds) (1995) *The Generic Book* (Chicago and London: University of Chicago Press).

Carston, R. (1988) 'Implicature, Explicature and Truth-theoretic Semantics', in Kempson, R. M. (ed.) (1988) *Mental Representations: The Interface between*

Language and Reality (Cambridge: Cambridge University Press), 155–81. Reprinted in Davis, S. (ed.) (1991), 33–51.

Carston, R. (1995) 'Truth-conditional Semantics', in Verschueren, J. et al. (eds) (1995), 544–50.

Carston, R. (1998) 'Informativeness, Relevance and Scalar Implicature', in Carston, R. and Uchida, S. (eds) (1998), 179–236.

Carston, R. and Uchida, S. (eds) (1998) *Relevance Theory: Applications and Implications* (Amsterdam: John Benjamins).

Castañeda, H.-N. (1967) 'Comment on D. Davidson's "The Logical Forms of Action Sentences"', in Rescher, N. (ed.) (1967), *The Logic of Decision and Action* (Pittsburgh: University of Pittsburgh Press).

Chierchia, G. and McConnell-Ginet, S. (1990) *Meaning and Grammar* (Cambridge, MA: MIT Press).

Chomsky, N. (1981) *Lectures on Government and Binding* (Dordrecht: Foris).

Chomsky, N. (1992) 'Explaining Language Use', *Philosophical Topics*, vol. 20, no. 1, 205–31.

Chomsky, N. (1994) 'Naturalism and Dualism in the Study of Language and Mind', *International Journal of Philosophical Studies*, vol. 2, no. 2, 181–209.

Clark, H. H. and Clark, E. V. (1977) *Psychology and Language: An Introduction to Psycholinguistics* (New York: Harcourt Brace Jovanovich).

Cole, P. (ed.) (1978) *Pragmatics* (*Syntax and Semantics* 9) (New York: Academic Press).

Comorovski, I. (1995) 'On Quantifier Strength and Partitive Noun Phrases', in Bach, E. et al. (eds) (1995), 145–77.

Comrie, B. (1976) *Aspect* (Cambridge: Cambridge University Press).

Comrie, B. (1985) *Tense* (Cambridge: Cambridge University Press).

Cruse, D. A. (1973) 'Some Thoughts on Agentivity', *Journal of Linguistics*, **9**, 11–23.

Cruse, D. A. (1986) *Lexical Semantics* (Cambridge: Cambridge University Press).

Crystal, D. (1966) 'Specification of English Tenses', *Journal of Linguistics*, **2**, 1–133.

Dahl, O. (1975) 'On Generics', in Keenan, E. L. (ed.) (1975), 99–111.

Davidson, D. (1967) 'The Logical Form of Action Sentences', in Rescher, N. (ed.) (1967) *The Logic of Decision and Action* (Pittsburgh: University of Pittsburgh Press), 81–120.

Davidson, D. and Harman, G. (eds) (1972) *Semantics of Natural Language* (Dordrecht: Reidel).

Davidson, D. and Hintikka, J. (1975) *Words and Objections: Essays on the Work of W. V. Quine* (revised edition) (Dordrecht: Reidel).

Davis, S. (ed.) (1991) *Pragmatics: A Reader* (Oxford: Oxford University Press).

Depraetere, I. (1995) 'On the Necessity of Distinguishing between (un)Boundedness and (a)Telicity', *Linguistics and Philosophy*, **18**, 1–19.

Diver, W. (1963) 'The Chronological System of the English Verb', *Word*, **19**, 141–81.

Dowty, D. R. (1977) 'Toward a Semantic Analysis of Verb Aspect and the English "Imperfective" Progressive', *Linguistics and Philosophy*, **1**, 45–77.

Dowty, D. R. (1979) *Word Meaning and Montague Grammar* (Dordrecht, Holland: Reidel).

Dowty, D. R. (1989) 'On the Semantic Content of the Notion of "Thematic Role"', in Chierchia, G., Partee, B. H., and Turner, R. (eds) (1989) *Properties, Types and Meaning* (Dordrecht: Kluwer), 69–129.

Dowty, D. R. (1991) 'Thematic Proto-roles and Argument Selection', *Language*, **67**, 547–619.

Dudman, V. H. (1991) 'Interpretations of "If"-sentences', in Jackson, F. (ed.) (1991), 202–32.

Emonds, J. (1975) 'Arguments for Assigning Tense Meanings after Certain Syntactic Transformations Apply', in Keenan, E. L. (ed.) (1975), 351–72.

Fillmore, C. J. and Langendoen, D. T. (eds) (1971) *Studies in Linguistic Semantics* (New York: Holt, Rinehart and Winston).

Fodor, J. D. (1970) *The Linguistic Description of Opaque Contexts*, Doctoral dissertation, MIT (New York: Garland, 1979).

Fodor, J. D. and Sag, I. A. (1982) 'Referential and Quantificational Indefinites', *Linguistics and Philosophy*, **5**, 355–98.

Frawley, W. (1992) *Linguistic Semantics* (Hillsdale, New Jersey: Lawrence Erlbaum).

Gärdenfors, P. (ed.) (1987) *Generalized Quantifiers* (Dordrecht: Reidel).

Gazdar, G. (1979) *Pragmatics: Implicature, Presupposition and Logical Form* (New York: Academic Press).

Geirsson, H. and Losonsky, M. (eds) (1996) *Readings in Language and Mind* (Oxford: Blackwell).

Gil, D. (1995) 'Universal Quantifiers and Distributivity', in Bach, E. et al. (eds) (1995), 321–62.

Goodman, N. (1944) 'The Problem of Counterfactual Conditionals', *Journal of Philosophy*, **44**, 113–28. Reprinted in Jackson, F. (ed.) (1991), 9–27.

Green, G. M. (1990) 'The Universality of Gricean Interpretation', in *Proceedings of the Sixteenth Conference of the Berkeley Linguistics Society*, 411–28.

Green, G. M. (1996) *Pragmatics and Natural Language Understanding*, 2nd edn (Mahwah, New Jersey: Lawrence Erlbaum).

Grice, H. P. (1975) 'Logic and Conversation', in Cole, P. and Morgan, J. L. (eds) (1975) *Speech Acts* (New York: Academic Press), 41–58. Reprinted in Davis, S. (ed.) (1991), 305–15.

Grice, H. P. (1978) 'Further Notes on Logic and Conversation', in Cole, P. (ed.) (1978) (New York: Academic Press), 113–27.

Gruber, G. (1965) *Studies in Lexical Relations*, Doctoral dissertation, MIT.

Grundy, P. (1995) *Doing Pragmatics* (London: Edward Arnold).

Halliday, M. A. K. (1970) *A Course in Spoken English: Intonation* (Oxford: Oxford University Press).

Harman, G. and Davidson, D. (eds) (1972) *Semantics of Natural Language* (Dordrecht: Reidel).

Hatav, G. (1993) 'The Aspect System in English: an Attempt at a Unified Analysis', *Linguistics*, **31**, 209–37.

Heim, I. (1982) *The Semantics of Definite and Indefinite Noun Phrases*, Doctoral dissertation, University of Massachusetts at Amherst.

Heyer, G. (1985) 'Generic Descriptions, Default Reasoning, and Typicality', *Theoretical Linguistics*, **11**, 33–72.

Higginbotham, J. (1983) 'The Logic of Perceptual Reports: an Extensional Alternative to Situation Semantics', *Journal of Philosophy*, **80**, 100–27.

Higginbotham, J. (1995) 'Mass and Count Quantifiers', in Bach, E. et al. (eds) (1995) *Quantification in Natural Languages* (Dordrecht: Kluwer), 383–419.

Hintikka, K. J. J., Moravcsik, J. M. E., and Suppes, P., (eds) (1973) *Approaches to Natural Language: Proceedings of the 1970 Stanford Workshop on Grammar and Semantics* (Dordrecht and Boston: Reidel).

Hitzeman, J. (1997) 'Semantic Partition and the Ambiguity of Sentences Containing Temporal Adverbials', *Natural Language Semantics*, **5**, 87–100.

Horn, L. R. (1984) 'Toward a New Taxonomy for Pragmatic Inference: Q-based and R-based Implicature', in Schiffrin, D. (ed.) (1984) *Meaning, Form and Use in Context: Linguistic Applications* (*Georgetown University Round Table on Languages and Linguistics 1984*) (Washington, D.C.: Georgetown University Press), 11–42.

Horn, L. R. (1989) *A Natural History of Negation* (Chicago: University of Chicago Press).

Horn, L. R. (1996) 'Presupposition and Implicature', in Lappin, S. (ed.) (1996), 299–319.

Hornstein, N. (1990) *As Time Goes By* (Cambridge, MA: MIT Press).

Ioup, G. (1977) 'Specificity and the Interpretation of Quantifiers', *Linguistics and Philosophy*, **1**, 233–45.

Jackendoff, R. (1983) *Semantics and Cognition* (Cambridge, MA: MIT Press).

Jackendoff, R. (1984) 'Sense and Reference in a Psychologically Based Semantics', in Bever, T. G. et al. (eds) (1984) *Talking Minds* (Cambridge, MA: MIT Press), 49–72.

Jackendoff, R. (1985) 'Information is in the Mind of the Beholder', *Linguistics and Philosophy*, **8**, 23–33.

Jackendoff, R. (1987) 'The Status of Thematic Relations in Linguistic Theory', *Linguistic Inquiry*, **18**, 369–411.

Jackendoff, R. (1988) 'Conceptual Semantics', in Eco, U., Santambrogio, M., and Violi, P. (eds) (1988), *Meaning and Mental Representation* (Bloomington, Indiana: Indiana University Press), 81–97.

Jackendoff, R. (1991) 'Parts and Boundaries', in Levin, B. and Pinker, S. (eds) (1991), 9–45.

Jackson, F. (1987) *Conditionals* (Oxford: Basil Blackwell).

Jackson, F. (ed.) (1991) *Conditionals* (Oxford: Oxford University Press).

Jespersen, O. (1932) *A Modern English Grammar on Historical Principles, Part IV* (London: George Allen and Unwin).

Johnson-Laird, P. N. (1982) 'Formal Semantics and the Psychology of Meaning', in Peters, S. and Saarinen, E. (eds) (1982), 1–68.

Johnson-Laird, P. N. (1988) *The Computer and the Mind: an Introduction to Cognitive Science* (Cambridge, MA: Harvard University Press).

Johnson-Laird, P. N. and Wason, P. C. (eds) (1977) *Thinking: Readings in Cognitive Science* (Cambridge: Cambridge University Press).

Kamp, H. (1981) 'A Theory of Truth and Semantic Representation', in J. Groenendijk *et al.* (eds), *Formal Methods in the Study of Language* (Amsterdam: Mathematical Centre). Reprinted in J. Groenendijk, T. Janssen and M. Stockhof (eds) (1984), *Truth, Interpretation and Information* (Dordrecht: Floris) pp. 1–41.

Kamp, H. (1995) 'Discourse Representation Theory', in Verschueren, J. et al. (eds) (1995), 253–7.

Katz, J. J. (1972) *Semantic Theory* (New York: Harper and Row).

Keenan, E. L. and Stavi, J. (1986) 'A Semantic Characterization of Natural Language Determiners', *Linguistics and Philosophy*, **9**, 253–326.

Keenan, E. L. (ed.) (1975) *Formal Semantics of Natural Language* (Cambridge: Cambridge University Press).

Keenan, E. L. (1996) 'The Semantics of Determiners', in Lappin, S. (ed.) (1996), 41–63.

Kempson, R. (1977) *Semantic Theory* (Cambridge: Cambridge University Press).

Kenny, A. (1963) *Action, Emotion and Will* (London: Routledge and Kegan Paul).

Klein, W. (1992) 'The Present Perfect Puzzle', *Language*, **68**, 525–52.

Kratzer, A. (1977) 'What *Must* and *Can* Must and Can Mean', *Linguistics and Philosophy*, **1**, 337–55.

Kratzer, A. (1988) 'Stage-level and Individual-level Predicates', in Carlson, G. and Pelleties, F. J. (eds) (1995), 125–75.

Krifka, M. (1992) 'Thematic Relations as Links between Nominal Reference and Temporal Constitution', in Sag, I. A. and Szabolcsi, A. (eds) (1992), 29–53.

Krifka, M., Pelletier, F. J., Carlson, G., ter Meulen, A., Link, G., and Chierchia, G. (1995) 'Genericity: an Introduction', in Carlson et al. (eds) (1995), 1–124.

Kripke, S. A. (1980) *Naming and Necessity* (revised edition) (Cambridge, MA: Harvard University Press).

Ladusaw, W. (1980) *Polarity Sensitivity as Inherent Scope Relations*, Doctoral dissertation, University of Texas at Austin. Distributed by Indiana University Linguistics Club, Bloomington, Indiana.

Ladusaw, W. (1988) 'Semantic Theory', in Newmeyer, F. (ed.) (1988), 89–112.

Ladusaw, W. (1996) 'Negation and Polarity Items', in Lappin, S. (ed.) (1996), 321–41.

Lakoff, G. and Johnson, M. (1980) *Metaphors We Live By* (Chicago: University of Chicago Press).

Lakoff, G. (1965) *On the Nature of Syntactic Irregularity*, doctoral dissertation, Indiana University. Published as *Irregularity in Syntax* (New York: Holt, Rinehart and Winston, 1970).

Lakoff, G. (1987) *Women, Fire and Dangerous Things: What Categories Reveal about the Mind* (Chicago: University of Chicago Press).

Lakoff, G. (1993) 'The Syntax of Metaphorical Semantic Roles', in Pustejovsky, J. (ed.) (1993), 27–36.

Lakoff, R. (1971) 'Ifs, Ands, and Buts about Conjunction', in Fillmore, C. and Langendoen, T. (eds) (1971), 114–49.

Lamarque, P. V. (ed.) (1997) *Concise Encyclopaedia of Philosophy of Language* (Oxford and New York: Elsevier Science).

Landman, F. (1996) 'Plurality', in Lappin, S. (ed.) (1996), 425–57.

Langacker, R. (1978) 'The Form and Meaning of the English Auxiliary', *Language*, **54**, 853–82.

Lappin, S. (1996) *The Handbook of Contemporary Semantic Theory* (Oxford and Cambridge, MA: Blackwell).

Larson, R., and Segal, G. (1995) *Knowledge of Meaning* (Cambridge, MA: MIT Press).

Leech, G. N. (1971) *Meaning and the English Verb* (London and New York: Longman).

Levin, B. (1993) *English Verb Classes and Alternations: A Preliminary Investigation* (Chicago: University of Chicago Press).

Levin, B. and Pinker, S. (eds) (1991) *Lexical and Conceptual Semantics* (Oxford: Blackwell). Reprinted from *Cognition: International Journal of Cognitive Science* vol. 41, nos 1–3.

Levin, B. and Rappaport Hovav, M. (1991) 'Wiping the Slate Clean: a Lexical Semantic Exploration', in Levin, B. and Pinker, S. (eds) (1991), 123–51.

Levin, B. and Rappaport Hovav, M. (1992) 'The Lexical Semantics of Verbs of Motion: the Perspective from Unaccusativity', in I. M. Roca (ed.), *Thematic Structure: Its Role in Grammar* (Berlin and New York: Foris).

Levinson, S. C. (1983) *Pragmatics* (Cambridge: Cambridge University Press).

Lewis, D. (1968) 'Counterpart Theory and Quantified Modal Logic', *Journal of Philosophy*, **65**, 113–26.

Lewis, D. (1970) 'General Semantics', *Synthèse*, 2, 18–67.

Lewis, D. (1973) *Counterfactuals* (Cambridge, MA: Harvard University Press).

Lewis, D. (1975) 'Adverbs of Quantification', in Keenan, E.L. (ed.) (1975), 3–15.

Lewis, D. (1979) 'Counterfactual Dependence and Time's Arrow', *Noûs*, 13, 455–76. Reprinted in Jackson, F. (ed.) (1991), 46–75.

Link, G. (1987) 'Generalized Quantifiers and Plurals', in Gärdenfors, P. (ed.) (1987), 151–80.

Löbner, S. (1986) 'Quantification as a Major Module of Natural Language Semantics', in Groenendijk, J., et al. (eds) *Studies in Discourse Representation Theory and the Theory of Generalized Quantifiers* (Dordrecht: Foris), 53–85.

Ludlow, P. and Neale, S. (1991) 'Indefinite Descriptions: in Defense of Russell', *Linguistics and Philosophy*, **14**, 171–202.

Lumsden, M. (1988) *Existential Sentences: Their Structure and Meaning* (Croom Helm). Published (1990) London and New York: Routledge.

Lycan, W. (1984) *Logical Form in Natural Language* (Cambridge, MA: MIT Press).

Malmkjaer, K. (1991) *The Linguistics Encyclopaedia* (London and New York: Routledge).

Martin, R. M. (1987) *The Meaning of Language* (Cambridge, MA: MIT Press).

McCawley, J. (1993) *Everything that Linguists have always Wanted to Know about Logic but were Ashamed to Ask*, 2nd edn (Chicago: Chicago University Press).

McCawley, J. D. 'Tense and Time Reference in English', in Fillmore, C. and Langendoen, T. (eds) (1971), 97–113.

McCawley, J. D. (1981) 'Notes on the English Present Perfect', *Australian Journal of Linguistics* 1, 81–90.

McConnell-Ginet, S. (1982) 'Adverbs and Logical Form', *Language*, **58**, 144–84.

Michaelis, L. A. (1994) 'The Ambiguity of the English Present Perfect', *Journal of Linguistics* 30, 111–57.

Milsark, G. (1977) 'Toward an Explanation of Certain Peculiarities in the Existential Construction in English', *Linguistic Analysis*, 3, 1–30.

Mittwoch, A. (1988) 'Aspects of English Aspect: on the Interaction of Perfect, Progressive and Durational Phrases', *Linguistics and Philosophy*, **11**, 203–54.

Mittwoch, A. (1995) 'The English Perfect, Past Perfect and Future Perfect in a Neoreichenbachian Framework', in Bertinetto et al. (eds) (1995), 255–67.

Moltmann, F. (1991) 'Measure Adverbials', *Linguistics and Philosophy*, 14, 629–60.

Mourelatos, A. P. D. (1978) 'Events, Processes and States', *Linguistics and Philosophy* 2, 415–34.

Munitz, M. K. and Unger, P. K. (eds) (1974) *Semantics and Philosophy* (New York: New York University Press).

Neale, S. (1990) *Descriptions* (Cambridge, MA: MIT Press).

Neale, S. (1992) 'Paul Grice and the Philosophy of Language', *Linguistics and Philosophy*, **15**, 509–59.

Newmeyer, F. (ed.) (1988) *Linguistics: The Cambridge Survey*, vol. 1 (Cambridge: Cambridge University Press).

Nute, D. (1984) 'Conditional Logic', in Gabbay, D. and Guenthner, F. (eds) (1984) *Handbook of Philosophical Logic*, vol. II (Dordrecht: D. Reidel), 387–439.

Ojeda, A. (1993) *Linguistic Individuals* (Stanford: CSLI).

Palmer, F. R. (1987) *The English Verb*, 2nd edn (London and New York: Longman).

Parsons, T. (1980) 'Modifiers and Quantifiers in Natural Language', *Canadian Journal of Philosophy*, **6**, 29–60.

Parsons, T. (1989) 'The Progressive in English: Events, States and Processes', *Linguistics and Philosophy*, **12**, 213–41.

Parsons, T. (1990) *Events in the Semantics of English* (Cambridge, MA: MIT Press).

Parsons, T. (1995) 'Thematic Relations and Arguments', *Linguistic Inquiry*, **26**, 635–62.

Partee, B. H. (1973a) 'Some Structural Analogies between Tenses and Pronouns in English', *Journal of Philosophy* **70**, 601–9.

Partee, B. H. (1973b) 'The Semantics of Belief-sentences', in Hintikka, K. J. J. et al. (eds) (1973), 309–335.

Partee, B. H. (1974) 'Opacity and Scope', in Munitz, M. K. and Unger, P. K. (eds) (1974), 81–101.

Partee, B. H. (1981) 'Montague Grammar, Mental Representations and Reality', in Kanger, K. and Öhman, S. (eds) (1981) *Philosophy and Grammar: Papers on the Occasion of the Quincentennial of Uppsala University* (Dordrecht: Reidel), 59–78.

Partee, B. H. (1982) 'Belief-sentences and the Limits of Semantics', in Peters, S. and Saarinen, E. (eds) (1982), 87–106.

Partee, B. H. (1984) 'Nominal and Temporal Anaphora', *Linguistics and Philosophy*, **7**, 243–86.

Partee, B. H. (1996) 'Semantics – Mathematics or Psychology?', in Geirsson, H. and Losonsky, M. (eds) (1996), 88–100.

Peters, S. and Saarinen, E. (eds) (1982) *Processes, Beliefs, and Questions* (Dordrecht: Reidel).

Pinker, S. (1989) *Learnability and Cognition* (Cambridge, MA: MIT Press).

Progovac, L. (1994) *Negative and Positive Polarity* (*Cambridge Studies in Linguistics* 68) (Cambridge: Cambridge University Press).

Pustejovsky, J. (ed.) (1993) *Semantics and the Lexicon* (Dordrecht: Kluwer).

Quine, W. v. O (1956) 'Quantifiers and Propositional Attitudes', *Journal of Philosophy* **53**. Reprinted in Quine (1976) *The Ways of Paradox and Other Essays* (Cambridge, MA: Harvard University Press), 185–96.

Reichenbach, H. (1947) *Elements of Symbolic Logic* (New York: The Free Press).

Reuland, E., and ter Meulen, A. (eds) (1987) *The Representation of (In)definiteness* (Cambridge, MA: MIT Press).

Richard, M. (1990) *Propositional Attitudes: An Essay on Thoughts and How we Ascribe Them* (Cambridge: Cambridge University Press).

Rijkhoff, J. (1991) 'Nominal Aspect', *Journal of Semantics* **8**, 291–309.

Rosch, E. (1976) 'Classification of Real-world Objects: Origins and Representations in Cognition', in Ehrlich, S. and Tulving, E. (eds) (1976) *La Memoire Semantique*

(Paris: Bulletin de Psychologie). Reprinted in Johnson-Laird, P. N. and Wason, P. C. (eds) (1977), 212–22.

Rosch, E. and Mervis, C. B. (1975) 'Family Resemblances: Studies in the Internal Structure of Categories', *Cognitive Psychology*, 7, 382–439. Reprinted in Geirsson, H. and Losonsky, M. (eds) (1996), 442–60.

Russell, B. (1905) 'On Denoting', *Mind*, 14, 479–93. Reprinted in R. C. Marsh (ed.) (1956) *Logic and Knowledge* (London: George Allen and Unwin), 41–56.

Russell, B. (1911) 'Knowledge by Acquaintance and Knowledge by Description', *Proceedings of the Aristotelian Society*, 11 (1910–11), 108–28. Reprinted in Salmon, N. and Soames, S. (eds) (1988), 16–32.

Ryle, R. (1949) *The Concept of Mind* (Hutchinson). Published (1963) Harmondsworth, Middlesex: Peregrine Books.

Saeed, J. I. (1997) *Semantics* (Oxford: Blackwell).

Sag, I. A. and Szabolcsi, A. (eds) (1992) *Lexical Matters* (Stanford: CSLI).

Salmon, N. (1986) *Frege's Puzzle* (Cambridge, MA: MIT Press).

Salmon, N. and Soames, S. (eds) (1988) *Propositions and Attitudes* (Oxford: Oxford University Press).

Sanford, D. H. (1989) *If P, then Q: Conditionals and the Foundations of Reasoning* (London and New York: Routledge).

Schlesinger, I. M. (1987) 'Instruments as Agents: on the Nature of Semantic Relations', *Journal of Linguistics*, 25, 189–210.

Schwenter, S. A. (1994) '"Hot news" and the Grammaticalization of Perfects', *Linguistics*, 32, 995–1028.

Segal, G. (1989) 'A Preference for Sense and Reference', *Journal of Philosophy*, 86, 73–89.

Sharvy, R. (1980) 'A More General Theory of Definite Descriptions', *The Philosophical Review*, 89, No. 4, 607–24.

Soames, S. (1987) 'Substitutivity', in Thompson, J. J. (ed.) (1987), 99–132.

Sperber, D. and Wilson, D. (1986) *Relevance* (Cambridge, MA: Harvard University Press). Revised edn, 1995.

Sperber, D. and Wilson, D. (1996) 'Précis of *Relevance: Communication and Cognition*', in Geirsson, H. and Losonsky, M. (eds) (1996), 460–86.

Stalnaker, R. (1968) 'A Theory of Conditionals', in *Studies in Logical Theory* (*American Philosophical Quarterly* Monograph 2), 98–112. Reprinted in Jackson, F. (ed.) (1991), 28–45.

Stalnaker, R. C. (1972) 'Pragmatics', in Harman, G. and Davidson, D. (eds) (1972), 380–97. Reprinted in Geirsson, H. and Losonsky, M. (eds) (1996), 77–88.

Steinberg, D. D. and Jakobovits, L. A. (eds) (1971) *Semantics: An Interdisciplinary Reader in Philosophy, Linguistics and Psychology* (Cambridge: Cambridge University Press).

Talmy, L. (1978) 'Figure and Ground in Complex Sentences', in Greenberg, J. H. (1978) *Universals of Human Language*, Volume 4: *Syntax* (Stanford: Stanford University Press) 627–49.

Tedeschi, P. and Zaenen, A. (eds) (1981) *Tense and Aspect* (*Syntax and Semantics* 14) (New York: Academic Press).

Tenny, C. L. (1992) 'The Aspectual Interface Hypothesis', in Sag, I. A. and Szabolcsi, A. (1992), 1–27.

Tenny, C. L. (1994) *Aspectual Roles and the Syntax-Semantics Interface* (Dordrecht: Kluwer).

ter Meulen, A. (1988) 'Linguistics and the Philosophy of Language', in Newmeyer, F. (ed.) (1988), 430–446.

Thagard, P. (1996) *Mind: Introduction to Cognitive Science* (Cambridge, MA: MIT Press).

Thompson, J. J. (ed.) (1987) *On Being and Saying: Essays for Richard Cartwright* (Cambridge, MA: MIT Press).

Ungerer, F. and Schmid, H.-J. (1996) *An Introduction to Cognitive Linguistics* (London and New York: Longman).

van Benthem, J. and ter Meulen, A. (eds) (1984) *Generalized Quantifiers in Natural Language* (Dordrecht: Foris).

van Valin, R. D. (1990) 'Semantic Parameters of Split Intransitivity', *Language*, **66**, 221–60.

van Valin, R. D. (1995) 'Role and Reference Grammar', in Verschueren J. et al. (eds) (1995), 461–9.

van Voorst, J. (1992) 'The Aspectual Semantics of Psychological Verbs', *Linguistics and Philosophy*, **15**, 65–92.

Vendler, Z. (1967) 'Each and Every, Any and All', in Vendler, Z. (1967), 70–96.

Vendler, Z. (1967), *Linguistics in Philosophy* (Ithaca, NY: Cornell University Press).

Verschueren, J., Östman, J.-O. and Blommaert, J. (1995) *Handbook of Pragmatics Manual* (Amsterdam and Philadelphia: John Benjamins).

Vlach, F. (1981) 'The Semantics of the Progressive', in Tedeschi, P. and Zaenen, A. (eds) (1981), 271–92.

Ward, G. and Birner, B. J. (1997) 'Response to Abbott', *Language*, **73**, 109–12.

Webster, N. (1789) *Dissertations on the English Language* (Menston, England: Scolar Press).

Westerståhl, D. (1984) 'Determiners and Context Sets', in van Benthem, J. and ter Meulen, A. G. B. (eds) (1984) 45–71.

Wettstein, H. (1991) *Has Semantics Rested on a Mistake? and Other Essays* (Stanford: Stanford University Press).

Wilson, D. and Sperber, D. (1986) 'Inference and Implicature', in Travis, C. (ed.) (1986) *Meaning and Interpretation* (Oxford: Blackwell), 45–75. Reprinted in Davis, S. (ed.) (1991), 377–93.

Wittgenstein, L. (1953) *Philosophical Investigations* (New York: Macmillan).

Woods, M. (1997) *Conditionals*, edited by David Wiggins (Oxford: Clarendon Press).

Wright, S. and Givón, T. (1987) 'The Pragmatics of Indefinite Reference: Quantified Text-based Studies', *Studies in Language*, **11**, 1–33.

Zwarts, F. (1983) 'Determiners: a Relational Perspective', in ter Meulen, A. G. B. (ed.), *Studies in Modeltheoretic Semantics* (Dordrecht: Foris).

Index